Hair Cutting Bible

The Complete Hair Cutting Masterclass Guide to Unlock Professional Techniques, Trendsetting Styles, and the Secrets of Precision Cutting

Aurora Cameron

Copyright © 2024 Aurora Cameron

All Rights Reserved

This book or parts thereof may not be reproduced in any form, stored in any retrieval system, or transmitted in any form by any means—electronic, mechanical, photocopy, recording, or otherwise—without prior written permission of the publisher, except as provided by United States of America copyright law and fair use.

Disclaimer and Terms of Use

The author and publisher of this book and the accompanying materials have used their best efforts in preparing this book. The author and publisher make no representation or warranties with respect to the accuracy, applicability, fitness, or completeness of the contents of this book. The information contained in this book is strictly for informational purposes. Therefore, if you wish to apply ideas contained in this book, you are taking full responsibility for your actions.

Printed in the United States of America

TABLE OF CONTENTS

- TABLE OF CONTENTS III
- PART I 1
- INTRODUCTION TO HAIR CUTTING 1
- CHAPTER 1 2
- INTRODUCTION 2
  - THE TOOLS OF THE TRADE 3
  - HAIR CUTTING SCISSORS | HAIRCUTTING SHEARS: CUTTING, TRIMMING, AND PERFECTING HAIRSTYLES 4
    - *Thinning Scissors | Texturizing Shears: Shape the Final Hairstyle* 4
    - *Straight Razors | Styling & Texturizing Shears to Create Volume* 5
    - *Hair Clipper Tools: Shorter & Cleaner Haircuts* 6
    - *Hair Trimming Tools: Perfecting the Final Hairstyle* 6
    - *Hair Comb: Controlling Hair While Cutting* 7
  - SETTING UP YOUR WORKSPACE 7
    - *Choosing the Right Location* 8
    - *Furniture and Layout* 8
    - *Tools and Equipment* 8
    - *Sanitation and Safety* 8
    - *Storage Solutions* 9
    - *Client Comfort and Amenities* 9
    - *Ergonomics and Personal Comfort* 9
    - *Personal Touches and Decor* 9
  - SAFETY AND HYGIENE PRACTICES 9
    - *Sanitation of Tools and Equipment* 9
    - *Workstation Cleanliness* 10
    - *Personal Hygiene* 10
    - *Client Protection* 10
  - HANDLING CHEMICALS AND PRODUCTS 11
    - *Electrical Safety* 11
    - *Ergonomics and Physical Safety* 11
    - *Emergency Preparedness* 11
- PART II 12
- BASICS OF HAIR CUTTING 12
- CHAPTER 2 13
- UNDERSTANDING HAIR 13
  - HAIR ANATOMY 13
    - *How does hair grow?* 13
    - *Hair growth cycle* 14
  - GROWTH PATTERNS AND FACE SHAPES 14
    - *Hair Growth Patterns* 14
    - *Cowlicks* 14

Hair Whorls	*14*
Natural Partings	*15*
Hairline Patterns	*15*
Face Shapes	*15*
Oval Face Shape	*15*
Round Face Shape	*15*
Square Face Shape	*15*
Heart Face Shape	*16*
Diamond Face Shape	*16*
CHAPTER 3	**17**
BASIC TECHNIQUES	**17**
HOLDING AND POSITIONING TOOLS	17
HOLDING AND POSITIONING TOOLS	17
Scissors	*17*
Combs	*18*
Clippers	*18*
Razors	*18*
TECHNIQUES FOR DIFFERENT HAIR TYPES	18
ERGONOMICS AND POSTURE	19
SECTIONING HAIR	19
Why is it important to section hair for haircutting?	*19*
What are the main steps in sectioning hair for haircutting?	*19*
THINGS TO AVOID WHILE SECTIONING HAIR	20
SECTIONING THE HAIR: 3 METHODS	21
Sectioning the Hair for Haircutting	*21*
Sectioning Of the Hair for Hair Rollers	*22*
Sectioning For Hair Straightening	*23*
ANGLES AND ELEVATION	24
Elevation	*24*
Angles	*25*
WOMEN HAIR TYPES	26
Straight Hair	*27*
Wavy Hair	*28*
Curly Hair	*30*
COILY HAIR	32
Thick Hair	*33*
Fine Hair	*34*
REASONS FOR HAIR TYPE CHANGES	35
MEN'S HAIR TYPES	36
Straight Hair	*36*
ADVANTAGES VS. THE DRAWBACKS OF STRAIGHT HAIR	36
Hairstyles for straight hair	*36*
Hair products for straight hair	*36*
Wavy Hair	*37*
ADVANTAGES VS. WAVY HAIR DISADVANTAGES	37

- *Hairstyles for wavy hair* 37
- *Hair items for wavy hair* 37
- COILED HAIR 38
  - *Advantages vs. drawbacks of coiled hair* 38
  - *Coiled hairstyles* 39
- KINKY HAIR 39
  - *Advantages vs. kinky hair drawbacks* 40
  - *Hairstyles for kinky hair* 40
  - *Hair products for kinky hair* 40

PART III 41

CUTTING TECHNIQUES 41

CHAPTER 4 42

HAIR CUT STYLES 42
- HOW TO TRIM LONG HAIR 42
- HOW TO HOLD THE SHEARS 43
  - *Horizontal rear trim* 43
  - *How to Trim Bangs* 43
- HOW TO FRAME SIDES OF LONG HAIR 44
  - *How to Frame Short Hair (Off the Ears)* 44

CHAPTER 5 46

HAIR CUTTING FOR DIFFERENT TEXTURES 46
- CUTTING CURLY HAIR 46
- CUTTING STRAIGHT HAIR 47
  - *Cutting Straight Hair At Home* 47
- HOW TO CUT SOMEONE ELSE'S STRAIGHT HAIR 49
- AFRO-TYPE HAIRCUTTING 50
  - STEP-BY-STEP AFRO-CUT 51
  - HOW TO CUT YOUR HAIR 51

CHAPTER 6 53

ADVANCED CUTTING TECHNIQUES 53
- TEXTURIZING AND THINNING 53
- CURRENT HAIR TEXTURIZING TRENDS YOU MUST KNOW .. 54
  - *Point Cutting* 54
  - *Internal Cutting* 54
  - *Twist Cutting* 54
  - *Slide Cutting* 54
- TEXTURIZING SHEARS PROBLEMS TO AVOID 54
  - *Over-Texturizing and Over-Graduating* 54
  - *Uneven Bob* 54
  - *Frizzy Hair* 55
- HAIR TEXTURIZING TOOLS 55

- *Straight-Edge Razor* 55
- *Hair Clipper* 55
- *Blending Shears* 55
- *Chunking Shears* 55
- *Finishing Shears* 55
- *Tail Comb* 55
- BLENDING AND FADING 56
- GUIDELINES 58
- BLEND FADE LINES 59

CHAPTER 7 61

LAYER CUTS 61

- LAYERING HAIR (DEFINED) 61
  - *Simple Long Hair "Shaggy Cut"* 61
  - *PROCEDURE* 61
- LIFTING HAIR WITH THE COMB 62
  - *Basic Layer Cut* 62
- HOW TO USE THINNING SHEARS 63
- CLIPPER CUTS 64
  - *Clipper Cuts* 64
  - *Clipper Attachments (Rakes)* 64
- COMMON RAKES 65
  - *How to Do a Buzz-Cut with a Rake* 65
  - *STEPS FOR BUZZ / BUTCH* 65
  - *Cut the buzz* 65
  - *EASY REGULATION STYLE CUT* 65
  - *Steps for Simple Marine Style Cut* 66
- STEP-BY-STEP TAPER 66
  - *Specialty Clipper Cuts* 67
- HOW TO DO A STANDARD FLAT TOP 67

CHAPTER 8 68

SPECIALIZED HAIRCUTS 68

- MEN'S HAIRCUTS 68
  - *Buzz Cut Styles* 68
  - *Crew Cut Styles* 68
  - *Thick* 69
  - *Gentleman* 69
  - *Classic* 69
  - *Fade* 69
  - *Side Part* 69
- FADE HAIRCUT STYLES 70
  - *Taper Fade* 70
  - *Low Fade* 70
  - *Mid-fade* 70
  - *High Fade* 70

- Undercut Haircut Styles 71
- Taper Haircut Style 72
- Side Part Men's Haircut Style 73
- Man Bun Hairstyles 74
  - *Full* 74
  - *Semi* 74
  - *Low* 74
  - *Undercut fade* 74
  - *The Lumberjack* 74
- Pompadour Haircut Style 75
- Quiff Style 76
- French Crop Haircut Style 77
- Faux Hawk Haircut Style 77
- Mohawk Haircut Styles 78
  - *Short* 78
  - *Fade* 78
- Children's Haircuts 79
- Keep the Natural Curls Carefully Sculpted 79
- Close Cropped Sides and Brushed Back Top Cut, Perfect for Fine Hair 80
- All-Over Short Buzz for Boys 80
  - *Bring Back the Long Locks* 81
  - *Completely Shaved Style for a Fresh Feel* 81
  - *Classic Crew Cut to Beat the Heat* 82
  - *A Rebellious Mohawk to Make a Statement* 82
  - *Short Hair Don't Care With This Pixie Haircut* 83
  - *Classic Bowl Haircut for Kids That Can't Sit Still* 83
  - *Short Scissor Cut with Fringe for a no-fuss Style* 84
  - *Chin-Length Bob with Bangs Is As Sweet As Can Be* 84
  - *Medium-Length Cut with Subtle Layers to Embrace the Mane* 85
  - *Long, Face-Framing Layers for the Kids Next Door* 85
  - *Classic Bob without Bangs for Your Mature Mini-Me* 86
  - *Long Layered Cut for a Soft Look* 86
  - *Natural Curls for a Beautiful Halo of Hair* 87
  - *Short Cut with Flipped Ends for a Vintage Look* 87
  - *Single Layer Cut with Side Swept Bangs Taking Center Stage* 88
  - *Edgy Stacked Bob with No Bangs* 88

CHAPTER 9 89

STYLING AND FINISHING TECHNIQUES 89

- Blow Dry Your Hair 89
- How do I get the perfect salon-quality blowout? 90
  - *Use a brush suited to your hair type* 90
- Invest in a high-quality blow dryer 91
  - *Apply styling products throughout your hair* 91
  - *Use a nozzle* 91
- Mistakes to Avoid When Blow-Drying Hair Straight Like a Pro 92

- *Using too high of a heat setting* 92
- *Using the wrong brush* 92
- *Skipping styling products or not applying them evenly* 92
- *Blow-dry the right way* 93
- *Avoid hair care products that are drying* 93
- *Not working from root to tip* 93
- *Moving too quickly* 93
- USING HEAT TOOLS 93
  - *The Basics: Curling Irons vs. Flat Irons* 93
- CURL YOUR HAIR WITH A FLAT IRON 94
  - *Start with healthy hair* 95
  - *Prep with a heat protectant* 95
  - *Start using the iron* 95
  - *Set it with hairspray* 96
  - *Be gentle* 96
- A FEW HELPFUL TIPS 96
- USING CURLING IRONS 96
  - *How to Use a Curling Iron with a Clamp* 98
  - *How to Use a Curling Wand* 98

PART IV 99

ADVANCED HAIR CUTTING AND PROFESSIONAL DEVELOPMENT 99

CHAPTER 10 100

CREATIVE CUTTING AND CUSTOM STYLES 100

- ASYMMETRICAL CUTS 100
  - *Asymmetrical Pixie Cut* 100
  - *Asymmetrical Bangs* 100
  - *Wavy Asymmetrical Bob* 101
  - *Asymmetrical Bob with Bangs* 101
- LONG ASYMMETRICAL HAIR 102
  - *Long Asymmetrical Hair with Undercut* 102
- ASYMMETRICAL SHAG 103
- ASYMMETRICAL UNDERCUT 103
- UNIQUE ASYMMETRICAL HAIRCUT 104
- ASYMMETRICAL LAYERED BOB 104
  - *Avant-Garde Hair* 105
  - *What Is Avant-Garde Hair?* 105
- THE RULES FOR CRAFTING AN AVANT-GARDE HAIRSTYLE 106
  - *Weight* 106
  - *Structure* 106
  - *Balance* 106
- SIMPLE AVANT-GARDE LOOKS TO STYLE YOURSELF 106
  - *Over-Teasing* 107
  - *A Wet Finish* 107
  - *Bold Faux Bangs* 107

Exaggerated Victory Rolls *107*
Big Updo *108*
AVANT-GARDE INSPIRED HAIRCUTS 108
Short Hair Ideas *108*
Color *108*
UPGRADE YOUR UPDO 109
THE PSYCHOLOGY OF HAIR: UNDERSTANDING CLIENT PREFERENCES 109
BUILDING A SOLID CLIENT BASE: HAIRSTYLIST'S DEFINITIVE GUIDE 110
Craft an Inviting Salon Atmosphere *110*
MASTER THE ART OF COMMUNICATION 110
Deliver Consistent Quality *111*
Personalize the Experience *111*
Leverage Social Media *111*
OFFER PROMOTIONS AND LOYALTY PROGRAMS 112
Attend Networking Events *112*
Stay in Touch through Email Marketing *112*
INVEST IN CONTINUED EDUCATION 113
ASK FOR REFERRALS AND REVIEWS 113

CHAPTER 11 114

COLOR INTEGRATION 114

BASIC STEPS FOR COLORING YOUR HAIR AT HOME 114
HAIR DYE BASICS 114
HAIR DYEING TUTORIAL: FROM FORMULA TO FINISH 114
Semi-Permanent *115*
Demi-Permanent *115*
Permanent *115*
Hair Dyeing Process *115*
Check for Irritants *115*
Prep Your Skin *115*
Strand Test *115*
DYE APPLICATION PROCESS 115
TECHNIQUES FOR INTEGRATING CUT AND COLOR 116
MAINTAINING HAIR HEALTH WITH COLOR SERVICES 118

CHAPTER 12 120

CONSULTATION AND CLIENT MANAGEMENT 120

EFFECTIVE CLIENT CONSULTATIONS 120
BUILDING AND MAINTAINING CLIENT RELATIONSHIPS 121

CHAPTER 13 124

BUSINESS AND CAREER DEVELOPMENT 124

SETTING UP A SALON OR HOME STUDIO 124
APPROXIMATELY HOW MUCH MONEY DO HAIR SALON OWNERS MAKE IN A YEAR? 127
How long does it take to complete cosmetology school? *127*

Continuing Education and Certification 127

CHAPTER 14 130

TROUBLESHOOTING AND CORRECTION 130

COMMON CUTTING MISTAKES AND FIXES 130
Ignoring Face Shape and Hair Type 130
Understanding Face Shapes 130
Working with Hair Types 130
Lack of Communication with Your Stylist 131
Not Considering Hair Maintenance 131
SKIPPING CONSULTATIONS AND RESEARCH 131
Being Influenced by Trends Alone 132
GOING FOR DRASTIC CHANGES WITHOUT PREPARATION 132
NEGLECTING REGULAR TRIMS AND MAINTENANCE 133
DIY HAIRCUTS AND OVER-RELIANCE ON ONLINE TUTORIALS 133
OVERLOOKING HAIRCARE PRODUCTS AND TOOLS 133
NOT EMBRACING PROFESSIONAL ADVICE AND EXPERTISE 134
ADDRESSING CLIENT CONCERNS AND FEEDBACK 134
MAINTAINING CUTTING TOOLS AND EQUIPMENT 135

PART V 138

MASTERY AND BEYOND 138

CHAPTER 15 139

STAYING CURRENT 139

TRENDS AND INNOVATIONS IN HAIR CUTTING 139
Current Trends in Hair Cutting 139
INNOVATIONS IN HAIR CUTTING 139
ADVANCED WORKSHOPS AND COURSES 140
Types of Advanced Workshops and Courses 140
Key Elements of Advanced Workshops and Courses 141
Notable Advanced Workshops and Courses 142
NETWORKING AND PROFESSIONAL ASSOCIATIONS 142
Importance of Networking and Professional Associations 142
Notable Professional Associations for Hair Cutting Professionals 143
STRATEGIES FOR EFFECTIVE NETWORKING 144

CHAPTER 16 145

MASTERING YOUR CRAFT 145

REFINING TECHNIQUES 145
UNDERSTANDING HAIR ANATOMY AND GROWTH PATTERNS 145
Mastering Basic Techniques 145
Advanced Techniques and Tools 145
Refining Techniques for Different Hair Types 146
Incorporating Technology and Tools 146

- Refining hair 146
- THE TOOLS YOU NEED! 147
  - *THE PREP* 147
  - *THE SOFT-CUT APPROACH* 147
  - *VERTICAL GRADUATION* 147
  - *SIMPLE THINNING* 148
- Developing a Signature Style 148
- Teaching and Mentoring Others 149

CHAPTER 17 152

PORTFOLIO DEVELOPMENT 152

- Creating a Professional Portfolio 152
- Compiling Your Best Work 152
- Organizing Your Portfolio 152
- Choosing the Format 153
- Enhancing Your Portfolio 153
- Photographing Haircuts 154
  - *Preparation* 154
  - *Camera Settings* 154
  - *Composition* 154
- Conclusion 154

INDEX 156

PART I
INTRODUCTION TO HAIR CUTTING

CHAPTER 1
INTRODUCTION

Hair cutting is a complicated mix of art and science that needs both skill and imagination to get the right result. When it comes to art, style, and fashion have a big impact on hair cutting. A hairdresser needs to know about the latest fashions because their clients often want to copy the looks they see on models or celebs. A stylist needs to know more than just what's in style. They also need to know how to make different styles look good on different face shapes. For example, a certain haircut might make a square chin look more defined or a round face look softer. This knowledge helps stylists make cuts that look good on each client, drawing attention to their best features and hiding any flaws they might see. A big part of the art of hair cutting is being able to show yourself. A haircut is more than just cutting hair short; it's about making a look that fits the person's attitude and way of life. This includes a long meeting where the stylist talks with the client about their tastes, lifestyle, and the image they want to project.

Some clients might want a bold, edgy cut that stands out, while others might want a classic style that will never go out of style. The stylist's job is to figure out what the client wants and give them a haircut that fits their idea. The artistic aspect also includes mastering various design and technique elements. Texturing and layering are two important techniques that can make a simple haircut look interesting and dynamic. When you layer, you cut your hair at different lengths to give it volume and movement, which is great for people with thin hair. Texturing, on the other hand, can give thick hair more bounce and make it feel lighter and airier by adding depth and less bulk. To do either method well, you need to know a lot about different hair types and how different cuts affect the hair's natural flow and fall. In terms of science, cutting hair needs a deep understanding of how hair grows and how it is structured. Keratin, a protein, is what hair is made of and gives each strand its shape. There are different ways to cut straight, wavy, curly, and coily hair because of the way their structures are built. For example, cutting wavy hair when it's dry can help it keep its natural shape and stop it from shrinking too much. On the other hand, cutting straight hair might need to be done while it's wet for better precision and control. The tools used for cutting hair also require a lot of technical skill. Scissors, razors, clippers, and thinning shears are all used for different things and need to be handled in a certain way. As an example, scissors are used to make straight cuts and fine details, while razors can make edges that are soft and feathery. For short, precise cuts, clippers are a must, especially when grooming men. Thinning shears are used to get rid of bulk and mix layers smoothly. You can get good at using these tools if you practice and learn how they affect different hair styles and types. Also, ergonomics and body mechanics are important parts of the science of hair cutting. For accuracy and health, hairstylists must keep their bodies in the right position and keep their hands in the right places. Doing the same things over and over or standing for long periods can cause pain and harm if they are not handled properly. Because of this, stylists are taught methods that reduce physical stress while increasing speed and accuracy. Along with professional skills, you need to have a deep understanding of geometry. The end look of a haircut is determined by the angles, lines, and shapes used in the cutting process. For example, to get the right stacked effect at the back of a graduated bob, it needs to be carefully sectioned and cut at certain angles. Stylists can make a lot of different styles, from smooth and polished to rough and full, by understanding how to change these geometric rules.

For both the artistic and science sides of hair cutting, it's important to keep learning and practicing. Trends and techniques change over time, and stylists need to stay up to date so they can give their clients the newest looks and techniques. Stylists can improve their skills and learn new ones by going to classes, seminars, and advanced training programs. To sum up, hair cutting is a complex skill that blends artistic vision with science accuracy. It requires learning about fashion trends, face types, and personal expression while also getting good at using different cutting tools and techniques. The stylist can make even more beautiful, unique haircuts by using the science of hair structure, mechanics, and geometry. When these things are put together, they make haircuts that not only look good but also fit the client's attitude and way of life.

The Tools of the Trade

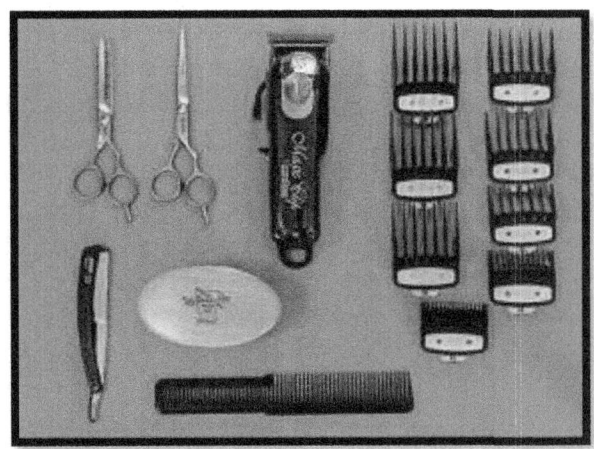

Hair Cutting Scissors | Haircutting Shears: Cutting, Trimming, and Perfecting Hairstyles

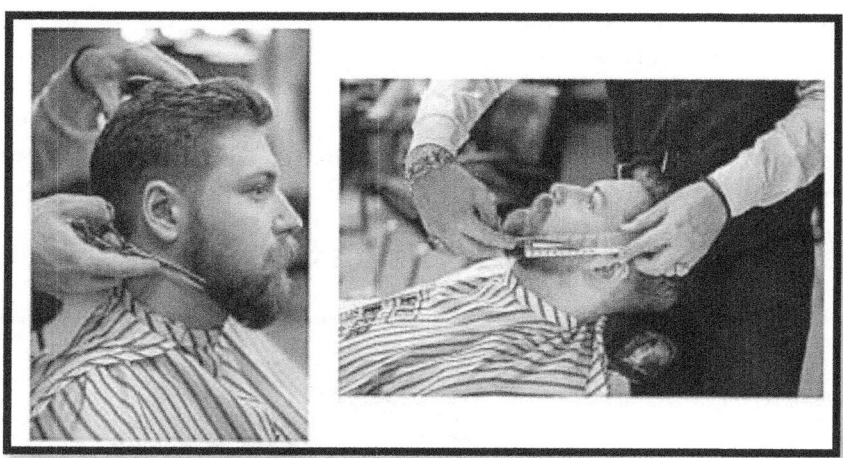

Shears are an important tool that is often used to cut hair, but they are more difficult than regular kitchen scissors. On the other hand, shears made just for cutting hair are more accurate and can be curved or beveled to allow for different ways of cutting hair. The pivot zone of the hair-cutting shear is also built with a certain amount of strain that is neither too free nor too tight. It has just the right amount of pressure to let you open and close the shears while you cut. Hair stylists use these scissors because they are made to cut hair and are the right size for their hands. They are usually 7 inches long and have a "tang" that lets the stylist have more control. These days' shears are made in a way that makes them easier on the stylist's arm, hand, shoulder, and back. This can help keep you from getting tendonitis, carpal tunnel syndrome, and bursitis. What change the design are the shears' shape, the finger holes' spacing, and the swivels that are built in. One of the best things about hair shears is that they cut straight through hair without twisting or breaking it. That's why they're so sharp. To keep them in good shape, they should be sharpened often. These shears are what you need for an exact cut or a sharp line style.

Thinning Scissors | Texturizing Shears: Shape the Final Hairstyle

Texturizing shears have two-finger blades that are the same as hair-cutting shears. However, on one or both sides of the blades, they have mixing teeth that are shaped like combs. Thinning shears are like cutting shears, but one or both of their blades have "teeth" cut out of them. The stylist can cut the hair shorter, smooth out the lines, or give the ends some texture. There are also different cutting methods they can use to add bulk. Also, don't forget that they can help you tame and mix hair that is hard to work with.

Different types of shears can do different things, just like anything else. Some of the things that affect the result are:

- The number of teeth present
- How much are the teeth separated
- The teeth can be found on the blades or both

Although thinning shears are mostly used to make hair thinner, they can also be used to make hair fuller if they are used correctly. For short hairstyles with layers, you can also use this type of shear to smooth out the line where the layers meet and the cuts made by your clipper and shear.

Straight Razors | Styling & Texturizing Shears to Create Volume

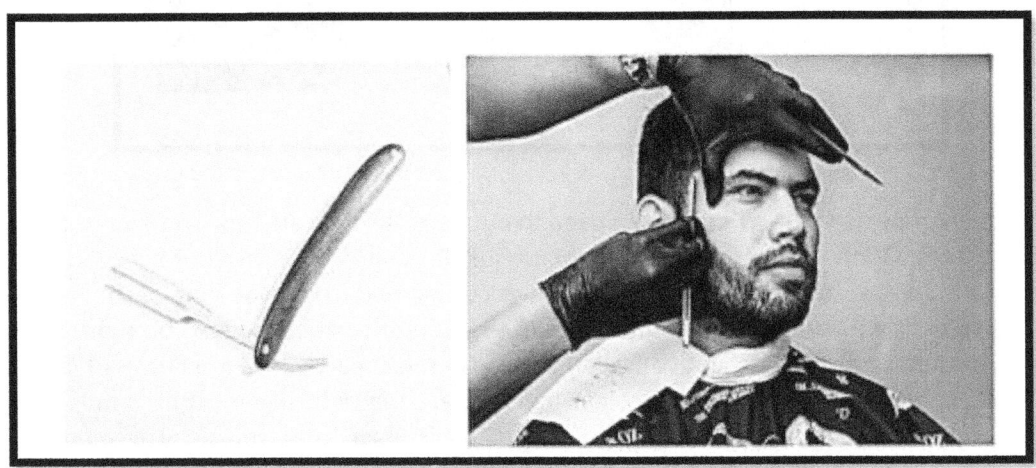

It was made so that this texturizing and feathering razor can give your hair style volume and layers. The design is better, and hair can't get in the way of the blade and guard while it cuts hair into tiny pieces that add volume and texture. Some people find that razor cuts are the best way to give their normal haircut more movement and structure. Shavers don't cut hair in straight lines, so this is the case. In the same way, they make the style look artificial and rough like it wasn't cut. You should tell your stylist that you don't like hard lines if you have any. One cool trick is to use scissors to cut the hair.

Then, go back to the hair and use razors to rough up the ends. That being said, depending on the cutting method used, a razor may still be able to make an exact cut. A styling razor, also called a straight razor, looks like a knife. They have different shapes, grinds, and handles to help you keep your hands from getting cut. Razor combs, on the other hand, are combs that have razors in them. Similar to thinning shears, they are used to make hair thinner when combs are used.

Hair Clipper Tools: Shorter & Cleaner Haircuts

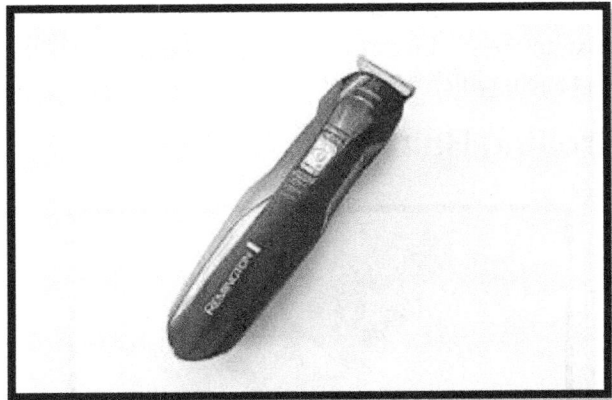

Hair clippers are often the most well-known tool used to cut men's hair. Clippers are mostly used to cut men's hair in styles like undercuts and buzz cuts, but women are also using them to make perfect end cuts that look like bobs or slow layers of hair. Clippers are often used to make very short haircuts like fades, military, and other styles. This may seem pretty obvious to some. They work like scissors, but they have two very sharp blades that move back and forth, cutting any hair in the passageway between them. The electric motor moves the blades from one side to the other in a straight line. The hair clipper is made up of two razors that are shaped like combs. Simply put the two blades on top of each other and slide them along to cut any hair in the middle. It works just like scissors.

Hair Trimming Tools: Perfecting the Final Hairstyle

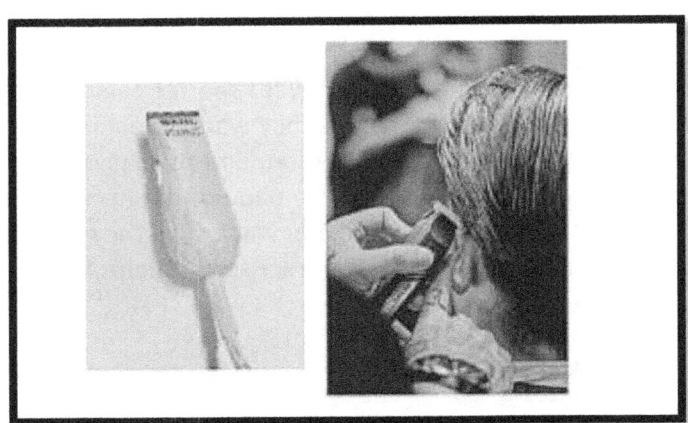

Hair clippers and hair trimmers go together surprisingly well. They look alike at first glance, but when you look more closely, you'll notice that trimmers have teeth that are narrower and less noticeable. It's the same with hair trimmers: they have two blades that cut hair. They can't cut through hair, though, because the blades aren't big enough. For exact and accurate work, the trimmers are made to smooth the edges of beards, sideburns, short cuts, hairlines, and necklines. The motor design is the most important part of the hair-cutting tool. The motor is linked to the piston, which has several small, sharp blades that look like comb teeth inside it. The blades move in a way that makes them touch, which lets them cut hair.

Hair Comb: Controlling Hair While Cutting

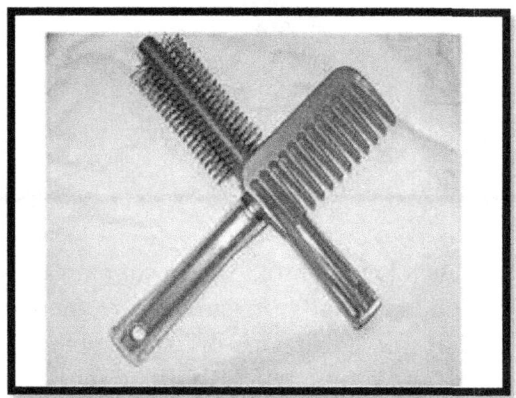

A comb has a shaft with teeth around it that are used to pull through the hair to remove hair, clean it, or style it. Combs have been used since ancient times. In Persia, they have been found in beautiful shapes in villages that are more than 5,000 years old. With this **home-styling razor comb**, you can get a close shave while cutting angles. It also changes the way your hair looks when you brush it. Shape, shave, cut, and reduce the hair. The razor comb has two edges and a regular hair comb on the other. It is simple and easy to use at home. This is because most barbers and stylists cut hair with scissors, which is why hair combings are so popular. One of the most common cuts barbers use is the scissor-over-comb cut. Mastering this method is important for making a wide range of haircuts for both men and women, especially for shorter hair. So, barbers can work close to the hairline and follow it to get the exact results they want. Clippers are good for cutting hair, but scissors make it easy to style your hair. People often do this to give their hair different forms or an effect that gets thinner on the sides and at the nape of the neck. You can style and shape the cut however you like by either cutting off the cut or smoothing the edges with thinner scissors. In this method, the comb does the same thing as the scissors: it helps lift the hair and shapes the cut.

Setting Up Your Workspace

Setting up your hair-cutting workspace is very important to make sure that both you and your client are safe, comfortable, and able to work quickly. An office that is well-designed and organized can make the process go more smoothly and be more fun. This can lead to better results and a more professional setting. For putting up the perfect hair-cutting workspace, here are the most important steps and things to think about:

Choosing the Right Location

Finding a good place to cut hair is the first thing that needs to be done to set up a hair-cutting workspace. The room should have a lot of natural light, as this helps you get a good idea of the hair's color, structure, and health. If there isn't enough natural light, make sure you have good lighting that can be adjusted to look like daylight. Instead of fluorescent lights, which can make shadows that don't look good, choose LED lights that give off clear, bright light.

Furniture and Layout

The way your workspace is set up should make it both useful and comfortable. Start with a strong hairdressing chair that can be raised, dropped, and tilted to fit clients of different heights and cutting angles. Patients should also be able to sit in the chair without pain because it should support their back and be padded. In front of the chair, put a big, full-length mirror. This lets clients see how their haircut is coming along and how it will look when it's done, which improves their experience and makes sure they're happy with the result. You can also use a smaller, hand-held mirror to show clients the back and sides of their heads. A strong, flat surface should be part of your workspace so that you can arrange your tools and goods. A beauty stand or a simple table with enough room for everything you need could be this. Make sure this area is at a good height so you don't have to bend or stretch too much.

Tools and Equipment

For cutting hair well, it's important to have the right tools and materials close at hand. Shears, razors, clippers, combs, brushes, and sectioning clips are some of the most common tools. Put these tools away in a way that makes them easy to get to and also keeps them safe to avoid accidents. For this, magnetic strips, tool belts, or drawer organizers can come in handy. To keep clippers and trimmers in good shape, clean and oil the blades regularly. To keep things clean, different combs and brushes that are used for different things should be cleaned after each use. To get clean cuts and keep hair from getting damaged, scissors and shears should be sharpened often.

Sanitation and Safety

In a salon, it's very important to keep the work area clean and germ-free. Use the right cleaning solution to disinfect all tools between clients. To keep things clean and comfortable, keep a stock of throwaway neck strips, capes, and blankets on hand. Keeping used tools in a closed bin and clean, sanitized tools in a different area helps keep them from getting dirty. To be safe, you should also keep electrical wires neatly arranged and out of the way so that people don't trip over them. Manage multiple tools that need electricity with power strips that have surge breakers. Also, make sure that all of your electrical equipment is in good shape.

Storage Solutions

Having good storage options is important for keeping your office clean and well-organized. You can store bigger things like hair dryers, style tools, and extra towels on shelves or closets. Organizers for drawers can help you keep small things like tools, clips, and combs in order and are easy to get to. Labeling storage bins can help you save time and avoid stress, especially when you're busy. You can quickly find what you need without having to dig through a bunch of boxes or bins if the containers are clear or have signs that are easy to read.

Client Comfort and Amenities

Making a place where clients feel welcome and at ease improves their general experience. Make sure the chair in the salon is nice and that customers can get water, books, or a place to charge their phones. Playing soft music in the background or giving the customer a choice of drinks can make them feel even more at ease.

Ergonomics and Personal Comfort

It's also important to you as a stylist that you're comfortable and healthy. Get an anti-fatigue mat that is comfortable to stand on. This will help your feet and back feel better. Make sure your tools are close at hand so you don't have to bend or stretch over and over again. During the day, make changes to your stance and workspace setting as needed to keep yourself from getting hurt or strained.

Personal Touches and Decor

By adding careful decorations and personal touches to your desk, you can make it feel friendlier. Pick a color scheme and decorations that show off your style and brand. Plants, art, and comfy chairs can make the room feel warm and inviting, which will make your clients want to sit back and enjoy their time in your chair.

Safety and Hygiene Practices
Sanitation of Tools and Equipment

Making sure that tools and equipment are clean is one of the most important parts of cleanliness in a hair salon. Every tool, like scissors, clippers, razors, combs, and brushes, needs to be cleaned and sanitized well between clients.

Here's how to keep things clean:

- **Cleaning**: After each use, wipe down tools to get rid of hair and other dirt. To get rid of any residue, wash them with soap and water.

- **Disinfection**: Soak tools in a disinfectant solution, like Barbicide, for as long as the directions say to. Make sure that every surface is fully covered.
- **Storage**: Put clean, dry tools away in a clean, dry case. Close the bottle before the next use to keep it from getting dirty.

Workstation Cleanliness

For keeping things clean, it's important to keep the whole workspace organized and clean. Clean these places after each client:

- **Chairs and Armrests**: The chairs and armrests should be cleaned with disinfectant wipes or sprays.
- **Mirrors and Surfaces**: Wipe down surfaces and mirrors to get rid of any smudges, hair, or product residue.
- **Floors**: After each client, sweep or clean the floor to get rid of hair. Use a disinfectant solution to mop the floor often.

Personal Hygiene

To set a good example for their clients and stop the spread of germs, stylists must keep up with good personal cleanliness. Some important habits are:

- **Hand Washing**: Use soap and water to wash your hands well before and after each client. If you can't find a place to wash your hands right away, use hand sanitizer.
- **Gloves**: When working with cuts or sores or doing other jobs that could come into touch with body fluids, wear disposable gloves.
- **Attire**: Put on clean, business-like clothes. You might want to use an apron or skirt that you can wash and dry often. If necessary, hair should be pulled back and neatly shaped so that it doesn't fall into the client's work area.

Client Protection

Client safety is very important. Take the following steps to make sure they are safe and comfortable:

- **Capes and Towels**: Give each client a clean cape and towel that has just been washed. You can also add an extra layer of cleanliness with disposable neck strips.
- **Neck Strips**: Wrap the client's neck in a new, single-use neck strip before putting the cape on it. This keeps the client's skin from coming into close touch with the cape.
- **Consultation**: Before starting any service, do a full review to find out if the person has any skin problems, allergies, or issues that might need special care.

Handling Chemicals and Products

To avoid mistakes and bad reactions, it's important to use hair products and chemicals carefully. Here are some rules to follow:
- **Labeling**: Make sure that all of the items you use are marked and kept in the right way. Keep hazardous chemicals in a different room with good airflow.
- **Usage Instructions**: For all hair products and chemicals, follow the directions on how to use them and how to get rid of them. Products should not be mixed unless told to do so.
- **Patch Tests**: To see if there are any allergic responses, do patch tests on new clients or when using new goods.

Electrical Safety

An area where hair is cut often has electrical tools like clippers, hair dryers, and curling irons. Follow these steps to keep electricity safety in check:
- **Regular Inspection**: Look for signs of wear and tear on cords and plugs regularly. Right away, replace any broken tools.
- **Avoid Overloading**: Don't use too many plugs at once. To keep track of many gadgets, use power strips with surge protection.
- **Safe Usage**: To avoid getting an electric shock, make sure tools are unplugged when not in use and out of water.

Ergonomics and Physical Safety

It is just as important to protect the stylist's health as it is to protect the clients. Use sensible techniques to avoid pressure and injury:
- **Proper Posture**: When you cut hair, make sure you keep a good stance. Place clients in chairs that can be adjusted so that they are at a comfortable height.
- **Supportive Footwear**: If you stand for long periods, wear shoes that are easy and support your feet.
- **Anti-Fatigue Mats**: Put anti-fatigue mats on the floor to soften it and make your feet and legs feel better.
- **Breaks**: Take breaks often to stretch and rest. This will lower your risk of getting injuries from repeated strain.

Emergency Preparedness

If you are ready for emergencies, you can keep small problems from turning into big ones. Make sure you have these things ready:
- **First Aid Kit**: Keep a first aid kit that is well-stocked somewhere that is easy to get to. Bandages, antiseptic wipes, and other simple emergency items should be in the kit.
- **Fire Safety**: Put in smoke alarms and always have a fire extinguisher nearby. Make sure that everyone who works there knows how to use it.
- **Emergency Contacts**: Put up a list of emergency contacts and what to do in a place where everyone can see it.

PART II
BASICS OF HAIR CUTTING

CHAPTER 2
UNDERSTANDING HAIR

Hair Anatomy

There is a hair shaft and a hair root in every hair. The hair that sticks out of the skin and can be seen is called the shaft. The root of the hair is in the skin and goes all the way to the lower layers of the skin. The hair shaft, which is made up of skin and fibrous tissue, wraps around it and is linked to a sebaceous gland. At the base of each hair shaft is a small muscle called an arrector pili that can make the hair stand up? Many nerves end at the hair follicle too. These nerves can feel even the tiniest draft and can tell when hair is moving. The hair root gets wider at the base of the hair and turns into a round hair bulb. Inside the bottom of the hair bulb is the hair papilla, which brings blood to the hair root. In the hair bulb, close to the papilla, new hair cells are always being made.

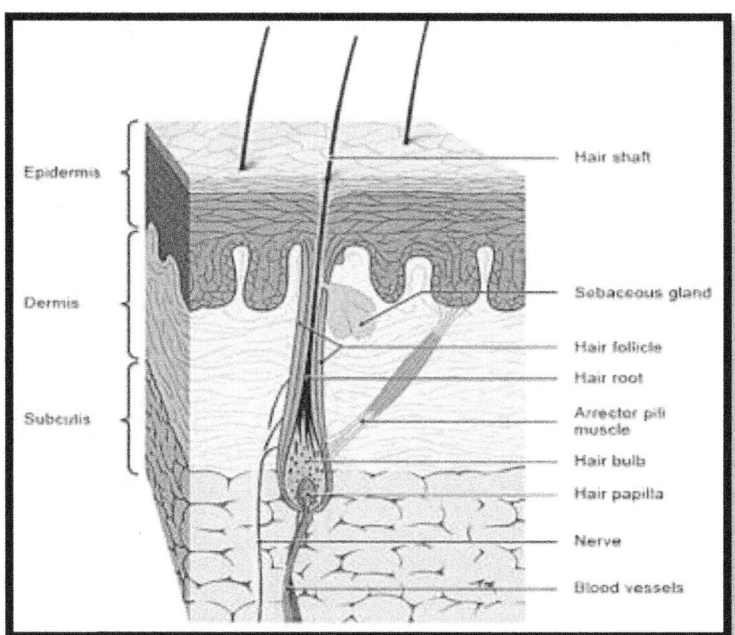

How does hair grow?

In the hair bulb, new cells are always being made. These cells get stiff and stick together. This group of rigid hair cells grows into a full strand of hair. The hair is slowly pushed up out of the skin because new tough cells keep sticking to it from below. One hair on your head grows at a rate of about 1 cm per month this way. Hair on the face, especially eyelashes, grows more slowly than hair on the body. How straight or curly it is will depend on how the hair is cut across. The skin is smooth and round hair grows right out of it. The hair will be curlier if the cross-section is more oval-shaped. The hair's color is based on how much melanin is in the hardened cells. There is a lot of difference between people in this, and it changes over time. As people age, their melanin levels drop, which means that more air gets trapped in their hair, which makes it lose its color and turn white. Then, the hair on their head goes gray or white, depending on what color their hair was to begin with and how many white hairs grow in.

Hair growth cycle

As long as there are new hair cells in the hair bulb, the hair will keep getting longer. The anagen phase is another name for this stage of growth. An average person has about 90% of their hair in this growth phase at any given time. Sometimes the growth phase lasts longer and sometimes shorter, depending on where on the body the hair grows. For example, hair on your head can grow to over a meter long if you don't cut it. For eyelashes, eyebrows, nose hair, and ear hair, the growth phase is very short. They can't get that long because hairs only grow for about 100 to 150 days. The hair root splits away from the papilla at the end of the growth phase. Then a process of change called catagen begins, which lasts for two to four weeks. When the hair is fully split from the papilla, the blood flow stops. This is the last phase of rest, which is also known as the telogen phase. Over time, the hair is pushed out of the skin and falls out. During this time, the body may rest for a few months. At the base of the "empty" hair shaft, new hair cells begin to multiply to make new hair. This starts the growth part of the hair growth cycle all over again.

Growth Patterns and Face Shapes

Hair Growth Patterns

Hair growth patterns show the way hair naturally grows and the direction it grows. When professionals know these patterns, they can work with the hair's natural movement to give clients cuts and styles that are easy to keep up and look great on them.

Key growth patterns include:

Cowlicks

Parts of hair that grow in a different way than the rest of the hair are called cowlicks. They usually look like a swirl or raised area. They often show up at the top, along the hairline, or at the back of the neck. When cutting and styling hair, stylists need to keep cowlicks in mind so that hair doesn't stick up or separate. Cowlicks can be managed by cutting the hair a little longer or using items to control the direction.

Hair Whorls

If you look at the top of your head, you can usually see hair growing in whorls. Some people have one or two whorls, which can change the way their hair grows and how much they have. When stylists know where hair whorls appear and how they behave, they can use these natural patterns to make styles that are balanced and orderly.

Natural Partings

The line where hair naturally splits is called a natural parting. It could be in the middle, off to the side, or even in a zigzag shape. Working with the natural split makes the look more natural and means you don't have to make as many styling changes. If a client wants a different parting, it's important to think about how flexible the hair is and which way it grows.

Hairline Patterns

It's the edge of the hair around your forehead, temples, and nape. Hairlines can be round, straight, or have widow's peaks. These patterns change how the face is framed and can help you choose the right bangs, layers, and edge styles. For example, if you have a widow's peak, you might need to cut and style your bangs differently to get a healthy look.

Face Shapes

Your face shape has a big impact on the hairstyles that will look best on you. There are five major face shapes: oval, round, square, heart, and diamond. Each has its traits.

Oval Face Shape

People with oval faces can wear their hair in a lot of different ways. Its dimensions are good, with a slightly bigger face and a slight shortening toward the chin. You can wear your hair in a lot of different ways, from short pixie cuts to long waves. The important thing is to bring out the natural balance without making the features look too busy.

Round Face Shape

People with round faces have big lips and a rounded chin. Their faces are soft and round. When you cut your hair to fit a round face, the goal is to make it look longer and narrower. Long layers, side parts, and styles that are high at the top can make the face look longer. By staying away from chin-length bobs and blunt bangs, you can keep your roundness from standing out.

Square Face Shape

A square face has sharp angles, a strong chin, and a wide forehead. To make the lines less harsh, hairstyles should add volume and curves. A more oval shape can be achieved with soft, layered cuts, waves, and side-swept bangs. Styles that end at the chin should be avoided because they can make you look square.

Heart Face Shape

A heart-shaped face has a wide forehead, high cheeks, and a chin that is thin and points outward. The goal is to make the body look more balanced by making the jaw area bigger and the face wider. This can be done with long layers, side parts, and chin-length bobs. Stay away from short, blunt bangs that make your forehead stand out.

Diamond Face Shape

People with a diamond face shape have wide cheeks and a narrow forehead. If your forehead and jaw are narrow, your hairstyle should try to smooth them out while drawing attention to your cheeks. This shape can look better with chin-length bobs, shoulder-length cuts, and styles that tuck behind the ears. Side hairstyles that are too full can make your face look wider, so stay away from them.

CHAPTER 3
BASIC TECHNIQUES

Holding and Positioning Tools

1. **Blunt Cutting**

When you blunt cut, you cut the hair across, making an edge that is clean and even. People often use this method to make bobs, one-length cuts, and bang trims.
- **Method**: Make sure the hair is tight between your fingers. Sharp scissors should be used to cut the hair straight across. Use your fingers to help you keep the line straight.

2. **Point Cutting**

Point cutting gives hair volume and softens the edges of a haircut, making it more moveable and less bulky.
- **Method**: Use the tips of the scissors to make small, vertical cuts into the ends of a piece of hair that you have held between your fingers. This gives the hair a more natural, curled look.

3. **Layering**

Cutting hair at different lengths to add volume, movement, and shape is called layering. Many people use it to give their hair more body and depth.
- **Method**: To cut hair, hold pieces at an angle and cut them along that angle. How long and how deep the layers are will depend on how you hold the hair.

4. **Texturizing**

Texturizing methods add depth and lessen the thickness of hair, making it easier to style and giving it a more natural look.
- **Method**: Cut the hair into different lengths and thinner sections with texturizing shears or razors.

5. **Thinning**

Thinning hair is to make thick hair easier to handle by reducing its thickness.
- **Method**: Use thinning shears to cut through the hair, taking out some strands but leaving others whole. This helps to cut down on bulk without changing the length.

Holding and Positioning Tools

Scissors

1. **Holding Scissors**
   - Your ring finger should go in the top ring and your thumb should go in the bottom ring. To hold on to the scissors, rest your index and middle fingers on the shank.
   - To make exact moves, make sure your grip is strong but not tight.
2. **Positioning Scissors**
   - Place the scissors so that the blade goes easily through the hair when you cut it. To make sure the cut is even, keep the blades straight to the hair you are cutting.

- Keep the length and angles the same by using your fingers as a guide.

Combs

1. **Holding the Comb**
   - Use your stronger hand to hold the comb and move it with your thumb and fingers.
   - Use the comb's wide teeth for detangling and its fine teeth to cut and smooth hair precisely.
2. **Positioning the Comb**
   - When you section hair, put the comb close to the head to make clean, even parts.
   - Lift and hold parts of hair with the comb while you cut them. This will keep the tension even so the cut is smooth.

Clippers

1. **Holding Clippers**
   - Take a tight hold of the clippers by putting your thumb on top and your fingers under it to keep it steady.
   - To move the clippers easily, keep your grip loose.
2. **Positioning Clippers**
   - When you use clippers, start at the base of the neck or the sides and work your way up, following the hair's normal growth pattern.
   - To get the length and mix you want, use different guard sizes.

Razors

1. **Holding Razors**
   - Use a strong grip on the razor, with your thumb on one side and your fingers on the other.
   - Make sure your grip lets you move smoothly and with control.
2. **Positioning Razors**
   - If you want soft, feathery edges, hold the razor at an angle to the hair.
   - Do not cut too much hair at once; use light pressure.

Techniques for Different Hair Types

1. **Straight Hair**
- For clean, straight lines, use blunt cutting.
- Layering and texturizing can give your hair movement and keep it from looking flat.
2. **Wavy Hair**
- Point-cutting can make natural waves look better.
- Layering helps define the wave design and get rid of bulk.
3. **Curly Hair**

- Cut your hair while it's still dry to see how it naturally curls.
- Point cutting and texturizing can help you get more curls and less bulk.

4. **Coily Hair**
- Sharp scissors are best for making clean cuts.
- Do not thin your hair too much, as this can make it frizzy and uneven.

Ergonomics and Posture

1. **Standing Position**
- Step forward and back so that your feet are shoulder-width apart.
- To prevent pain, keep your back straight and bend your knees if you need to.
2. **Hand and Arm Position**
- Do not bend your arms. Keep them straight. This will keep them from getting hurt.
- It's better to use your arms and shoulders instead of just your wrists to control your moves.
3. **Client Position**
- Make sure the client's chair is at a comfortable height for both cutting and styling.
- Make sure the client's head is in the right place for each section you're working on.

Sectioning Hair

Why is it important to section hair for haircutting?

Here are the three most important reasons to know how to section hair for haircutting:

1. Easy handling while cutting or styling hair.
2. Application of hair products like conditioner or color in the same way every time.
3. Damage avoidance and better hair control.

What are the main steps in sectioning hair for haircutting?

Sectioning hair is an important part of hairstyling that you need to do to get exact and regular results. It's important to have clean, dry hair that is completely detangled before you start sectioning. Pick a starting place for the sectioning based on how you want to style it, like the back of the neck, the crown, or somewhere else that makes sense. Make a clean part in the hair with a rat-tail comb, making sure it is straight and well-defined. As soon as the first part is done, use clips or ties to keep one side of the hair out of the way. Keep parting the hair carefully, taking into account natural splits such as the center part, side parts, or ear-to-ear sections.

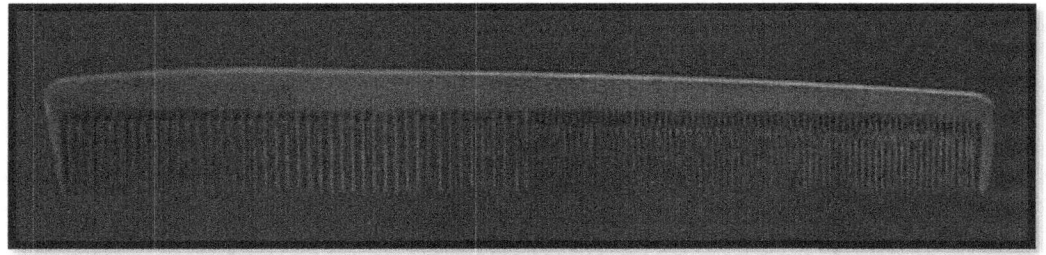

As you work on each area, tie back the hair that hasn't been worked on yet to keep your workspace neat and easy to use. This keeps the hair from blending, so you can work on one area at a time. Working through each part in a planned way gives you more control and makes sure the results are the same every time. It's important to make sure that the parts are the right size for the style or method you are using. For accuracy, smaller parts are often better, while bigger sections may be better for faster use. You can make the styling go more smoothly by using the hair's natural splits and growth patterns as you go through the process. Check and re-evaluate your parts from time to time to make sure they are even and have clear edges. As you go along, making any changes that are needed improves the quality and regularity of the final haircut.

Things to Avoid While Sectioning Hair

When sectioning hair, hairstylists should try to avoid making these mistakes:

1. **Uneven Sections:** Don't make uneven sections because it can make your haircut or style look bad. To keep sections separate and in order, use clips or hair ties.
2. **Too Large Sections:** It can be hard to handle and style the hair correctly when you work with too big of sections. For accuracy, smaller pieces that are easier to work with are usually better.
3. **Inadequate Clipping:** Make sure that each section is properly held in place with hair ties or clips. When you don't clip properly, hair from different sections can mix, which can make the results uneven.
4. **Sectioning Wet Hair Incorrectly:** If you're working with wet hair, don't section it in a way that lets water fall on other parts. This could make hair color or style tools less effective, which would change the result.
5. **Rushing:** Don't cut or style your hair quickly when you're sectioning it. Take your time. In a hurry, you might make mistakes and get an uneven result. Don't rush hairstyling; it's an art.
6. **Inconsistent Tension:** Keep the tension even while sectioning, especially when you're cutting or styling. Uneven lengths and textures can happen when tension isn't kept the same.

Sectioning the Hair: 3 Methods

Sectioning the Hair for Haircutting

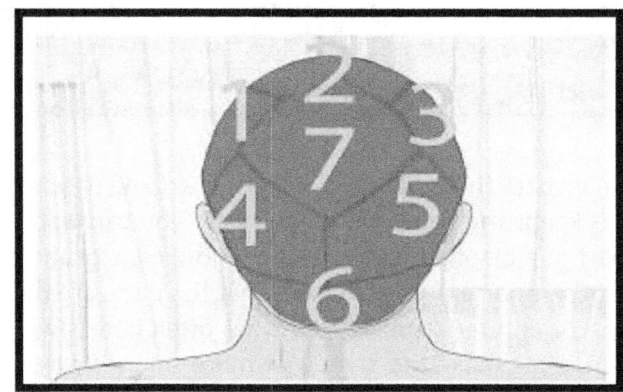

- By sectioning the hair, you will achieve a clean and neat style of cut
- When it comes to haircutting, you should section it in a way that makes the result even and perfect. So that can happen, the hair needs to be split up in this way:
- You will have better control when cutting your hair if you divide it into seven sections: the top, the right, the left, the right crown, the left crown, the right nape, and the left nape.

Step 1: Sectioning the front
- To section the front of the hair, pick out and part the hair above one ear from one side to the other side in the same place above the other ear with a comb. Separate the front part of the hair from the rest of it, and then comb the hair that you just separated forward.

Step 2: Separate the hair on top of the head
- Take out the top third of the hair that was pulled forward and sectioned in the last step. To make the sectioned hair on top of the head tighter, twist and clip it with a butterfly clip.

Step 3: The right and left side of the hair
- In a way similar to the last step, use the butterfly clip to keep the right and left sides of the sectioned hair together.

Step 4: Partitioning the hair in the back of the head
- To make a clean and even separation of the back hair, start with a piece of hair in the middle of one ear and run it across to the same spot behind the other ear. For the crown of the head, the top part of the sectioned hair will be used.

Step 5: Dividing the right and left crown of the hair
- The top part of the hair that was split in the previous step needs to be split down the middle into the right and left crowns. A butterfly clip can also be used to pull these two sections of hair together.

Step 6: Creating the nape-sectioned hair

- Once the right and left crowns have been separated, gather the remaining hair air at the bottom, which is toward the nape section, and do the same thing you did for the crowns. Use a butterfly clip to hold the sectioned hair in place.

Sectioning Of the Hair for Hair Rollers

- If you divide your hair into sections before using hair rollers, you will get good results.
- As we already said, each hairstyle needs a certain way of sectioning to keep it balanced. Before you use a hair roller, you need to divide your hair into three sections: the crown, the nape, and the top of your head. In the next steps, these parts will be split up even more and rolled into place:

Step 1: Sectioning into three parts
- With a comb or pick, divide the hair into three sections. The top of the head should go from the top of one ear to the bottom of the other. The second section should go from the middle of one ear to the bottom of the other. The third section should be the hair at the very bottom. This sectioned hair will not only make rolling your hair easier but will also make sure that the curls fall in the best place.

Step 2: Further sectioning the sectioned hair
- The hair that has already been sectioned needs to be split up even more. Using a comb or pick, make a 2-inch wide strip in the middle of your hair that includes hair from your forehead and hair from your forehead to the back of your head, or the nape of your neck. Clip this strip in place with a butterfly clip.

Step 3: Sectioning the remaining hair
- Make left and right ponytails with the hair that's left over. You can use either a butterfly clip or a rubber band to hold these pieces of hair together.

Step 4: Sectioning to the size of the hair roller
- Pull the hair away from the head after rolling the sections into place. The roller should be tied together and rolled toward the head. After the hair has been tightly rolled, it needs to be held in place with hairpins.
- For sections of hair, like the hair at the nape of the neck, the fourth step is what you should do. After the hair is rolled up, it should be left on for two to three hours or overnight with

a shower cap or bed cap on top. This will help keep the hair from getting damaged or frizzy.

Sectioning For Hair Straightening

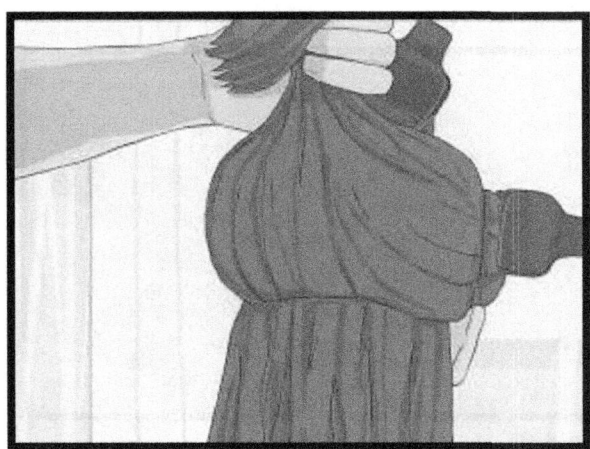

- When you straighten your hair, you should split it into three sections, just like when you roll your hair. The only different thing is where the sectioning is placed. It is easier to get the best results if you divide the hair into three layers or parts. The 3 layer sectioning method does not work for all hair types, though. If the person has thicker hair, it can be split into four or six layers, depending on what they want.

Step 1: Sectioning into 3 layers
- Use a butterfly clip to separate the hair into three layers: the left and right hair, and the top part of the head.

Step 2: Defining the sectioned hair portions
- Put your thumbs behind your ears and pull your top hair up. Then, slide your thumbs across the back of your head until they meet in the middle. This will give your hair more shape and straightness. To make the top layer, twist the sectioned hair and clip it in place.

Step 3: Sectioning the sides of the hair
- Do the steps above again to separate and fix the top hair's left and right sides.

Step 4: Straightening the hair
- You can leave the bottom of the hair free and start making it straight from there. For the best results, take small pieces of hair and straighten them over twice. Once the bottom action is fully straight, remove the clips from the other section of hair and straighten it the same way. This means taking a lock of hair and straightening it until it is straight.

Angles and Elevation

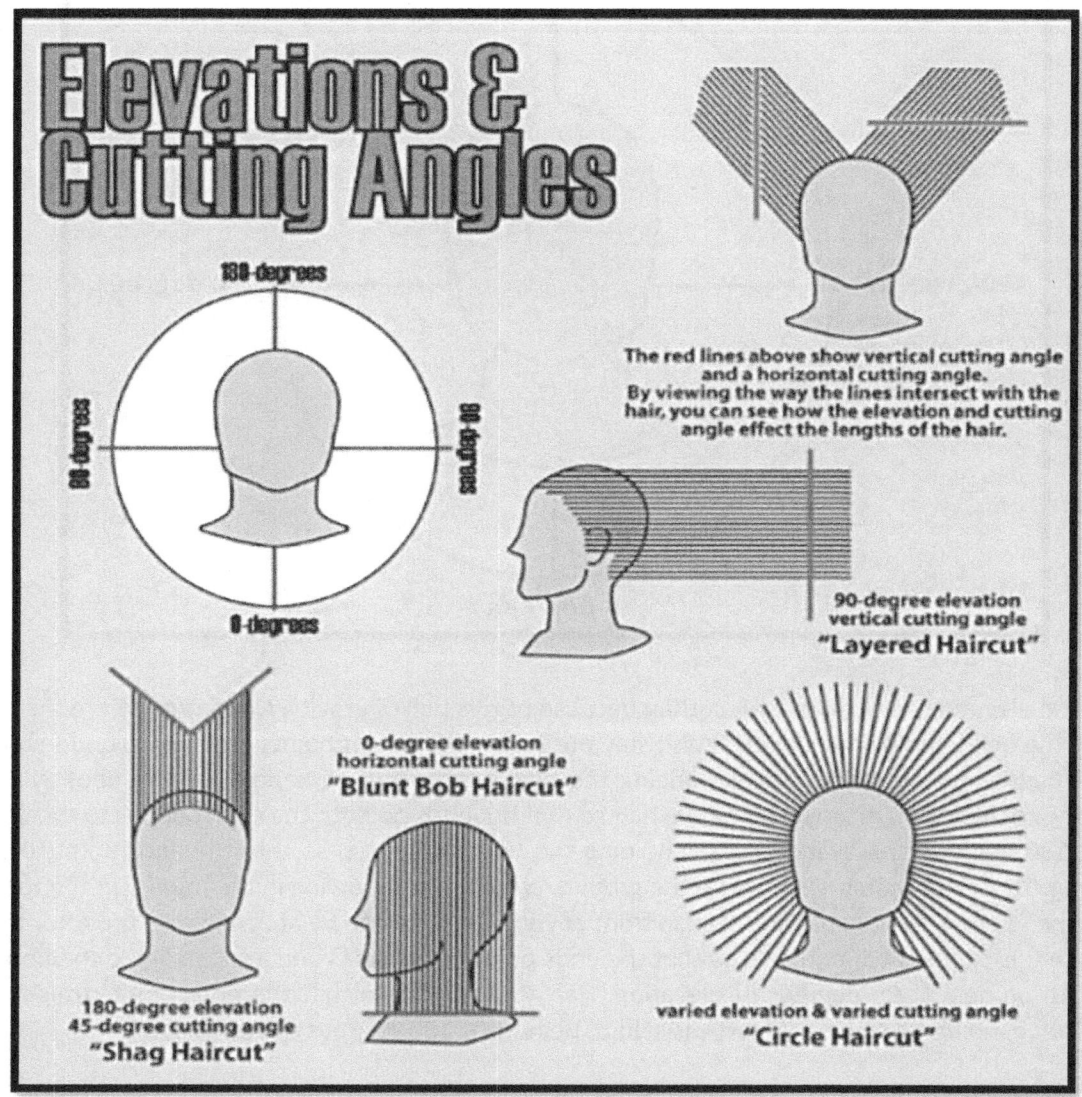

Elevation

There is a pull to everything in the world. The end of a piece of string that you hold will hang down and point to the ground. The string's length and weight will make the endpoint down, even if you hold it so that it comes out from between your fingers and starts to point up. More or less, hair always acts the same way. Hair will eventually end up with the ends pointing down, but this will depend on its texture, length, and wave pattern. For some hair types, especially coarse and kinky hair, this might need a lot more length than the hair can reach.

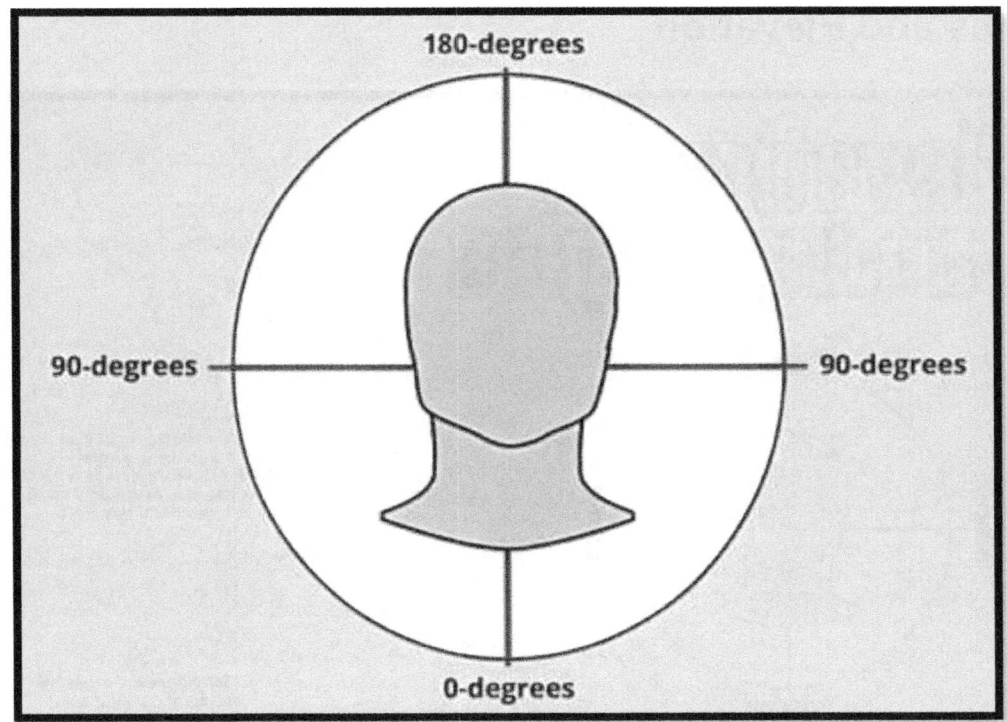

We use elevation as a part of hair cutting because of this pull of gravity. No matter where the hair is on the head, the degrees of elevation stay the same. The height points are easy to understand: Zero degrees of elevation means hanging the hair so that the ends point to the floor. Ninety degrees of elevation means holding the hair so that the ends point to the side, parallel to the floor. And 180 degrees of elevation means holding the hair straight up so that the ends point to the ceiling. Thus, hair that is lying flat on the ground, whether it is growing in the middle of the top of your head or on the side of your head in front of your ear, is said to be at zero elevation. After that, hair that is combed out and held so that the ends point to the sides and are parallel to the floor is said to be held at 90 degrees of elevation. Hair that is held so that the ends point straight up overhead, no matter where it starts, is said to be held at 180 degrees of elevation.

Angles

Angle is another part of haircutting that a lot of people get mixed up with. When a stylist talks about the angle, they're talking about where the scissors are in their hand concerning something else, usually the floor. Some people naturally understand these ideas. When they look at a haircut, they can "see" where the cuts need to go and what angles and heights are needed to make them. For some, it takes longer to learn how these different roles work together and change how the cut turns out.

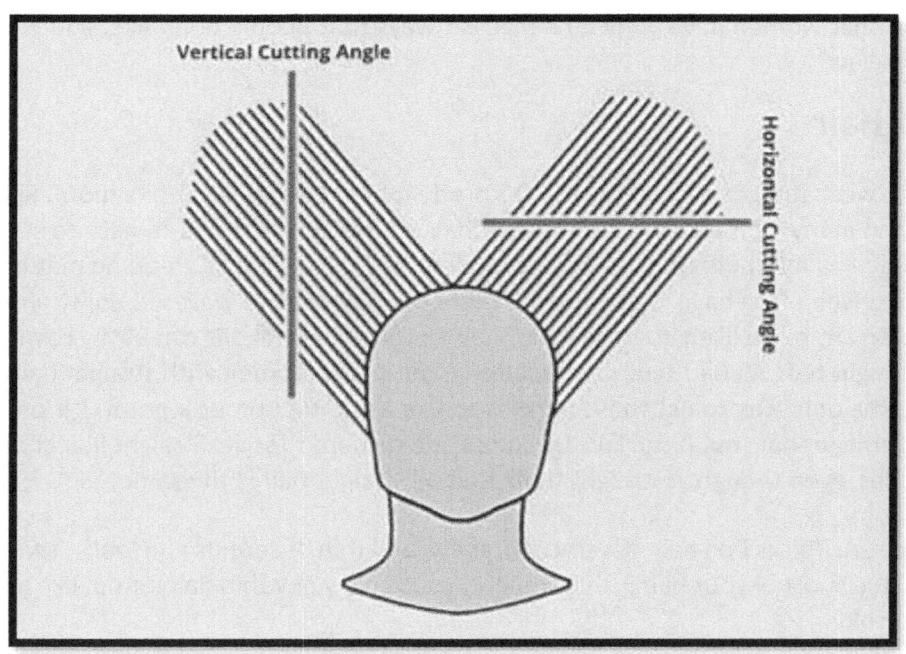

From style to style and even hair type to hair type, the angles used to cut hair will be very different. So, there's no real reason to make things more difficult than they need to be. As long as the cutting directions don't say otherwise, "the hair is cut at X-degree angle" means that the scissors are held at an angle of X degrees to the floor. To cut at a 45-degree angle, for example, you would hold the scissors halfway between being completely horizontal (flat on the floor) and completely vertical (upright against the floor). A stylist can make a lot of different looks by using angles and elevation. Most of the time, the cut will be less layered and flat if the slope is low and the cutting angle is straight. Changing the cutting angle and slope will make the hair have more layers if you do either or both of them. For example, a classic blunt bob is cut with the hair held at 0 degrees of elevation and cut horizontally. A long-layered "shag" haircut is made with the hair held at 180 degrees of elevation and cut at a 45-degree angle to make layers that get shorter as you move from the middle of the head to the edges. Each style and cutout is just a different take on the theme, which is made by mixing angles and elevation in different ways around the head.

WOMEN HAIR TYPES

The hair of one woman and that of the other is very different, even though we both have it and sometimes it looks very much the same. The type of hair we are born with is completely determined by our genes, just like our natural hair color. In other words, you can't change the type, texture, or structure of your hair. You can, however, make the most of what you've been given by treating it as well as you can. Along with that, you should take precautions to make sure that your hair stays strong and safe as you go through everyday life. Learn about the different types of hair that women have, why it changes in ways that people don't like, and what you can do about it below!

Straight Hair

Being able to wear straight hair is the best. It's pretty much ready to go after a morning brush. One reason why so many women want this type of hair so much is that it is so easy to style. You can wear your hair in a lot of different ways, and straight hair usually looks great, no matter how long, short, or in between. You have straight hair if there are no bends or waves in the strands. Straight-haired women are more likely to have "oily" hair because natural oils can easily cover the whole strand of straight hair. All hair types are beautiful, but many women with straight hair want curls and waves. The only way to get these looks is to use a curling iron or a perm. It's pretty easy to take care of straight hair, but it can lack thickness and be hard to style. Straight hair comes in three different styles, even though you might think that all straight hair is the same.

- **Type 1A:** This is fine hair. It's smooth, shiny, and thin. It sounds and looks "sweet," but it's still too short. If your hair is this straight, you can try any thin haircut tip, like a layered cut and color.

- **Type 1B:** Type 1B straight hair is a little thicker than fine hair. It can be used better because it has a longer range. Many beautiful, classy hairstyles, like an updo or a slicked-back look, look great on women with Type 1B hair. Not so thick that it's hard to style, and not so thin that you can see a lot of skin.

- **Type 1C:** Type 1C hair is the roughest and thickest of all straight hair types. It can be tough to work with, and curling it is the hardest part. Styles that are easy to do with this type of hair are long, layered cuts. Some things need to be done to keep short cuts in good shape.

Wavy Hair

A lot of people look great with their hair wavy. A lot of lucky women who naturally have this look did hit the hair jackpot. Soft, wavy hair always looks good, even if you've been running your hands through your hair a thousand times during a stressful day or are walking home in gale-force winds. Also, soft waves are great for almost any braid, updo, bun, or chignon because of the way their structure and natural volume make hair look. There is no doubt that wavy hair has curly strands, but they are curled in a way that looks more like an "S" than a spiral. Many people with wavy hair

have both straight and curled hair at the same time. Wavy hair is usually neither too oily nor too dry. Like straight hair, wavy hair comes in different styles. What kind of wavy hair does it have?
Type 2a: Many women with straight hair use a curling iron and a lot of hair cream to get the look of "beachy hair," which is what type 2a wavy hair has. The hair shaft in Type 2a is slightly bent, and it doesn't get as frizzy as other hairstyles.

For best results, cut this type of hair so that it's about shoulder-length. This method works best for fine hair.
Type 2b: Type 2b hair waves are a bit tighter and clearer than type 2a waves. Type 2b waves can get frizzy, but the right hair product can make it easier to deal with.

Type 2c: If you have type 2c wavy hair, it might look like you have curled hair because the curls may be loose and spiral around each other. A "healthy hair day" means that your waves are probably getting a lot of praise. But frizz can be your worst enemy.

Curly Hair

You don't see as many people with real curly hair as you might think. Corkscrew curls that spring back up when pulled straight are what make this type of hair different from its wavy cousins, which have soft waves. Curly hair looks great, but it takes a lot of love and care to keep it in good shape. It can be hard to enjoy this style of hair because of the knots that are hard to get out or the time it takes to dry air. On the plus side, the curls that come out of a simple ponytail look amazing. There are a lot of women who spend a lot of time, effort, and money trying to get their beautiful curls cleaned out. Curly hair has more "real" curves than wavy hair. Curly-haired women might have tight curls or ringlets. Like other hair types, curly hair comes in different styles that depend on how thick and big the curls are. Curly hair is dryer than straight hair, so you don't need to wash it every day. When you go to a hairstylist, make sure they have a lot of experience cutting curly hair. You can get a lot of different styles and cuts.

Type 3a: Type 3a curly hair is the best because it has the biggest and loosest curls. Because the curls are so big, it's the easiest to work with, but it does frizz easily like all curly hair does.

Type 3b: If you have curly hair type 3b, you have ringlets that other women wish they had. It's not too thin or too thick for your hair. With the right moisturizer, you can keep your curls looking great.

Type 3c: Curls Type 3c hair has a mix of loose and tight corkscrew curls. For people with type 3c curls, the curls are likely to be rough and not as smooth as you'd like. If you use the right product, your curls might become a little less curly.

Coily Hair

Now for a very important message: hair that is coily looks beautiful! There's no reason to hide those pretty locks. Without a doubt, oily hair is the best when it comes to taking care of it. Because true coils don't have as many cuticle layers as straight or softly wavy hair, air is naturally bad for them. Put away the curling iron and blow dryer and enjoy the look of your hair as it is. As you can see, frizzy hair needs a lot of moisture to stay springy. Use deep conditioners, leave-in conditioners, and lotions in your hair care routine to see results. Coily hair, also called kinky hair, is a type of curled hair. Women with coily hair may have curls that are shaped like "Z"s and "S." Women with curly hair often cut it short because they don't want to deal with it or are afraid of what will happen if they do. But many styles look great. Like other types of hair, coily hair comes in three different styles.

Type 4a: The hair in type 4a coily is fine and can look "wiry" at times. This kind of coily hair looks rough because the s-curls are so tight. Women with Type 4a curls may not want their curls to stay the way they are but put the dryer down and let the curls do what they want to do.

Type 4b: Type 4a coils have a Z-shaped pattern instead of an S-shaped design. Because it is thinner and less dense, this type of coily hair feels soft when you touch it.

Type 4c: Different types of coily hair look a lot alike. The main difference is that type 4c hair has more z-shaped curls, which gives the whole head of hair a shape (like an afro). When you have coily hair, it's often better to let the curls be as they are than to try to tame or control them.

Thick Hair

A lot of us want thick hair more than anything else. There is no way to get this kind of hair if you were not born with it. It's best to start with thick, coarse hair for many cuts and styles. If you're a lucky woman with this hairstyle, enjoy it! A lot of hair makes most people think their hair is thick. That might be true for all women, but it's not the same. Not sure how thick or thin your hair is? You could ask your stylist, but a quick way to find out is to put a strand of hair between your thumb and fingers. If you can feel the strand, you have thick hair. Grab a strand of hair like you're about to put it up in a clip. This is another easy way to tell if your hair is thick. Your hair is thick, and you can barely see your head. Women with thick hair can also have hair that is straight, curly, or wavy. Many women have different combinations of thickness and texture in their hair, so there are no "rules" about what styles to wear. Women all over the world often wish they had thick hair, but it can be hard to handle and feel heavy. Cutting your hair into layers or a bob will bring out the best in your thick hair while also making it easier to curl and style.

Fine Hair

People often think that having fine hair is a curse instead of a gift. Okay, that's not always the case. Let's start with the bad news: Not like with thick hair, you can't change the way your hair looks. On the other hand, you can do a lot of things to thin hair to make it look fuller! You can blow-dry your hair over a circle brush, try out the curling iron, do a stacked wash, use bulking shampoo, and play around with hair products. The best thing about it is that you won't have to spend as much on beauty items as your friends do. There aren't many style products that should be part of your daily hair care routine because they make your hair oilier and flatter. Carefully stop brushing your hair too much too! Don't spend hours brushing your hair; it won't help if you have thin hair. Also, some cuts and styles don't look as good on thick hair as they do on fine hair. Like, a long bob is the best cut for fine hair.

Wispy bangs always look great! You can do all of the "tests" we talked about earlier to find out if you have thin hair, which is sometimes called "normal" hair. If your results are the opposite of someone with thick hair, you have thin hair. People with thin hair don't necessarily have a lot of hair loss or go completely bald. It just makes you look like you have a lot less hair on your head than you do. There are hundreds of hair-thickening products and recipes out there that claim to make your hair thicker. Be careful with any products that say they can do that. Your genetics may cause your hair to be thin, but you can try to make it thicker by living a healthy life and eating a well-balanced diet. Vitamins may also help. If you want to try some natural home treatments to make your hair thicker, you can, but keep in mind that they don't always work. Many women with thin hair look great with a layered cut with some color added. This style makes the hair look thick. To get the most out of your hair, use rich oils on it and take extra care of it at night. Your hair will stay safe and tangled if you sleep on a soft scarf or a silk pillow.

Reasons for Hair Type Changes

There are many reasons why hair patterns can change. They don't have to be signs of getting older, and they usually aren't just linked to getting older.

- **Hormonal Changes**: The most obvious reasons for changes in hormones that can cause hair changes are puberty, pregnancy, changes that happen after giving birth, menopause, and hormonal birth control that goes on and off. If you notice a change in your hair type and can rule out the other reasons listed above, you might want to get your thyroid checked. In particular, hair loss is often caused by a low thyroid, which many women experience as they age. In any case, hair changes that you can't explain should make you pay attention and maybe make an appointment for a full check-up at the doctor.
- **Lifestyle Nutrition:** This is one of the most common (and easy to fix) reasons why hair changes, especially hair loss. Not getting enough of certain minerals, especially iron, could be a big reason why you lose your hair early (or at all). Eating right and working out regularly will keep your hair healthy and shiny.
- **Other Causes**: Stress is another common reason why hair health goes down, and it can also cause hair loss. Especially long times of high stress can be bad for your hair, whether it's from relationship problems, problems at work, or just life throwing too many things at you at once. Stress-related hair loss can happen up to three months after the stressful time, and you may still see the effects long after the stressful things have been taken care of.

If you're sick, your hair's color, length, or structure may also change. Loss of hair or changes in hair color is signs or side effects of many diseases and medicines. Take good care of your locks if your health allows it to help you feel better and avoid or lessen the obvious signs of your problems. Too much sunshine and too many chemical treatments are two things that can hurt your hair. If you tend to (over)use blow dryers, straightening or curling irons, bleaches, and other similar tools, you might want to take a step back and let your hair heal if it starts to split, thin, or fall out.

MEN'S HAIR TYPES

Men's hair comes in 4 different styles, and you need to make sure that your grooming and style work with your hair type. Here is the coolest guide to the guy haircut you can find on the Internet. Men may have four kinds of hair. Do you know which one you have? Why do you need to know this to get cool haircuts and hairstyles?

Straight Hair

As you just read, straight hair is hair that comes straight out of the scalp. Because hair naturally wears down and is styled with tools like combs and heat, if enough length is grown in a straight lock, there will be some small curving. The bending will be very light, though, and you'll only be able to see it when the hair is long—i.e., more than 6 inches long. To make it easy for you to find your hair, I added a length mark 3 inches from the head to this guide. You can use this mark to tell if your hair is straight or not. If, from the head to the first three inches of its length, your hair doesn't bend, you have straight hair. If it does bend, you should move on to the other styles to properly identify your hair type, as it may be wavy, twisted, or kinky. Guys with straight hair, like Tom Cruise, Brad Pitt, and our friend Justin Bieber, are examples. Brad Pitt with his hair straight and styled in a shaggy way. Brad Pitt has changed his hair a lot throughout his work to make himself look even better, and who wouldn't?

Advantages vs. the drawbacks of straight hair

One of the best things about straight hair is that it is the easiest to shape and style. If you want to copy Justin Bieber's hair fringe flip from back when we couldn't tell if he was a boy or a girl (we still can't, but at least with his brush-up hairstyle, we can believe he has some XY in his DNA), straight hair often falls with only a few inches of length.

Hairstyles for straight hair

Men with straight hair look best with short hairstyles that can be styled into different shapes and long hair that is between the jaw and shoulder length. If you have straight hair, a Faux Hawk that needs a short haircut and the above hairstyle brush-up both work pretty well. For the brush-up, make sure to use a hairdryer.

Hair products for straight hair

If your hair is straight, the best things to use for your form are hair wax, pomade, hair mousse, hair spray, and a hair dryer. You can get a lot of other hair treatments for guys, but these five should be your mainstays. This is also important if your hair is medium length or longer (more than 2 inches). You should use a daily conditioner at least once a week.

Wavy Hair

Wavy hair is hair that bends a little as it comes out of the hair shaft. When it's long enough, it looks like waves, which is how it got its name. Some people think that short hair (up to 1.5 inches) is straight hair, so you should wait until your hair is at least 3 inches long to be sure of your haircut. When you look at your hair, if it bends in the first three inches but doesn't coil up all the way, then it is wavy.

Advantages vs. wavy hair disadvantages

It could be said that guys should have wavy hair. Wavy hair can be styled in the same simple way as straight hair, but it also has the natural texture of curlier hairstyles. When worn at medium lengths, wavy hair can look like a real lion's mane. When hair is long and wavy, it always looks good. It doesn't have that strong "look at me" twisted and kinky hair look (trust me, after a while, women will stop asking you about your hair care routine).

Hairstyles for wavy hair

If you have wavy hair, you can try medium-length hairstyles like side parts and messy hairstyles. Also, wavy shoulder-length hair will look pretty cool, and wavy hair can often look nice during the whole growth stage to get to shoulder length. This isn't the case for coiled or kinky hair, which I call the "awkward stage" because these hairstyles usually look awkward or funny during the growth stage to shoulder length (though this won't be the case).

Hair items for wavy hair

A leave-in conditioner should be used most days of the week on your curly hair, even though it is wavy. Also, wavy hair needs a regular conditioner more often, and if your hair is longer than 2 inches, you should use a regular conditioner a few times a week. However, if your hair is medium-length or longer, you should have a good style cream on hand for when it looks frizzy and to better define and shine your waves. You can still use hair waxes and pomades. You can also use a hair dryer, but make sure it has a diffuser attached to it. Get the same hair dryer that you used for straight hair, but add the diffuser. The diffuser is attached to the hairdryer's tip with a clip and helps the heat spread.

Coiled Hair

Most of you, but not all, would say "coiled hair" when you hear the phrase "curly hair." Coiled hair grows in coil-like shapes that are easy to spot. Because it curls, wavy hair often grows in a coiled shape. However, because it takes so long to finish a coil, wavy hair looks "wavy" instead of coiled. Still, when hair is curled, the distance to the coil is shorter, which changes its shape. Coiled hair can make coils in the first two inches of growth. When hair is wavy, you can only see the first three inches of curls. But when hair is coiled, the first two inches of hair will be marked by clear coils. Troy Polamalu, David Bisbal, and indeed yours (aka "that" guy with the awesome profile... kinda, sorta, maybe...) are all guys with coiled hair. A problem that many men with coiled hair will think about is whether to grow their hair long or let it stay short.

Advantages vs. drawbacks of coiled hair

Coiled hair that has been cared for properly (note the word "properly") would stand out in a good way. Some people have defined curls, also known as coils. Medium to long curls attract kids like honey attracts flies (or, as the songs say, like a "milkshake taking all the boys to the yard"). I can tell you that. Girls with wavy hair want to ask you the same hair care questions over and over again, but girls with straight hair want to play doctor and nurse with you. Shapely, shiny coils give off a very sexual vibe, and as a dude, it would be a major crime if you didn't use this swag ability. The Issue? It's hard to have nice-looking coils (i.e., an amazing mane), and most men with coils don't know how to take care of their hair, so they look more like Sideshow Bob or Will Ferrell than like Fabio with curled hair. One big problem with coiled hair is that it's hard to style, especially if you don't take good care of it or groom it, which is the case for most guys with curly hair. When styling your curly hair, you should always use a broad-tooth comb. You can also style your coils with your fingers. But for the love of Bambi, don't use a regular comb! I still see this with curly guys who don't know why their hair looks like tumbleweed (hint: 90% of the time, it's the comb). Coiled hair is indeed hard to style, but it does naturally have a lot of volume, so you don't have to do any fancy hairstyles (like straight-hair guys) to enjoy some awesome hair volume. This wild volume is part of coiled hair's sexual appeal, but again, you can only enjoy this benefit if you take care of your coiled hair.

Coiled hairstyles

Short military haircuts and shake-and-go styles for medium-length hair look good on coiled hair. When you have curly hair, it can be upsetting, so only try to grow your mane long if you are ready to stick with it no matter what, even if that means learning more about your curls (within reason; don't grab the Cosmopolitan magazine of your lady). The good news is that coiled hair that is shoulder-length can look really good, so waiting a few years to let that mane grow out to shoulder length will be worth it in terms of looks. A deep conditioner is another hair care tool that you should use. A normal conditioner does not condition hair as well as a deep conditioner does, so use the deep conditioner only once a month or every two weeks. Hair styling products: Don't use hair wax, and then use a good styling cream to keep your haircut. One more thing: a leave-in conditioner can also be used to style your hair, especially if you want the Shake & Go look or have long hair. Lastly, you can paint the tips of your coils with natural butter and oils to hide them and give them a deeper meaning. Yes, please get a wide-tooth comb while you're at it.

Kinky Hair

This is the last of the four hairstyles for curly hair. It is also the curliest of the three hair types. Kinky hair, which is also called afro-textured hair, is most common in black men. However, people of other races and ethnicities can also have kinky hair. It takes so little length to curl kinky hair that the curls (i.e., kinks) would look like straight curves. When looking at the first half-inch of hair, kinky hair is easy to spot. It is also the hardest of the four hair types to tell apart. To tell if your hair is twisted or kinky, stand about 3 feet away from it and look at yourself in the mirror. Try to tell the difference between the curls on your head. Do you see your curls, or do you just see your hair as a mess of curly hair? If the second is true and you can't tell the curls apart, you have kinky hair. So, men like Barack Obama, Will Smith, and Morgan Freeman have kinky hair. That guy in the back there is Barack Obama when he was younger and wore an Afro haircut.

Advantages vs. kinky hair drawbacks

Kinky hair is by far the fullest type of hair. The only problem is that it takes over 6 years to grow enough hair length to naturally hang down your kinky hair. This is a problem that many women who are growing their natural kinks long have. For most people, though, the problem is that their curls aren't defined enough. By default, kinky hair isn't defined as much as coiled hair, and it's much harder to get defined curls in kinky hair because the curls are so close together and short.

Hairstyles for kinky hair

Because kinky hair is so strong, it's great for cutting with a hair clipper. You can get epic Afro hairstyles with kinky hair because it naturally has a lot of volume. No other hair type can grow epic Afros as well as kinky hair can. Again, though, because it is thick, kinky hair looks great with high hairstyles like the High-Top Fade and the Fade haircut, where the sides and back of the head are cut very short and the hair on top is shaped with a hair clipper.

Hair products for kinky hair

For people with kinky hair, hair wax and pomade are not recommended. You could use a little pomade every once in a while, but other than that, leave-in conditioner, style cream, and natural butter are better choices. An everyday conditioner should be used most days, and every two weeks you should use a deep conditioner. To take care of your kinky hair, use the same conditioner that you would for straight, wavy, or twisted hair.

PART III
CUTTING TECHNIQUES

CHAPTER 4
HAIR CUT STYLES

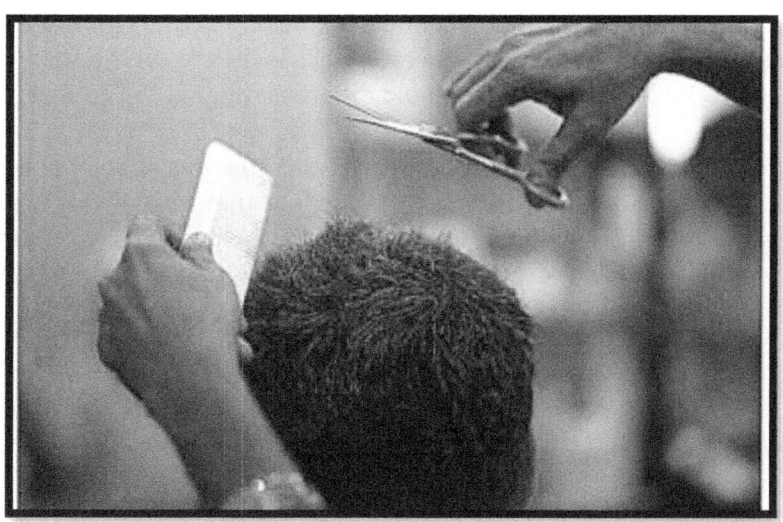

How to Trim Long Hair

Here is a simple, step-by-step guide on how to trim long hair. If the hair isn't too thick, this might be very simple.

- **STEP 1:** Get the patron ready by setting up the chair cloth drape, cleaning, etc. This is the first step for every cut.
- **STEP 2:** We need to get ready very badly. Make sure you can comb hair as quickly as a knife can cut soft butter. Also, make sure there are no knots or hairs in the hair that haven't been combed out. Some hair types, like dry, broken, or thick hair, need more time to do this. First, shampoo, or wash thick hair. You can make it easy to cut your hair when it's wet. This is because the hair can stick together. It also looks like the hair blows around less. The main problem with cutting hair while it's wet is that you can't be sure how short it will get, especially if you have "cowlicks." Because of this, thick hair might be easier to cut while it's still wet. It can be easier to cut off bangs with "cowlicks" and fine hair. After getting the hair ready for Step 3 by brushing out all the knots and picking how much to cut, you are ready to go.
- **STEP 3:** Part your hair down the middle and brush it all backward.
- **STEP 4:** Have the person lean their head forward and look at the floor. By cutting at this angle, you will "undercut" the hair. That is, after you cut your hair, the hairs on top of your head should be a little longer than the hairs near the nape of your neck. This will make it look like the hair is turning in instead of out.

HOW TO HOLD THE SHEARS

- **STEP 5:** You need to learn the right way to hold the shears before you can make any cuts. You can put the shears on either the left or right side. Through the bigger hole, put your thumb into the handle. Use the smaller hole on the other hand to put the ring finger (third finger) into the handle. The little palm (4th finger) will rest on the shears if you put your hand on them. This is the best way to hold the shears so that the cutting edge is under the most strain.
- **STEP 6:** Begin cutting on the side that feels best to you. In a straight line, start cutting off about 1/4" more than you need. Take into account that hair will likely shrink a bit. Less cuts are easier to work with than a lot of small chops. The trim looks "choppier" and more even when there are fewer cuts.
- **STEP 7:** Start cutting until you've cut the back diagonally all the way along.

Horizontal rear trim

- **STEP 8:** Make sure the cut is right. One way to do this is to check that the line you cut is straight across from the hair.

Note: Hair should be cut straight across. Check again to make sure that all the hair is gone. Always keep in mind that no deep ends are safe.

How to Trim Bangs

Get these things ready before you start cutting your bangs: You will need a comb, a few big hair clips, and a pair of metal scissors that are about 6.5 inches long and have sharp points.

1. **First, Dry and Style Your Bangs.**

Cut your bangs while they are still wet because hair shrinks when it dries. If you do this, your bangs might be way too short. Dry your fringe with a hair dryer and style it the way you normally do, whether that's straight down or swept to one side. When you trim, the shape of your bangs and the lines that were cut at the beginning will help you a lot. Divide the bang section into two parts. Clip the rest of your hair out of the way and away from your face. Because most bangs have a little extra length on each side, you can just cut these ends off too. They won't be in your eyes.

   2. **Get Your Bangs Ready.**

Use your comb to smooth the fringe into place, putting it where you normally do it. Leave the comb aside and put the bang part between your less-used middle and pointer fingers. To keep the bangs in place, slide your fingers down to your eyebrows and rest them there. (Don't pull the hair back too far; that could make the bangs too short.) When I cut my hair, I always use my fingers as a guide. It's much easier to work with my fingers than with a comb and scissors in each hand. You can also keep your face safe from the sharp scissors with your wide fingers.

   3. **Cut the Length.**

With the other hand, hold the scissors horizontally and cut the hairs that are hanging below your fingers. Cut these in two or three short cuts, like you would a piece of paper. Always cut less than you think you need to, about a quarter of an inch at most, and make sure the bangs stay just below the brow. Hold your fingers at that angle and put them on your face if your bangs are slightly to one side. Once more, use your fingers to help you cut the hairs below that line at that angle.

   4. **Chip Into the Ends to Soften the Line.**

Once you're happy with the length, grab the fringe section again with two fingers and hold the scissors vertically. Cut tiny V-shapes across the ends. "Don't go too far; just cut those tips off a little!" This adds some texture to the bangs and lowers the line if they aren't cut straight.

How to Frame Sides of Long Hair

If you need to do lateral framing, read and follow these steps. It's not always necessary, especially if the hair is all the same length and, as we already said, the back has been cut.

- **STEP 1:** Separate the hair on each side from the back of the ears up.
- **STEP 2:** Face the skipper. The patron will either bend their head left or right forward depending on which way you cut.
- **STEP 3:** Trim the hair into the shape you want without holding it.

How to Frame Short Hair (Off the Ears)

- **STEP 1:** Brush the hair well to get rid of any knots or snarls.
- **STEP 2:** For now, start in the back. Once you know the move, you don't have to start in the back all the time. Cut a straight line in the back.
- **STEP 3:** Cut down from the top of the head and add the right back corner to the front. Do not be afraid to bow your head. The oars can be used for many things.
- **STEP 4:** Comb the back left part of the hair to the front and then start cutting up from the nape of the neck to the mouth. Do not be scared to bend your head again.

- **STEP 5:** Check each corner to make sure the angle is the same.
- **STEP 6:** Get rid of the hair around your ears. At this point, it's important to make sure that there's no hair hiding behind the ears.
- **STEP 7**: Cut the patron's hair out of their left ear very small. Cut from the back of the neck to the front. When you need to, bend the ear.
- **STEP 8**: Move the person whose hair you cut to the right side. Cut off hair on the right ear. Cut backward from the front of the head. When you need to, bend the ear.
- **STEP 9:** Comb the hair away from the ears and look around to see if you missed any loose hairs when you trimmed around the neck. Steps 5, 6, and 7 will need to be done again.
- **STEP 10:** Face the skipper.
- **STEP 11:** Blend all the hair forward from the eyebrows to the sideburns, and cut the corners on the right and left.
- **STEP 12:** Don't touch the front of your hair; there should be plenty to comb back. If it's very long, a little bit might be cut off at the end. Comb and cut the hair forward, but don't go above the eyebrows.
- **STEP 13:** Use the small clippers to make lines around the head, on the arms, and the cheeks.

You can also use a razor or beard trimmer to do this. When trimming hair, the most important things are

1. Having sharp razor shears,
2. Make sure the hair is smooth, and
3. Not cutting too much.

After following those easy steps and practicing, you can cut hair like a pro. When hair is very thick, it may need to be cut one part at a time. This can be done by pulling the hair up and slowly lowering it to be cut in sections, which cut down on the amount of hair that needs to be cut all at once.

CHAPTER 5
HAIR CUTTING FOR DIFFERENT TEXTURES

Cutting Curly Hair

Cutting curly hair has its own set of rules and standards. It can feel like you need to learn a whole new language to understand and follow your curly hair. And these rules aren't just for dressing; curly hair also needs different rules for sleeping and cutting. Want to know how to cut curly hair? Before you cut those beautiful locks, here are five things you should know.

1. **Trim Often**

Trim curly hair off often. More often than other hair types need. Curly hair is more likely to break and split ends because of its beautiful twists and bends. Because wavy hair tends to get dry faster, cutting it off more often will help keep any split ends at the ends from moving up the hair shaft and drying out the rest of your hair too. If your curls are getting less stable, that's another sign that it's time for a trim. Curly hair should be cut about every 6 to 8 weeks as a general rule. Making regular visits to your favorite salon is a good way to make sure you get a new trim every so often.

2. **Stick to Dry Hair Trims**

This is up to each person, but in general, curly hair should be cut when it's dry. Each curl has its design, and curls on the same head of hair can have more than one. When hair is dry, it's easier to separate it into the different curl shapes it has and treat each one separately. When cutting curly hair, each curl should be cut separately, not all at once like when cutting straight hair. You can also see the curls' spring factor (how much each curl will spring back into shape after being pulled down) better when the hair is dry. It's hard to tell how much hair bounce back will when it's dry when it's wet because it has to be pulled down to be cut. This is a bad idea that could lead to hair being cut way too short. Another part is density. When hair is wet, it sticks together, which makes it hard to tell how thick something is. This will have a big effect on how much hair might thin. Girls with curly hair know that "density" means "puff factor." Sometimes curls need to be tamed and stepped down a notch, but it would be terrible to lose too much volume by taking out too much density. We've always said that curly hair is special, and one of its special needs is to be cut dry instead of wet.

3. **Find Someone Who Gets *Your* Hair**

How often do you get your hair cut? If so, does your stylist change every time you go? You don't have to be friends with your stylist, but it will be helpful to work with the same person. See the same stylist every time. That way, they'll get to know your curls and understand what makes them unique. There are a lot of stylists who say they "specialize in curly hair," but everyone's curls are different. It's possible that the way a stylist handles curly hair on someone else might not be the best way to handle your own. Find someone who understands your hair and who likes it.

4. **Or Become Your Hair Expert**

You may have always cut your hair short, or maybe being in lockdown made you discover your inner stylist. No matter what, we admire your skill—cutting curly hair is not an easy job.

Take these things into account when you cut your hair to make sure you do it safely and correctly:

- You need to make sure you have the right tools. Please note that kitchen or office scissors will not work for this task.
- Make sure you cut your hair in a well-lit area close to a mirror. A simple background will help you see how your hair will frame your face and what shape it will have when it's done.
- Don't forget to cut your curly hair after it's dried.
- The best time to trim hair is two or three days after washing it when it's back to its normal state. If you recently used heat to style your hair, you should wait until it's naturally curly again to see how it looks when it's not dressed.
- Give your head a good shake and let your hair fall where it naturally falls before you pick up the scissors.
- If your hair is longer than your shoulders, pull it forward so you can see the whole length of it.
- When you trim, remember that you can go back and take off more, but you can't go back if you take off too much at first. It's better to be safe than sorry, so be careful and take it slow.

Cutting your hair is fun, and you can decide how it will look in the end. If you cut your hair for the first time and don't like how it looks, it's not the end of the world.

5. Use the Right Products

Your whole hair care procedure should be based on how your curls are shaped. It's important to remember that curly hair is unique and should be treated as such. Care for your hair and cutting it will go more smoothly if you use items made just for curly hair. If you use the right nourishing shampoo and conditioner, split ends won't be able to grow up the hair shaft, so you won't have to cut off as much.

Cutting Straight Hair

Cutting Straight Hair At Home

If you want to cut your straight hair at home like a pro, here are the steps you need to take. For those who are scared, cutting your hair is possible if you go slowly and steadily.

1. Comb Your Hair Thoroughly

Detangle your hair by combing it the right way so there are no knots left. Cutting straight strands of hair can be done with dry hair, but if your hair is thick or wavy, you should wet it before cutting.

2. Bind Your Hair In A Ponytail

Comb your hair back and tie it in a low ponytail. You need to make sure that your hair is smooth and that an elastic band holds all of it in place.

3. Tie An Elastic Band A Little Down

Once you have an elastic band around your hair, go down a few inches and wrap another one around it. It will help you figure out how long your hair is and how short you want it to be. No matter what you like, you can add more bands below the second one.

Putting a rubber band around your hair gives you the freedom and power to cut your hair in a controlled way, so you don't end up cutting it too short by accident.

4. Decide The Length (Where You Want To Cut)

Once you decide the size you want after the cut, the next step is cutting them down. To do that, put your hair between your two fingers. You can make a V shape with your middle and forefingers. To get a round edge, slide your fingers down.

5. Start Cutting Your Hair

When you have your knot held in place with your fingers, cut your hair off. Professional barber tools that are sharp are needed for easy and quick cutting. When you cut your hair, never use regular scissors because the cut will look bad. Kitchen, cloth, art, and general scissors are all types of regular scissors. If you cut your hair with regular scissors, you will damage the ends, which will lead to split ends, hair that is hard to style, and damage to your overall look.

6. Check The Length And Shape After The Cut

It's time to check your hair for problems after cutting it straight. Take the ponytail out.

- For a better look, turn around with all of your hair in the back, or get two mirrors that face each other.
- Your hair will have a curve or be round at the bottom, but you can move on to the next step if you want it to be straighter.

7. Part Down Your Hair From The Middle

Take your hair out of its knot and split it down the middle. Now, put the left side of your hair on your left shoulder and the right side of your hair on your right shoulder. To make things easier for you, it's like making pigtails.

8. Choose The Length

Once your hair is split into two sections, you can choose how long it will be. Either side can pick to go first. Like before, use your index and middle finger to pinch your hair. After the cut, slide them down to the length you want.

9. Position Your Hair At A Cutting Angle

Pulling your fingers down will give them a slight angle. After you cut off your fingers, they should be longer than the length you want. In a slightly upward angle, place your fingers. Your fingers should be pointing toward your shoulder.

- This is the right way to cut your back hair shorter. Before you cut, you should always make sure that the hair in the back is close to the outside of your shoulder.

10. Cut Your Hair

Once you have your hair held in place with your fingers, it's time to cut it off. When you cut, always keep your hair and hand close to your arm.

- If your hair is thick, it's best to divide it into sections and cut each one to fit the others.
- You can keep track of the numbers by measuring the first part and then lining up the next one with the first one.

11. Repeat The Process On The Other Side

After cutting the straight hair on one side, you can move on to the other side. Measure the hairs to make sure you cut them all the same length. Compare your hair that hasn't been cut to hair that has been cut. The inside strands are all you need to do that.

- Find the middle strands on both sides and mark where the cut ends meet the hair that hasn't been cut.
- To get a good idea, pinch the space between your fingers.

How to Cut Someone Else's Straight Hair

Are you going to cut someone else's hair? Or do you want to know how to cut straight hair? In either case, the rule for cutting someone's hair is right below.

1. **Dampen Your Hair (Don't Soak)**

Wet the hair with a spray bottle. Make sure you don't soak the hair when you dampen it. For a fine cut, we only need the strands to be under control and easy to work with. To make cutting easier, make sure the person's head is at a good height.

2. **Make A Hair Bun**

First, you need to make the bun and split the hair into three equal parts. To do this, you will need a rat-tail comb to divide the hair into neat sections. Once you have a piece of hair, pull it back and put it in a bun on top of your head. Clip or tie the bun in place to move it out of the way. Leave the hair on the bottom of the head free for the cut after you tie the hair on top.

3. **Pinch The Hair Between Fingers**

With your middle finger and thumb, make a V shape. Now, pinch a strand of hair between these two fingers. The strand should be about 1 to 2 inches wide when you pinch it. A rat-tail comb can help you get rid of the strand. The rat-tail comb will help you cut the hair into even pieces.

4. **Evaluate The Hair Length**

As soon as you pinch the hair strand between your two fingers, move your fingers down to the spot where you want to cut it. Keep your hand close to your back at all times. Do not pull them away to make an angle, as this could change the shape of your cut and cause gradation. Keep your fingers straight out from the strand and the floor.

5. **Start Cutting Hair**

Now get the real shears and cut the hair off below the fingers. To get a clean, exact cut, the shears used for haircuts should be very sharp.

- The person getting a haircut needs to sit up straight. If there is any lean in the stance, the haircut would not be right.
- You can make a clean cut if you sit up straight and keep your head straight.

6. **Evaluate The Length And Shape**

After cutting the first piece of hair, take another part and cut it the same way you did the first. Compare a ½-inch hair strand to the one that has already been cut. Now pinch the line between your fingers once more and cut it out. Your fingers need to go down the strand until they hit the end of the cut strand.

7. **Keep Sectioning And Keep On Cutting**

This is how it's done: cut the part, then take another area, measure its length with the cut section in mind, and cut off the hair. Let go of that piece and measure another piece against the cut piece to see where to cut it. Pulling the hair away from the back of the person shouldn't be done while cutting. To keep the hair a uniform length and style, keep it as close to the back as possible.

8. **Continue With The Layering And Cutting**

After cutting the hair at the bottom, check to see if there is a change between the left and right sides. If both parts are the same, it's time to move on to the next pile of hair. Take out the hair clips or ties. A rat-tail comb can be used to separate the hair into sections. Take a hair on your finger and measure how long it is. Pull the hair that's left back into a bun.

9. **Measuring The Upper Layer With The Bottom One**

The top layer that we can grab with our finger needs to be compared to the hair that was cut off before. To do this, match a piece of hair from the new layer with some hair from the old layer. When the new strand hits the bottom of the old strand, cut the hair off.

10. **Keep On Sectioning And Layering**

Now use this method again to cut all the hair. All you have to do is compare a hair from the new part to one from the old one, then cut them both off. When you compare the new layer to the old one, you can see where you need to cut. Do these steps over and over until all the hair is gone.

11. **Blow-Dry And Final Adjustments**

Once the cut is done, the hair needs to be dried and the cut needs to be improved. To make more changes, blow-dry the hair and then cut off any ends or edges that need it. Otherwise, you can wash your hair first and then blow-dry it to get rid of all the mess.

Afro-Type Haircutting

The hair would be passed down. Everyone has their unique hair. As a result, haircutting is not always done in a planned way. Just like no two thumbprints are the same, no two men's hairs are the same. Their hair looks most like that of their parents and other close relatives. When cutting "Afro-style" hair, the same rules apply as when cutting any other type of hair. What makes them different is how they cut Afro-type hair.

To get hair that is smoother and less wavy, follow the steps already given for cutting it in the way you want. When you trim hair that has a very tight curl, you have to use a fork comb to keep pulling it out of your head. You can cut "Afro-type" hair all the same length by using the rake attachment on the clippers. In Afro-hair cutting, you shape or mold the hair. You can use the same steps to trim beards as well. The haircutter and customer decide what kind is needed. Following is a step-by-step guide to "designing" Afro hair.

STEP-BY-STEP AFRO-CUT

- **STEP 1:** You should always make plans. Before you start to do a good job, you should wash, condition, and dry the hair. Conditioning your hair is very important. You don't have to get rid of all of the conditioner. If you leave a little conditioner in your hair, it can be smoother and easier to work with.
- **STEP 2:** This is the most important thing to do. Use a fork comb to pull all the hair out of the head. This process goes on all the time and needs to be done several times during the cut.
- **STEP 3:** Cut the hair with scissors or electric clippers. Form the way you want. No need to use a comb at the same time as cutting. Keep in mind that it gets softer every time the hair is cut. The hair has to be pulled back out all the time.
- **STEP 4:** Use shears or clippers to cut: Do steps 2 and 3 again. Go over the entire scalp, and shape it however you like.
- **STEP 5:** Use a small clipper to outline the whole head, including the front, back, and sideburns. As with every haircut, don't cut into the hairline.

HOW TO CUT YOUR HAIR

Cutting someone else's hair is a good way to get better at cutting your own before you try it on yourself. You can cut your hair once you understand some of the ideas in this book. You only need to learn a few things.

From this book, you can choose any of the ways to cut your hair into the style you want. Just remember these four things:

1. You need two mirrors. One mirror will be in front of you and the other will be behind you.
2. When cutting, put down the comb and pick up the shears. Then, use the same hand to cut all the hair, if you'd rather.
3. When you frame, the cut should be facing the opposite way when you look at it in the mirror.
4. When you shape the back of short hair, put your hand on your neck and use your middle finger to make sure you don't cut into your hairline.

CHAPTER 6
ADVANCED CUTTING TECHNIQUES

Texturizing and Thinning

Using scissors to thin hair and change its texture are important ways to add dimension, reduce bulk, and make hairstyles feel soft. For these methods to work, you need to be very precise and know a lot about the hair's nature and the look you want.

Here's how to use scissors to thin hair and give it texture:

1. **Thin and Texturize Strategically:** To make the hairdo look better without changing its general structure, you should thin and texturize it strategically. Pay attention to places where the hair looks too thick or heavy.
2. **Use the Right Scissors:** Use texturizing or thinning scissors that are made for these tasks. The sides of these scissors are pointed or sharpened, which makes it easy to cut hair.
3. **Section the Hair:** Use clips or hair ties to separate the hair into parts. When thinning and texturizing, working with small pieces gives you more control and accuracy.
4. **Consider Hair Type and Thickness:** Change the way you thin and texturize your hair based on the type and thickness of your hair. If your hair is thin or fine, be more careful not to let it thin too much.
5. **Gradual Thinning:** Make small, quick cuts in the hair to fine it out over time. Don't add too much grit at first; add more as needed.
6. **Use a Light Hand:** As you cut with the thinning scissors, be gentle and smooth. Do not use too much force to avoid random results and forceful shaving.
7. **Point Cutting for Softness:** Use point cutting and thinning scissors together to make the look softer and more natural. Cut the ends of the hair with a point to make the edges soft and wavy.
8. **Blend and Layer:** To mix hair of different lengths and layers, use methods like texturizing and thinning. This helps make the shift between hair parts look smooth and natural.
9. **Texturize Curls and Waves:** Texturizing curly or wavy hair can bring out its natural structure and make it less bulky. To keep the curl pattern, only use the thinning scissors on certain sections of hair.
10. **Step Back and Assess:** As you thin and texturize your hair, take a step back and look at how the style looks generally in terms of balance and volume. As needed, make changes to get the look you want.

Current Hair Texturizing Trends You Must Know

Point Cutting

To use this method to add texture to a client's hair, hold the ends of the sectioned hair between your fingers and cut it into pieces with the scissors facing the hair.

Internal Cutting

Internal cutting is the best way to get a modern, smooth look because it gets rid of sections while adding depth. Freehand divides the hair into sections and chips at each one. Use a tail comb to help you separate the hair properly and trim it where you want it.

Twist Cutting

For longer hair, twist cutting is a great way to add depth. Cut the hair into sections, and then twist each one. To make the hair more interesting, cut the curled strand in half down the middle with shears.

Slide Cutting

Run a blade along the hair section to thin it out and make the cut smooth. For a softer look, slide-cutting hair texturizing methods can also be done with a razor.

Texturizing Shears Problems to Avoid

Adding texture to hair can make a haircut look great. However, hair texturizing can be bad for your hair if you don't do it right. Texturizing hair the wrong way can make it look too thin, wavy, or uneven. If you want to escape making these mistakes when texturizing cut, read on.

Over-Texturizing and Over-Graduating

Adding a little graduation to a bob can give hair a lot of body in the end. But if the graduation is put on too high, the haircut might look too thin. To avoid this mistake as much as possible, we suggest making a point cut with a wide-tooth comb and hair texturizing shears. Do not cut more than ½ inch to 1 inch into the hair. This will keep the line of your bob smooth.

Uneven Bob

The bob's line is what draws people in, so this line must be straight. Use a straight blade to make a straight line. Place the shears so that the pointy end is facing down and the toothy side is against the skin. In turn, this lets the shear's teeth hold the hair in place so you can cut the line straight.

Frizzy Hair

No one wants their hair to be frizzy. A smooth result, not a wavy one, is what texturizing methods are meant to achieve. To keep this from happening at all, remember to cut your hair very slowly, carefully, and precisely.

Hair Texturizing Tools

Without the right tools, you won't be able to make beautiful, custom-textured hair. Here are some hair texturizers that every stylist should have on hand before they start working.

Straight-Edge Razor

To make hair more interesting, a straight-edge razor is great. But please be careful not to cut off too much hair or parts that aren't even.

Hair Clipper

Hair clippers are a type of hair texturizer that is different from a razor and scissors because they can be changed to cut hair of different lengths. A clipper is mostly used on longer hair because it doesn't cut as close to the skin as a razor or groomer would.

Blending Shears

You can make your hair look beautiful by texturizing it with blending shears or thinning shears. Blending shears have a shear blade on one side and a blade on the other. This lets you cut hair without cutting the whole piece.

Chunking Shears

Bitching shears are similar to blending/thinning shears in how they work. The main difference is that chunking shears are made to cut off more hair than thinning shears. This tool works especially well for people with thick, curly hair.

Finishing Shears

Finishing shears is the last tool you'll need to change the texture of your hair. You use them after you've changed the texture with the method of your choice to clean it up and make it more even. With finishing shears, you only need a small amount of hair to get a clean look.

Tail Comb

Tail combs are the best tools for giving hair texture. You can easily section, manage, and be exact with this tool, which helps you give precise haircuts.

Blending and Fading

When it comes to fading, it's important to know how the different parts of your blades can change how long they cut. **We'll start with the most popular and simple clipper setup, which is:**
- Fade blade clipper
- Clipper closed cuts to 0mm.
- Clipper open cuts to 1.5mm

I'm going to quickly go over how these work with each other and how they fit in. You need to know this to get a better sense of when we fade.

Here's how they work...

Guard	Inches	Size (mm)
#1/2 or 0	1/16"	1.5mm
#1	1/8"	3mm
#1 1/2	3/16"	4.5mm
#2	1/4"	6mm
#3	3/8"	10mm
#4	1/2"	13mm
#5	5/8"	16mm
#6	3/4"	19mm
#8	1"	25mm
#10	1" – 1 1/4"	32mm
#12	1" – 1 1/2"	38mm

If you have a #1 guard (3mm) and the lever is closed (0mm), it will cut hair to the exact length of 3mm. But if you had a 1 guard (3mm) and the clipper lever open (1.5mm), it would now be 1 ½ = 4.5mm. If the lever is open, 1.5 mm of hair is added, but if it is closed, leaves 0 mm of hair. These numbers give you a good idea of how the guard and lever work together, but they are not exact because there are differences. Then, put on the real 1 ½ guards (4.5mm) and close the clipper lever (0mm). This will give you the guard's real cutting length, which is 1 ½ (4.5mm). Also, if you open the lever up 1.5 mm and have a 1 ½ guard (4.5 mm), it changes to a #2 guard (6 mm). If you put on the real #2 guard (6mm) and close the lever, it will cut to that length. If you then open the lever + (1.5mm), you'll have a 2 ½ guard (7.5mm). The small details don't mean much after this point...

But can you see how one way to move the cutter lever can make each guard slowly blend into the next? Plus, it doesn't matter what guard you have; you can always figure out what guards you need to make a certain cut by knowing the guard and the length of your blade. #1 guard plus open lever equals 3mm plus 1.5mm or 1.2mm (if gapped zero). This gives you a cutting length of 4.5 mm, which is about a 1 ½ guard. Start with a 1 guard with the lever closed. If you had two guidelines, one at 3 mm of hair and the other at 4.5 mm of hair. You could start at the 4.5 mm hair level and slowly close your lever as you move down to the 3 mm guard level. This way, by the time you get to the bottom of the 3 mm level, the two lines will be flush. Fading is just an organized way to do this process. You must know how to use levels and a clipper guard to fade between tracks if you want to fade. As you watch, I'll show you how to blend hair from #2guard guideline 6mm in length down to a zero.

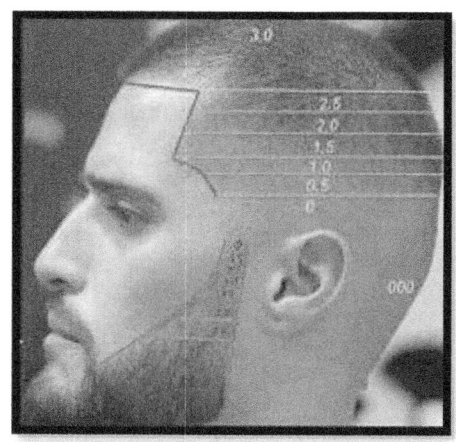

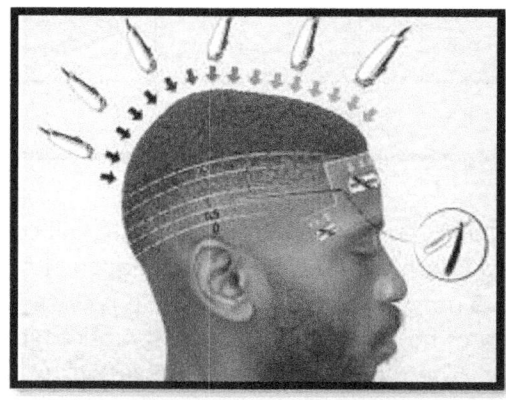

First, though, what is a guideline? Each line will serve as a base from which to replace the previous guard with a new one that will cut to the same length. The new guard can get shorter as you close the lever, which means you cut more hair, which gives you a fade as you move down a guideline. What's a guideline? Next, we'll talk about this.

Guidelines

These are guidelines.

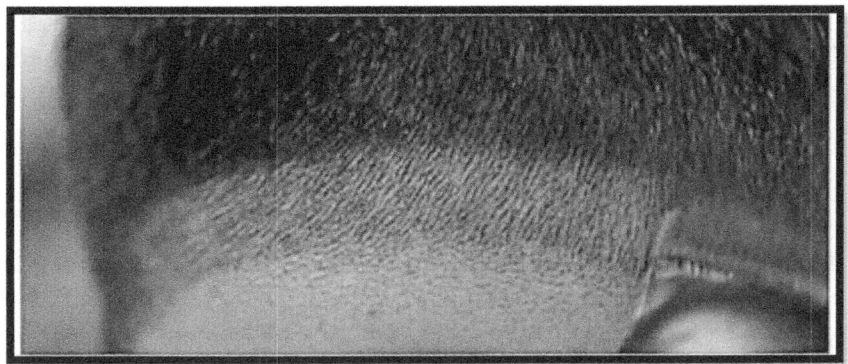

A guideline is a clear, sharp line that is drawn between hairs of different lengths. When the length you're cutting leaves more hair than the length below it, you have one of these. Look at how they slowly go up and each line gets thicker. They are usually about an inch long, but it depends on the style. The more room you leave, the better the mix. As you close your lever, you will cut more hair, making a fade. It will start bigger overall and longer when cutting. As you do this, you should be fading out the guideline until you get to the bottom, which will be the beginning of the new one. When you set guidelines you go up to leave the hair and make the guideline, **then you put on the right guard and lever setting to take it out and blend.**

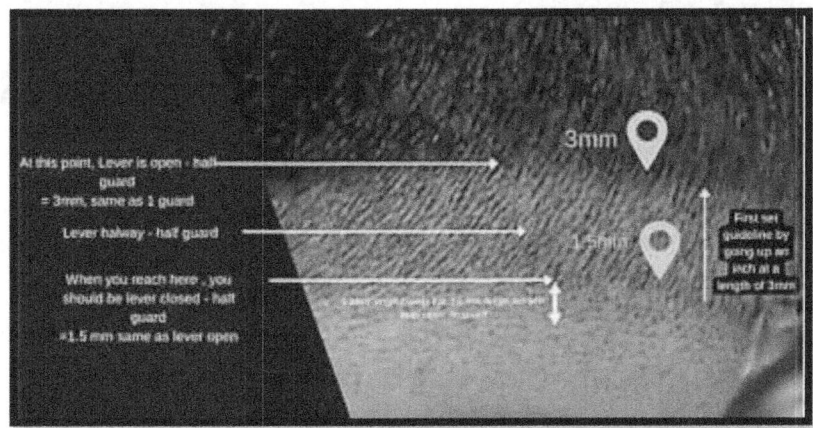

BLEND FADE LINES

This is how you fade from a #2 guard (6mm) to a 0. How does your present cutting fit with the next rule (the best way to fade)? I'll explain it in more detail below. When your lever is halfway down and you want to get rid of hair in the middle of the guideline, this is called flicking. I'm not going to tell you the exact length you cut to because

1. It gets confusing
2. The exact length is up to you and your sense of what the middle is.

But just try to be as close to the middle as you can. You should now brush your hair down as you fade to get a better idea of how it looks as you fade. To make things less likely to go wrong, I'll be making my way down from the longest piece of hair.

Let's begin at the top...

At this point, you'll meet the 1 ½ (4mm) guideline. Then, start at the 1 ½ (4mm) guard line if you want to pop on your 1 guard (3mm) lever open (1.5). Halfway turn the lever and flick off the middle of this guideline. Then with the 1 guard (3mm) lever closed (0mm) your clippers now cut true to the 1 guard (3mm). That's when you'll come across the 1 (3mm) guard guideline.

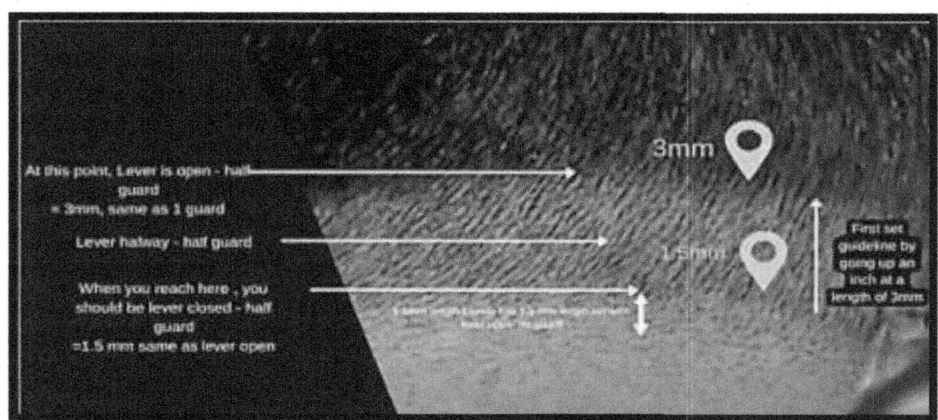

Then, put on your ½ guard or 0 guards (1.5 mm) with the 1.5 mm lever open and start on the 3 mm 1 guard guideline. Halfway turn the clipper lever and flick in the middle of this guideline. Then, when the ½ guard (1.5 mm) lever is closed (0 mm), it will cut exactly that length.

And that's where the ½(1.5mm) guard line comes in.

At this guideline, you set your clipper with the lever open and no guards in place. You can now take your clippers and slowly close them as you move down this guideline. Then it'll get to a point where you'll.

Meet the 0 guideline

This is an exact zero, and it's the guideline you made with your trimmers. So, take out that last guideline while your clippers are fully closed and there is no guard on them. That was it! You were able to blend hair from the #2 guard length down to a 0.

That's how you'd blend fade lines.

You can make the space between the blend's top and bottom much bigger. You can also make it longer or shorter, based on your guess. But all in all, you now have the tools to fade your skills. Just line up your cut now.

CHAPTER 7
LAYER CUTS

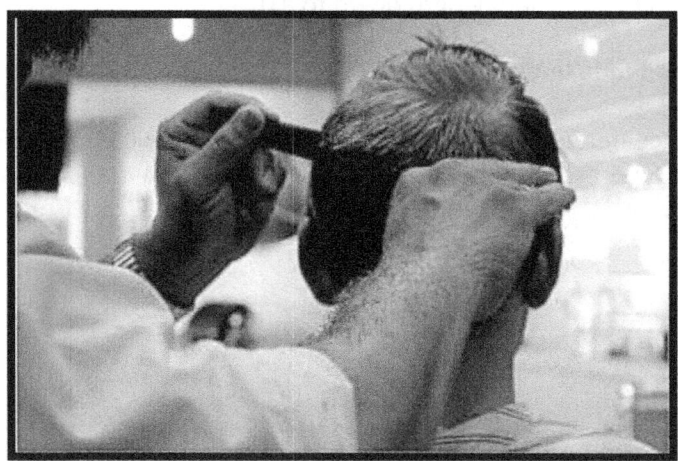

Layering Hair (Defined)

For haircuts, "layering" is the most common method used. When the hair is brushed back, you can still see the scissor lines, which is why this is also called "feathering." Adding layers to your hair also makes it less bulky. If you want to layer your hair, you might have to cut the hair off of your whole head instead of just the end. Imagine a magnet pulling the hair straight out of the head at a 90° angle. That's the best way to explain it. Even better, think of a movie where the character gets shocked and his hair stays straight at the end. To layer hair, wrap small pieces of hair around your head and cut off some. When you add at different points or on different parts, you can make different styles. When cutting layers for shorter haircuts, bend them more inward, like in the pictures. When cutting layers for longer hair, bend them in a way that lets more hair cover the face. In a "rooftop" style, the hair should be cut in layers.

Simple Long Hair "Shaggy Cut"

Long haircuts look good with a shaggy cut. It works great for long hair that is naturally curly. You'll pick out and cut small pieces of hair for the next layer cuts. In this method, you'll cut the hair all at once, even though it's still a layer cut.

PROCEDURE

- STEP 1: Pull all of your hair down to the middle of the top of the head.
- STEP 2: Use a rubber band to hold the hair in place.
- STEP 3: Cut the hair straight off the top of the head at least 5 inches.

- STEP 4: Take off the band and let the hair fall. The hair is now styled in a "shaggy cut." To see an example of a "shaggy cut," picture the patron hanging upside down.
- STEP 5: Preferential frame

LIFTING HAIR WITH THE COMB

Before you go any further, you need to know how to use the comb to pick up hair and hold it with the first two fingers of the other hand.

The comb can be used in three different ways to pick up hair:
- push the comb into the hair and lift it,
- move the comb toward you and raise it, or
- To start, hold the comb in your preferred hand (right or left) and push or pull a small piece of hair apart with it. At the same time, use the index and second fingers of the other hand to grab the hair under the comb. The only difference between the push and pull methods is that the push method moves hair away from you and up with the comb, while the pull method forces hair upwards toward you. I like to use a mix of both push and pull techniques, but instead of randomly moving through the hair with the comb, I pick up the hair parts one at a time. If you're just starting, practice will help you understand these strategies better.

If you learn how to do these steps, you can start cutting the layer in front of you and then work your way back. It doesn't matter where you start and end the break. Keep in mind that haircuts aren't always planned out. Everyone's hair is a little different, which is one of the things I love most about cutting hair.

Basic Layer Cut

- **STEP 1:** Picture what the hair would look like when it stands out at the end.
- **STEP 2:** Comb out all hair so there are no knots. It might be easier to wet thick hair first.
- **STEP 3:** Always cut into the person's face when cutting their hair. Remember this! When cutting the top front and left side of the patron, you must face the patron. (For left-handed people, cut into the right side instead of facing the patron.) This is the best way to get to the part of the head you're layering.
- **STEP 4:** Finally, keep the scissors and comb in the hand you prefer. Lift a small section of hair with the comb in front of you. This is similar to how you section off bangs; you should pull it up instead of combing it back. Grasp the section of hair you just pulled up with the first two fingers of the other hand. Once you have a hold on it, move the comb to the hand that has the grip on it and hold it between your thumb and first finger. Do not switch hands with the scissors.
- **STEP 5:** Cut the hair you are lifting to start layering. **Note:** Don't cut shorter than 3" unless the person whose hair you cut uses a product to keep their hair in place or you want the hair to stand up a bit. As a general rule, cutting less than a 3" layer is too short. Cut the hair above your second knuckle so that you can get a good grip on the bulk of it. You will

be cutting your hair in the next row of parts. The first cut, which leaves the hair at the same length as the second finger, is called the "guideline."

- **STEP 6:** Move the comb a little further back into a segment than the one you just cut. The hair will pull up, and you should also try to pull a small amount of hair from the previous segment. This will allow you to see the guidelines from the previous cut.

Note: There are three ways to find the guideline when layering hair:
1. By looking at or "seeing through" the hair from the previous rule;
2. By measuring how long the first section has been cut, which is done by feeling; and
3. Practice, practice, practice.

- **STEP 7:** Repeat steps 5 and 6 back to the crown of the head, then start a new line following the same cycle. The crown is where the hair, shaped like a tornado, comes out of the scalp at the top back of the head. Be extra careful not to cut this hair too short, or it will stick up.
- **STEP 8:** Once you've cut all the pieces for the top, you can lay the left side (or the left side). Begin by meeting up with the host. Use the comb to pull out a small section of hair from the left front to follow the line from the top. Keep the pew at the same angle as the head leg. All hair must be picked out from where it grows and cut straight out. Cut in rows again from front to back.
- **STEP 9:** Move to the back of the person whose hair you are cutting. If you are cutting the left and back of the head, you should stand in front of the person. If you are cutting the right side and back of the head, you should always stand behind them.
- **STEP 10:** Lay the right side and the back over using the same method. It doesn't matter how you do it as long as you pick up all the hair in small pieces and cut them all the same length. You don't have to layer from front to back; you can start at the back and work your way forward, or even go in a different direction, like from side to side. This is also a good way to make sure the cut is even all around.
- **STEP 11:** Once the layering part of the cut is done, the hair can be trimmed or framed to the length you want. Many stylists like to trim the hair first and use that length as their first guideline. Remember that there is no right or wrong way to do things; what matters is the result. After layering, I like to trim (or frame), so there is less hair to cut.
- **STEP 12:** Don't give up. If the haircut looks "choppy" or you can see "lines" from the scissors' chops, try back on those parts.

To change the direction of your cuts, think about going from side to side instead of front to back.

HOW TO USE THINNING SHEARS

If the cut still looks choppy, you may need to use thinning shears to make the hair look smoother or more natural. If you can, use the comb to lift the hair out of the head where it looks choppy. The thinning shears should hit flat against the outside of the comb. Cut the thinners in half an inch or less. Thinning shears never get too close to the head. For most cuts, you don't even need to use these tools. Thinning shears work best on blonde hair because scissor lines stand out more on lighter hair. Thinning shears can cut just 1/2 "or less.

- **STEP 13:** Outline the arms and sideburns with a small trimmer or razor.

These 13 steps can be used for any layer cut. The sheet can be cut in different ways, and those cuts are only used in certain places. Even if your hair gets thinner in some places, you should still protect it. If you have thin hair, a "box cut" pattern is usually best because it leaves more hair in the smaller places. Getting ready is the most important thing when it comes to layering hair. It's like learning to type or play an instrument: the more you do it, the better you get at it. Many students have told me they understand the layering principle but can't find the guidelines. There are three ways to find the guideline: by looking, measuring, or thinking.

CLIPPER CUTS

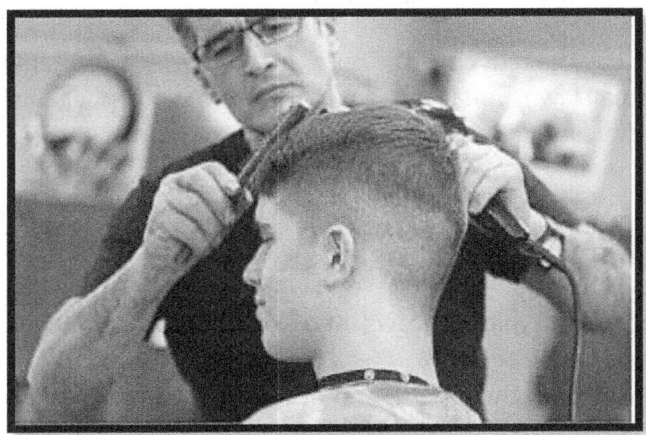

Clipper Cuts

Framing or hair trimming is similar to paper pattern cutting. To layer hair, you have to picture the "electrified" hair that sticks out on top. This segment will talk about another way to cut hair with electric clippers. Clipping hair is more like slicing hair with the clippers. You can cut hair in many styles with the clippers, from flat tops and Mohawks to military cuts governing.

Clipper Attachments (Rakes)

Clipper attachments, which are usually called rakes, fit onto the clipper head. There are different types of rakes to account for the different sizes of the clipper blades. Some brands of clippers, like all of one device, have the rakes built into the blades. Rakes usually can't be switched between brands of clippers. Different sizes of rakes are made to cut hair at different lengths. The most common sizes are #1, #2, and #3, with #1 being the smallest. They clip on blades with electric clippers.

Common rakes

Up until the 1990s, it was harder to get hold of attachments in sizes #4 through #8. Now, only attachments are needed to cut a man's hair. Follow the steps below carefully. The attachments need to go over the hair in many different directions. To make sure you didn't miss a segment, you'll have to do the cycle more than once. If you use a higher number on top than on the sides and back, you'll need to blend or taper the middle part with a clipper and comb. Finally, you'll have to cut the sideburns and the neck. There is one form of rake known as a rake called "taper." A "taper" rake has a right rake on the right side of the head and a left rake on the left side. The bottom of these rakes is cut down tighter than the top and made at an angle. You shouldn't use this type of rake unless you have practiced with it. These rakes are supposed to make thinning hair easier, but they don't usually work right. The same is true for many other grooming tools on the market that are made for beginners.

How to Do a Buzz-Cut with a Rake

First, let's look at a very easy haircut called a "buzz" or "butch." It's very simple and easy to do. It's kind of like mowing a small lawn; you just have to make sure you cut against the grain of the hair. For this cut, a # 2 rake attachment might work best. For really fine hair, a # 3 rake might be better, so the hair gets a little longer. For a close break, use a # 1 rake.

STEPS FOR BUZZ / BUTCH

STEP 1: Create the patron saint. You don't have to wash your hair first.
- Keep in mind that hair typically grows forward on the face and neck.

STEP 2: Put the right rake on the clippers.
- Cut the hair back along the length, and always clip hair that is growing in the opposite direction.

STEP 3: Do step 2 a few times to make sure you cut any hair that got tangled.

STEP 4: Cut sideburns and arms with a small clipper or razor. Remember not to cut into the hairline, as this is where hair starts to grow from the head.

Cut the buzz

Let's try something a little more difficult. That cut looks more like it was done by a regulator.

EASY REGULATION STYLE CUT

- **STEP 1:** Use rake attachments #1, #2, or #3 to clip the back and sides to the part of the head that is just before it starts to curve.
- **STEP 2:** The top layer is about 3 "thick. 3 "is the average layer cut in thickness. Quite fine hair can be cut one inch shorter in the layer. Quite thick hair typically sticks up when less than 2 3/4 "layer is removed. Be extra careful that the sheet doesn't cut the "cowlicks"

too short. A cowlick is a small spot on the head where hair doesn't grow in the same way as the rest of the hair.
- **STEP 3:** Use thinning shears to make the top fit in with the back and sides. With the comb, the hair is pulled away from the head and cut straight across from where it grows with thinning shears. If you use shears to thin, they will go past the comb. Thin shears should not be used too close to the head. No need to cut off 1/4 "to 1/2"
- **STEP 4:** Use thinning shears to draw the neck and sideburns with a small clipper or razor. Don't go too close to the hairline.

Steps for Simple Marine Style Cut

- **STEP 1:** Do not use any mounting rake on the clippers. To avoid this, place the clipper's head flat against the sides and back, and then bend the head up.
- **STEP 2:** For the top of the head, use rake attachment #2 or #3.
- **STEP 3:** Use the razor to shave around the mouth and the neck. Tapering The Hair (Shingling)

When you taper, you get an even hairline. Some of the hair is cut off between the neck and the head. Near the top of the head, the hair gets longer over time. This is thought to be tapering with the men's haircut. When it comes to girls, the same method is called "shingling." This kind of cut would be a military haircut rule, which is not the same as a navy cut but more like the classic men's cut from the 1950s. When it comes to guys, a tapering haircut is a little different from a shingle haircut. For women, you will only taper the back of their cut and not the arms. The "tapers" of women are not cut as high as those of men. For women, "tapers" are often done with scissors and a comb instead of electric clippers. This next section shows you how to use an electric clipper to cut your hair in a tapered style, step by step. Before you try this step, you should get used to using the clippers with the rake attachments.

STEP-BY-STEP TAPER

- **STEP 1:** Set up the patron
- **STEP 2:** Put something over the top hair to cover it.
- **STEP 3:** Use the clipper and comb to start at the hairline at the nape of the neck. Put a little of the comb into the head and tilt it back. They should stay in your favor pocket. Cut the hair in an arc shape by angling the blade forward and pressing the hair against the outside of the blade. The comb will be farther away from the head the higher you clip. Keep in mind that sounds like "slicing" hair.
- **STEP 4:** If necessary, smooth out the curve with the thinning shears.
- **STEP 5:** Make the sideburns and collar stand out.

As I always do, I will stress the old proverb "Practice makes good."

Specialty Clipper Cuts

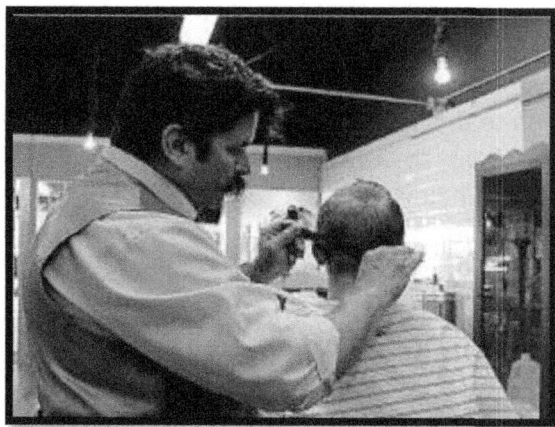

It would take a lot of practice to use the clippers to make flat tops, step haircuts, mohawks, and other unique cuts. Most people should go to the barbershop to see how pros do their jobs. A flat-top comb, which is a long, thin comb, would be very helpful for these kinds of cuts. There's also a flat-top comb that is very big and shaped like a big fork... with a level on top. This comb is made to cover the whole top of the head. Most of the time, you can only buy this comb at big chain haircut shops.

How to Do a Standard Flat Top

- **STEP 1:** Cut the sides and back of the hair with a # 1 or # 2 rake up to the curve of the head clipping. This is done against the grain of the hair.
- **STEP 2:** If the top is long enough to be cut by layering, do so. If the top is short, skip this step.
- **STEP 3:** Wet the top part of the hair and blow it back hard until the hair strands stand up. Extra hair spray can help this process.
- **STEP 4:** Stand in front of the person and put the flat-top comb into the front of their hair. Clip the front of their hair at an angle to make it a little longer.
- **STEP 5:** Slide a flat-top comb through the hair a little further back than in step 4. Use the front cut as a guide. Keep doing this, moving the comb a little further back each time, until you reach the crown of the head. Clip over the top and pebble until it looks good.
- **STEP 6:** At this point, the haircut will start to take shape. The corners of the head will be full of extra hair. Cut those corners off at an angle of 35 to 45 degrees using the same sliding-comb method.
- **STEP 7:** Use a small clipper or razor to cut the sideburns and change the neck.

A lot of people wear this look with their sideburns completely shaved off. Avoid giving up. Learning how to use clippers isn't easy the first time. Remember the type of cut you want to learn. It took me at least 20 tries to make a "flat-top" cut that I was proud of.

CHAPTER 8
SPECIALIZED HAIRCUTS

Men's Haircuts

Buzz Cut Styles

This popular hairstyle for men called the "military cut," has been around for more than 100 years and is still very popular today. The buzz cut is exactly what it sounds like a short, buzzed haircut that is cut very close to the scalp. Read on to learn how to do a quick and easy buzz cut.

How to Get It:
Before you start, make sure your hair is clean and dry because wet or dirty hair won't cut well with clippers. Next, follow the barber's rule of thumb: 6-4-2. This means using a 15mm/.59 in guard (usually a #6 guard) on top of your hair, a 12mm/.47 in guard (usually a #4 guard) on the sides, and a 6mm/.24 in guard (usually a #2 guard) to trim the edges. Because buzz-cut hair is defined by its sharp lines, make sure to trim the edges as precisely as possible.

Crew Cut Styles

The crew cut is a type of buzz cut that became popular among college rowing teams because it is easy to maintain and very short. This is where the nickname "Ivy League" comes from. Men's crew cuts are very simple and consist of a fade from the forehead to the crown of the head (where the top of the head starts to curve downward to the back of the head) with shorter sides. The longer hair on top can be styled in many ways, such as with bangs, spikes, a pompadour, or a side part just a few examples. Currently, these are the 5 most popular crew cut styles:

Thick

The sides of this style are thicker, which makes the fade less clear.

Gentleman

The gentleman's cut is all about how the edges mix. Men like it the most because it works with almost all hair types and hairlines.

Classic

For a more traditional man, the standard cut is best because the hair on top is shorter and the hair on the sides is longer. It doesn't fade, so it's a good choice for him.

Fade

A high and tight fade crew cut is exactly what it sounds like a very short fade that goes around the head and up into the crown.

Side Part

A crew cut with a side part is added for a more polished look. This is the side part cut.
How to Get It:
To get a crew cut, start by tapering the sides and back of your hair. To do this, use the longest-numbered guard and cut your hair once on the sides and back. Next, switch to a 9mm/.35 in guard (usually a #3 guard) and do the same thing again, but this time stop an inch below the first pass. Finally, switch to the shortest numbered guard and blend your hair from the bottom up to contrast. You can leave the top of your hair as long or short as you want.

Fade Haircut Styles

The US Military made the fade haircut popular in the 1940s and 1950s. It has made a huge comeback in recent years as both a trendy style for young people and a classy haircut for the office. The fade style is when the hair on the sides and back is cut as close together as possible with clippers, and the hair on top "fades," or tapers, up into any length. There are many variations on the fade, but these four are the most popular right now.

Taper Fade

A taper fade is the smallest and softest fade of all the types. It is often used to fade a beard into the hairline or to give the sides of the hair more length.

Low Fade

When you want to do a low fade, you need to decide where you want the fade to start. For the sides and top, start with higher edges and move down on them as you get closer to the base of the neck.

Mid-fade

The mid-fade starts halfway up the head, about one-third to two-thirds of the way down the side of the head. This is usually just above eyebrow height and can make the eyes look great. If you have a longer head, this is about the highest height you should go because a high fade can make the head look even longer.

High Fade

This is the hardest of the four fades, and the high fade can start anywhere in the last third or so of the head. When worn high and tight, it can almost reach the top before getting longer.

How to Get It:
The first step in any fade haircut for men is to trim your hair with scissors. If your hair is already the length you want, you can move on to the fading. As with the low fade haircut, the most important thing is to decide where you want the fade to start. Next, choose a guard size (we suggest starting on a lower guard and working your way up, but if you are a beginner, you can do it the other way around). Starting at the neck, gently sweep your hair clippers upwards. Be sure to work slowly and make sure that the layer lines are straight. After a few touch-ups, style as you desire.

Undercut Haircut Styles

The undercut is a short to medium-length haircut for men where the top is longer than the sides. The sides and often the back are buzzed short, making the top and sides stand out. The undercut is very popular because it's a classic style that looks classy and sophisticated. There are many variations of the undercut hairstyle, but the main idea is that the sides are buzzed short and the top is longer. Men with diamond-shaped or square faces look best with this style because it makes the face look less rigid.

How to Get It:
You can have an undercut with hair that is any length. The sides can be buzzed as short as a 9mm/.35 in guard (usually a #3 guard) or as long as a 21mm/.82 in guard (usually a #10 guard). This makes it perfect for most people because it is flexible, easy to maintain, and can be customized.

Tip: If your hair on top is 5 cm/2 in, a 12mm/.47 in guard (usually a #4 guard) on the sides will look best. If your hair on top is 12-15 cm/5-6 in., a 24mm/.94 in (usually a #12 guard) would look best. When you have a haircut, it's pretty easy to style. All you need is a good pomade and hair that is wet and towel-dried. Rub the pomade in your hands and run it through your hair, styling it however you like.

Taper Haircut Style

The tapered cut, also called the businessman cut, might be the most confusing hairstyle. A tapered haircut shortens the hair about a centimeter above the ear and around to the nape of the neck, while a fade haircut shortens the back and sides from the temple down to a length anywhere below a 6mm/.24 in guard setting (usually a #2 guard). The tapered haircut has clean lines that follow the shape of the head and works with any hair type, but it takes away weight from thick or wavy hair.

How to Get It:
To get the classic taper haircut, first decide how long you want your hair to be and where you want the taper to end. Then, pick the longest hair clipper guard. The clipper setting can be as short as a 6mm/.24 in guard (usually a #2 guard) or as long as an 18mm/.70 in guard (usually a #8 guard), depending on your preference. Run your hair clippers around your head, starting at the ears, to get the first level of the fade. Then, switch the hair clipper guard to the next shortest length and do the same thing below the next level. Do this 1-2 more times, keeping the guard number going down until you reach the nape of the neck. Make sure your hair is blended well enough so that you can see the taper.

Side Part Men's Haircut Style

This hairstyle is a clean, short cut with a trendy side part, as the name suggests. It has been thought of as the perfect gentleman's haircut for a long time because it looks so classic and traditional.

How to Get It:

The general rule for this look is to let your hair grow out about 5–10 cm/2-4 in. You don't need to cut your hair unless it's much longer than 10 cm/4 in, because clipping is a big part of this style. To get the sides, use a hair clipper with a guard between 9mm/.35 in (usually a #3 guard) and 15mm/.59 in (usually a #6 guard). You should curve or fade the sides and collar so that the cut goes in gradually. You can also do a "hard part," which is a shaved line that makes a clear part. This makes the haircut stand out and contrasts the top with the sides. Now that you have a side part fade, how do you style it? To style a side-part haircut, you need a good pomade to keep the style in place. Apply the pomade to hair that is wet and towel-dried. Next, decide which side of your head you want the side part to start on and comb all the hair from that side over to the other side. To get a little pompadour look, comb the front part of your hair towards the back. Once all the hair is back, comb down the sides. Finish by spraying a little hairspray on the style to keep it in place.

Man Bun Hairstyles

The man bun is a trendy haircut that has become very popular over the last few years. It looks exactly like it sounds: a ponytail or bunch of hair is put together on top of the head. **Here are some ways to rock a man bun.**

Full

All of the hair is pulled back into a single bun at the top of the head.

Semi

Only the hair on top of the head is used to make a small bun at the crown of the head.

Low

The only difference between this and the full-man bun is that this one covers less of the head.

Undercut fade

It looks like a half-bun with a trim fade on the sides and back of the head.

The Lumberjack

Putting on a beard with any kind of man's hair.
How to Get It:
You'll need hair ties and practice to get this look. If you don't already have long hair, you should grow it out until it's at least 15 cm/6 in long. That's the minimum length needed for a good man bun, and not having enough will make it hard to tie up all of your hair. To get a man bun, first decide where you want to put it. For most styles, this is the top of the head. Next, pull your hair

back into a ponytail and run it through the hair tie once with your free hand. On the second pass, stop halfway through to get a bun. If the hair tie is extra stretchy, you can also run the hair through the band twice and make the bun on the third pass.

Pompadour Haircut Style

The pompadour hairstyle is named after Madame de Pompadour, who was King Louis XV's mistress. It involves sweeping hair up and away from the face and wearing it high on the forehead. Pompadour hair comes in many styles, from retro 1950s to modern and trendy. The pompadour fade is a popular variation of the pompadour style that adds a side fades.

How to Get It:
To get this look, you should first fade your hair. Next, cut the top part of your hair. Once you know how long you want it to be, grab sections of hair between your index and middle fingers and stop when they reach the length you want. Then, use hair scissors to cut straight across your fingers as a guide. Do this until all the sections are cut, making sure that each one is cut an even length.

Quiff Style

Before the quiff haircut came out in the 1950s, there was the strict military buzz cut and the flat top haircuts of the 1940s. The quiff hairstyle quickly became a sign of rebellion and confidence, especially among rock-and-roll musicians (think Elvis) and fans. What is quiff hair? It's a mix of the pompadour and the side part, with short sides and back and longer hair on top that is swept up and back at the front. The main appeal of the quiff hairstyle is that it is less structured and glossier than the pompadour, with pieces of hair falling over the forehead.

How to Get It:

The only difference between a pompadour and a quiff is how it is styled. To get a pompadour haircut, first blow dry your hair and pull it away from your roots with a comb or brush to give it as much volume as possible. Next, warm up a coin-sized amount of pomade and work it into your hair, starting at the roots and working your way forward to the ends. Make sure to spread the pomade evenly. Finally, blow dries your hair again to give it more definition and volume. For extra hold, mist with hairspray.

French Crop Haircut Style

The French crop is a standard haircut for guys. It has a short fade or trim and a long fringe on top. The best thing about the French crop haircut is how easy it is to take care of. Touch-ups are only needed every 6 to 8 weeks. Not only that but styling a men's French crop is very easy. If you want more structure, you can add a little hairspray or pomade. The French crop fade is the most famous way to wear French crop hair. The French crop fade is a classy French crop with a tight fade on the back and sides.

How to Get It:
To start, fade or trim the sides of your hair. After you're done with this, start cutting the top part of your hair. Lightly point cut the front of your hair by pulling it forward toward your face with your index and middle fingers. You should keep this part of your hair longer than the rest of your hair because this style needs a "fringe." Do the same thing to the back of your head until all of your hair is textured.

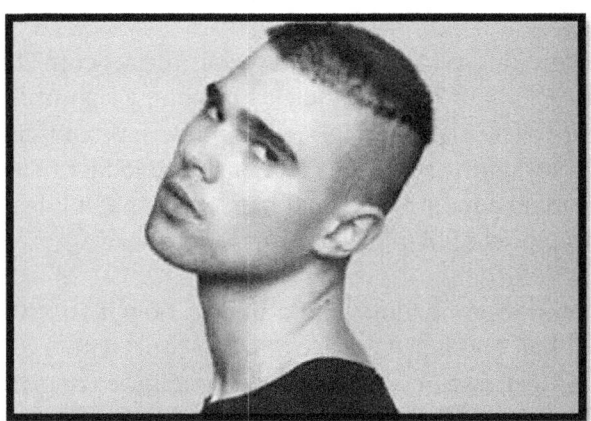

Faux Hawk Haircut Style

The fake hawk hairdo is a mix of a pompadour and a mohawk. The sides are shaved, and there is a strip of longer hair that is styled freely in an inward, jutting forward motion. People say that the fake hawk haircut is more stylish than a pompadour and less crazy than a mohawk, making it appropriate for a job interview or the office. Many different styles exist, such as the shaggy fake hawk and the bald faux hawk. However, the faux hawk fade is one of the most famous. The fake hawk fade, which is also called the short mohawk fade, is all about making sure that the sides are the right thickness for the spiked top. The fake hawk fade is not as sharp as a real hawk fade. It is softer and fits in better with the big strip of hair on top.

How to Get It:
First, decide how wide you want your fake hawk to be on dry, clean hair. You can measure this from one outer eye to the other, but if you want it to be narrower, you can measure it from center eye to center eye. Next, use a comb to divide your hair into three equal parts. Start at the front of your hairline and move down to the nape of your neck on both sides of your head. This will form

a C shape. The start and end points of the part are the same as the start and end points of the width. Start cutting both sides of your hair in the way you want, depending on whether you choose to fade or trim your sides. Once this is done, you can start cutting the middle part. Grab pieces of hair with your index and middle fingers, working your way up from the base of your neck. Use your fingers as a guide to cut straight across with hair scissors. Do this again and again until all of the hair is cut off. Make sure that your hair has been evenly cut.

Mohawk Haircut Styles

In a mohawk haircut for guys, the sides are shaved, and there is a larger strip of hair on top. The Native American Mohawk group came up with this edgy and very modern haircut. During World War II, the American Air Force wore it as a sign of power. **The mohawk haircut comes in two main styles:**

Short

People think of the shorter style as the standard one, but the top is cut shorter. Usually, the sides of the hair are spiked inwards to style it.

Fade

The mohawk fade is a haircut with buzzed, curved sides and a long strip of hair in the middle. It is a little less dramatic than the standard.
How to Get It:
The mohawk haircut is similar to the fake hawk haircut in that you have to shave the sides of your head off and leave the top long. To shave the sides, use the hair clipper's guard with the lowest number. If you want to style your hair in spikes the right way, you may need to trim it often, and depending on how fast it grows.

Children's Haircuts

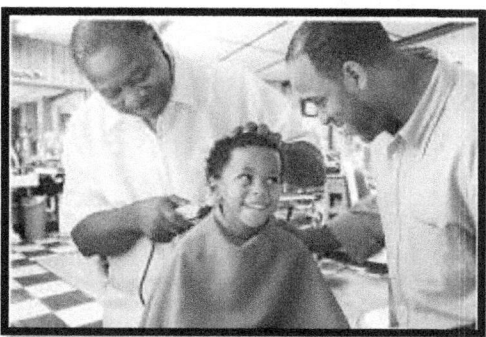

Hairstyles for kids should be easy to take care of so that you don't have to take them to the salon every two weeks, but they should also be cool enough that your kids feel like they can show off their personality and tastes. Your child can get a haircut that looks good on them no matter what length or type of hair they have. Here are some of the best haircuts for kids of all types, from basic cuts to styles that set trends.

Keep the Natural Curls Carefully Sculpted

Boys with naturally curly hair might not want a very short chopped haircut or to let it grow out and wear it long, but shaping their curls low around the head is a great way to control the volume until they're old enough to do their hair care. Going to a stylist who hasn't cut curly or natural hair before is, of course, one of the worst things you can do. If they do it wrong, they can ruin the curl pattern and give your child a weird look for weeks. So, make sure you talk to the stylist about your curly haircut before you decide on one.

Close Cropped Sides and Brushed Back Top Cut, Perfect for Fine Hair

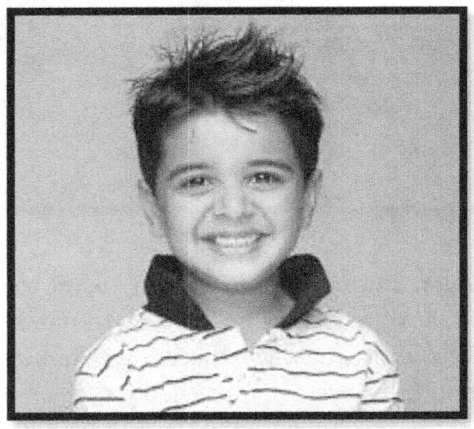

Some extra length should be left on top of a standard haircut for kids with fine, straight hair. The sides and back should be closely shaved. If you don't want their hair too short, you can ask the stylist to use clippers with bigger guards (6 or 7 sizes) so there is more hair to work with. After cutting off some length on top, they can add body by running some gel or wax through it. In general, this style is very simple to copy at home.

All-Over Short Buzz for Boys

One of the most standard haircuts for young guys is cutting it short all the way around. This looks a lot like a Caesar haircut, with a clear high fringe. They won't feel like they're going to military school after getting their hair buzzed with a 3 or 4 guard, but it will be longer between trips to the salon.

Bring Back the Long Locks

Some boys want their hair longer, and some parents don't want to deal with the care of getting their son's hair cut all the time. For these parents, an easy trim is a great way to keep the messy look. If your child's hair is naturally curly or wavy, this cut will look good on them because it has a body and won't look flat around their eyes. If your child has thick or different types of hair, you may need to use a hair product like flexible pomade to keep it under control.

Completely Shaved Style for a Fresh Feel

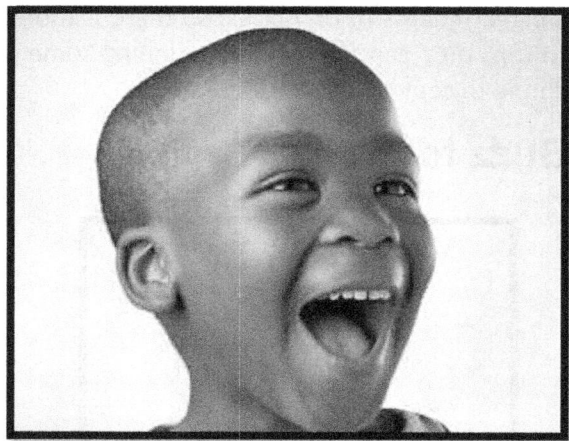

What could be easier for a kid than a shaved head? It's easy to make at home and doesn't need to be styled, so even the youngest kids can wear it. It's great for kids who have trouble sitting still in a stylist's chair, and it's also one of the best choices for places where it's very hot all year. It will look fine for a while if you don't let it grow out, but you'll need to do more touch-ups, which you can do at home with clippers and a razor.

Classic Crew Cut to Beat the Heat

When it comes to kids, the basic crew cut is another great style for those who don't like hair in their face or who need shorter hair because of sensory issues. This style needs hair clippers instead of a comb and scissors because the hair is short all over and only a little longer on top. It's not as short as a shaved style. It's a good choice for boys who want neat hair, but it will need to be trimmed often to keep it looking its best.

A Rebellious Mohawk to Make a Statement

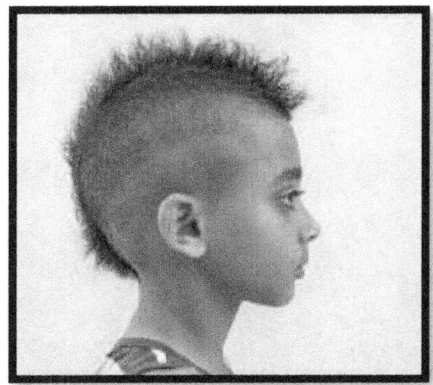

A mohawk is a great haircut for kids who like to make a statement or who want to try new things with their style. The mohawk is a bold look for a bold child, even when it's not gelled into spikes. Kids no longer have to work up to getting this haircut because you don't need a lot of length to begin with like you did in the past. Even better, you don't have to shave the sides down. For an even more rock 'n' roll look, you could have a cool skin fade from the ends to the collar.

Short Hair Don't Care With This Pixie Haircut

Girls' basic pixie cuts are cute, and they don't need much care when it comes to washing and dressing. Thin or fine hair works best with it. Hair that is very thick or twisted might not hold its shape as well. A pixie cut is usually very short, but a girl could choose to have it a little longer in the front for more styling choices. For a cool retro look, she could also add baby fringe as Mia Farrow did in Rosemary's Baby.

Classic Bowl Haircut for Kids That Can't Sit Still

The standard bowl haircut is named after the way it looks on kids' heads, like a bowl around them. Most of the time, the bowl cut has longer hair on top that slowly slopes down the sides and rests behind the ears in a circle around the head. This haircut has been popular for kids for a long time. It looks good on most face shapes and hair types, but it might not look good on kids with very curly hair. It's not always the coolest style, but it's great for kids who have trouble with their hair and want to get it out of the way, or for kids who can't sit still for a complicated chop.

Short Scissor Cut with Fringe for a no-fuss Style

This basic cut is sweet and easy, so it doesn't need much work. It's a constant length because it's pretty short all over, and the breezy look that can be achieved with a little cutting keeps the casual vibe. It looks great as is, but kids can make it their own by adding styling products to make spikes on the head, slicking it back, or giving it a ducktail or bouffant shape.

Chin-Length Bob with Bangs Is As Sweet As Can Be

Some people think that the Karen movement stole the bob haircut, but many parents still give their kids this style. It looks classic and easy, and it keeps their hair out of the way while it grows. Also, fringe is always in style, and since this style can be washed and worn again, it's a must-have for kids who are always on the go. The kids can also make it more fun by adding barrettes, a headband, shiny lines that clip in, and a lot more.

Medium-Length Cut with Subtle Layers to Embrace the Mane

A chop that skims the shoulders is a great choice for kids who are old enough to start taking care of their hair. Even so, if their hair has any kind of body or curls, they need to add some minor layers. This will take some of the weight off the ends so that it doesn't hang too low around their neck and face. It will also keep it at a length that they can handle.

Long, Face-Framing Layers for the Kids Next Door

If your child has long hair, keep the ends cut and add a few face-framing layers to draw attention to their face. Ever-classic styles, the layers that start at chin level and get longer until they meet the longest pieces are angled. This gives hair a fun structure, especially for people with straight or fine hair, and the style grows naturally.

Classic Bob without Bangs for Your Mature Mini-Me

And finally, a bob cut without bangs is always in style. The ends can be shaped to turn just a little under toward the face, or they can be left alone. It can be split down the middle or on the side, based on what the child wants. This haircut, the shoulder-length to chin-length bob, can work for almost any hair type and shape as long as it's cut by the right stylist. It's also pretty easy to keep up.

Long Layered Cut for a Soft Look

Adding soft, gentle layers can help thick hair stay in place and give a naturally wild and wavy look a little more control. There are soft layers all over this cut that give the hair body and dimension without being too noticeable. But if the layers feel too heavy, you can also get the hair cut. The layers are what make the look. In the same way, this haircut stays in shape for a long time, making it one of the best ones to let grow out.

Natural Curls for a Beautiful Halo of Hair

A girls' haircut that ends just above the shoulders and is about medium length is a pretty way to show off natural curls. It can also work for most other hair types. Girls can style it with hair items because it's long enough, but not too long that it's hard to take care of or style. In the same way, letting your kids' hair grow out naturally without cutting it short gives them the option of longer haircuts when they are old enough to take care of it themselves, without having to start from scratch.

Short Cut with Flipped Ends for a Vintage Look

A girl's haircut that looks fun and a little retro is a single-layer cut bluntly just above the chin. This cut can make a cute flip at the ends, which looks especially cute if your child's hair naturally waves. But even kids with straight hair can get this cute look by rolling the ends of their hair a little with a straightener or curling wand.

Single Layer Cut with Side Swept Bangs Taking Center Stage

People from the millennial generation and their children often wear side-swept bangs. These styles look great on people with thick hair or big foreheads. The bangs don't need to be cut all the time to look great because the style is casual and relaxed. They also look good on hair of all lengths and types, but the best thing about them might be how easy they are to grow out. Side bangs are a good balance because they don't look too harsh on elementary school kids. If you've ever had full fringe grow out, you know how bad it is.

Edgy Stacked Bob with No Bangs

People love the stacked bob haircut, which has a shorter back and a longer front. It's become a social media star. You can make this style a little more edgy and cool than a regular bob by adding layers or cutting the hair very unevenly from the back to the front. You can wear fringe or not. Moody kids are great candidates for this style of haircut.

CHAPTER 9
STYLING AND FINISHING TECHNIQUES
Blow Dry Your Hair

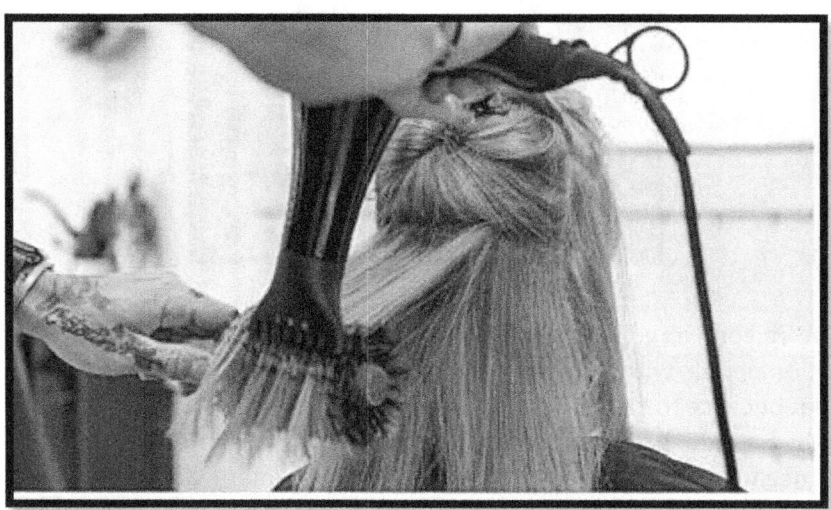

Step 1: Pat hair dry with a towel
It takes a long time and makes hair frizzy to blow-dry hair that is dripping wet. Since you asked, "Why does my hair look frizzy after I blow-dry it?" this is most likely the answer! When you start with hair that is completely wet, it becomes dry and tough. People hurt their hair with heat most of the time when they blow dry for too long. If you have time, you can let your hair dry naturally for a while, but this is not the best way to get it done. Towel drying cuts down on the time it takes to blow-dry, so your hair is less likely to get frizzy and dry. But be careful not to rub your hair too hard with a towel. This will cause the towel and your hair to rub against each other, which will break the cuticles. Take a microfiber towel and squeeze out the extra water near the ends. Then, pat the hair dry.

Step 2: Follow with a general blow-dry, until the hair is about 50% dry
To shape hair, it needs to be between damp and dry, NOT damp, so get rid of any extra water first, and don't waste time or effort here. Instead, use your fingers to rough dry. Use a heat protectant and your best straight hair product to get your hair ready. Then, rough dry your hair until it's almost completely dry. Take your time with the rough dry and don't point the spray down yet. Dry the hair from the roots up with a hair dryer. If you want a rough dry, keep moving your hairdryer around the whole time. Focusing on one spot for too long will damage your hair with heat, and you're not trying to style it yet. If your hair is frizzy or wavy, do this until it's about half dry. If your hair is straight, try for 80 to 90% dry. This should be done until your hair is about 80% to 90% dry if it's straight and about 50% dry if it's curly or wavy.

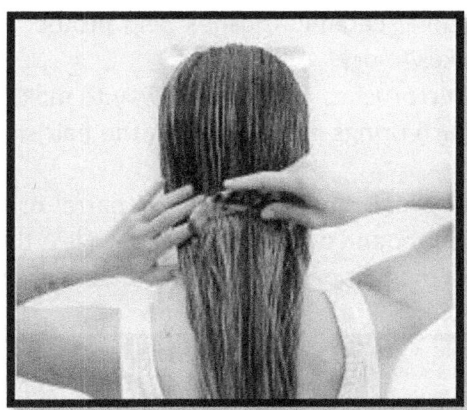

Step 3. Divide hair into small sections
People often mess up their at-home blowouts by dividing their hair into parts that are too big. If there is too much hair on your hairbrush, it can make your hair flat or frizzy. Using parts that are too big can also make it hard to focus your brush, which can cause breaking (this is especially true for curly hair). For easy styling, split your hair into small pieces that are about 1 to 2 inches wide. Make a horseshoe shape with your hair from your temples to the back of your head. Then, part your hair down the middle to make four pieces. Next, work on one area at a time while the hair is clipped up.

Step 4: Dry each section by pulling it with a brush and using a nozzle that focuses hair on the shafts in the section
When it comes to getting a blowout that lasts, tension is key. It's very important if you want your hair to dry easily, especially if you have cowlicks or hair that is naturally curly. To keep hair from flying around, always use a vent to direct air over the bristles of your brush, about five inches away from tight hair and pointing downwards. Dry your hair slowly and in small parts so that you can seal the cuticle. Dry the hair from the roots to the ends.

Step 5: Put on your finishing touches
Once each area of hair is dry, give the whole head a quick blast of cool air to set the blowout. When you're done and your hair is cool, use your fingers to lightly rake it through. Shake your head around a bit, and then flip it back over. After you're done with your look, don't touch your hair. Mist it with your best shiny hair products.

How do I get the perfect salon-quality blowout?

Use a brush suited to your hair type

Pick out a brush based on your hair type and the results you want. These are the most popular hair brushes:

- **Round brush:** Use a round brush that is between 1" and 2 ½ inches" in diameter, based on how much curl and volume you want. The hair will be smoother if the brush is bigger.
- **Ceramic brush:** The heat from ceramic brushes is just right for the heat style. The hair stays soft and is simple to style. Blow-drying is needed to make heat, which speeds up the

drying process. Over time, ceramic brushes help protect hair from damage by cutting down on the time it takes to dry.
- **Boar-bristle:** Boar bristle brushes are the best way to make your hair look smooth. They massage the head, which brings more blood to the hair shaft. This is great for hair that needs some TLC.
- **Ceramic-coated barrel brush**: A ceramic-coated barrel brush is great for all hair types because it holds heat better and dries hair faster with less damage. The brushes are made in a special way to help the hair dry faster and with less damage from heat.

Invest in a high-quality blow dryer

Yes, you can blow-dry your hair every day. If you do, you should get a good hair dryer with features that protect your hair and help you dry your hair faster. A good dryer has ionic air technology, multiple heat levels, and a cool shot to close the ends of the hair. If you don't want to spend a lot of money, there are also many choices that your stylist will suggest that won't break the bank.

Apply styling products throughout your hair

Always use the right style products on all of your hair before styling it, and make sure you spread them out evenly. When you use hot tools on your hair, you should always use heat protectants, a smoothing serum for frizzy hair, or a texturizing liquid for volume, and you should work the products through your hair from the middle of the shaft to the ends using your fingers or a comb while the hair is still wet. This spreads them out evenly across the area.

Use a nozzle

The blow dryer comes with a flat tip piece that sends direct, focused heat down the hair shaft. This makes damaged hair smooth and shiny. To close the cuticle and give the hair a shiny look, always point the tool down along the hair shaft. Finish with a blast from below for a more textured and messier look.

Mistakes to Avoid When Blow-Drying Hair Straight Like a Pro

Using too high of a heat setting

To get the job done faster, you might think about blow-drying your hair in the hottest setting. However, this is bad for your hair. Depending on the type of hair you have, you should change the heat setting and the speed setting on your blow drier. A level with low to medium heat and wind works best for hair that is fine or thin. Thicker hair can handle a little more heat and less movement. No matter what heat setting you use, make sure to add shine with a blast of cool air.

Using the wrong brush

For a straight blowout, the strands need to be pulled tight. The hair shaft will spring back to its original shape if the brush bristles are too far apart for your hair type. This means that the hair will dry in place. When your hair is wet, a round brush can damage it because it puts a lot of stress on the hair strands. A lot of round brushes have metal centers that get hot from the dryer and can do even more damage. Use a brush with a lot of surface area to get the best finish. A big brush will let your hair dry while still making it easy to brush out parts. You can choose either a boar bristle brush or a nylon bristle brush.

Skipping styling products or not applying them evenly

Before you blow-dry your hair, you should at least use a heat protectant to get it ready. Not protecting hair from heat is one of the main causes of hair loss. Our heat protection tools keep your hair healthy and strong by protecting it from heat. Also, use a mousse or blow-dry prep that adds volume. When styling thick hair, divide it up into parts. If your hair is thin, put products halfway down the ends to keep it from looking greasy.

Blow-dry the right way

Should you have hair loss, blow drying it every day can be drying. Find a blow dryer with ionic technology to keep damage to a minimum. Make your hair fuller with mousse and a heat protection spray. Then, turn your head upside down and blow air at your roots. This will give your hair a lot of thickness, hiding any hair loss.

Avoid hair care products that are drying

Stay away from style items with plastics, chemicals, and solvents if you have thin hair. These can take away the natural oils that your skin and hair need. They can make hair that is already thin look even stringier.

Not working from root to tip

When you blow dry your hair, you should work from the roots to the ends because that's how your hair grows. Working against it opens up the hair shaft's cuticles, which makes it more likely to get tangled and frizzy. To make your hair shine, always blow dry your hair from the roots to the ends.

Moving too quickly

It takes time to blow-dry your hair straight. If you move too quickly, a blowout might not last long. If you let your hair cool a bit on the brush before going on to the next area, it will set, which will make your hard work last longer. Your smooth, shiny hair will last up to two days if you take your time. Have dry shampoo on hand to make it last even longer.

Using Heat Tools

The Basics: Curling Irons vs. Flat Irons

It's important to know the difference between curling irons and flat irons before we get into the important tips and tricks. Even though they look alike, they are used for different things and need different methods. The curling iron is a barrel-shaped tool used to curl or wave hair in beautiful ways. The curls will be tight or loose depending on the size of the barrel. It has a clip or clamp that holds the hair in place while the heat is coming on. A flat iron, which is also called a hair straightener, has two hot plates that move through the hair to make it look smooth and straight. It's great for getting rid of frizz and leaving your hair smooth and shiny. Let's get to the good stuff now that we've got that cleared up.

Tip 1: Protection is Key
The most important thing to remember when heat styling is to always use heat protectant spray. The scorching heat can't damage or break your valuable strands because this magical potion protects them. We promise that it will be good for your hair. Spray a lot of heat protectant spray

all over your hair before you use a curling iron or flat iron. Spread it out evenly so that every strand is covered. Putting this on will protect your hair from heat damage and make the styles you use last longer.

Tip 2: Temperature Control
Most new flat irons and curling irons have temperature settings that can be changed. It may be tempting to turn up the heat to get things done faster, but it's important to use the right temperature for your hair type and the style you want. Keep the temperature between 250°F and 300°F (120°C and 150°C) for hair that is fine or damaged. Between 175°C and 205°C, 350°F to 400°F is a good range for hair that is thick or tough. A good rule of thumb is to start with a lower temperature and raise it slowly if needed. Never forget that being careful is always better than risking damaging your hair!

Tip 3: Section, Section, Section
"Divide and conquer" is the key to the heat style that works. Not only will working on small pieces make the process easier, but they will also make sure that each strand gets the care it needs. Start at the bottom and work your way up with curling irons. Put your hair back with clips so it doesn't get in the way. Place the curling iron close to the roots of a 1-inch piece of hair and wrap it around the barrel, away from your face. Hold for a few seconds, then let go, and a beautiful curl is born! When you use a flat iron, it works best to work with small pieces of hair. Start putting the small piece between the plates as close to the root as you can. Hold on tight as you slowly slide the iron down the hair shaft. Do this again and again until your head is smooth and straight. Now your hair will look so good that people will want to steal it.

Tip 4: Practice Makes Perfect
Let's be honest: it takes time and practice to get good at heat style. Don't give up if your first try doesn't make the red carpet! You'll be a pro soon enough if you keep trying new things. If you've never used heat style before, start with a lower heat setting and help from a friend. To do this, start slowly and build your confidence as you go. Remember that even the best hairstylists started as newbies. Enjoy the process, and have fun making beautiful hairstyles!

Tip 5: TLC for Your Tresses
Finally, hair that has been treated with heat needs a little extra care to stay healthy and bright. If you use heat tools on your hair often, they can dry it out and make it break easily. To stop this from happening, give your hair a deep conditioning treatment and a hydrating mask once a week. These powerful products will bring back the wetness your hair lost and make it healthy again. You can also avoid split ends and keep your hair looking its best by cutting it regularly. You'll see a huge change if you get your hair cut every 6 to 8 weeks. As of now, you know how to safely use curling irons and flat irons since we reviewed the basics. So, my fellow hairstylists go out there and make some hair magic!

Curl Your Hair with a Flat Iron

Take a moment to think about the famous people you see walking the red carpet. The ones whose curls look so beautiful and natural that you wonder, "Could my hair do that?" We've all been there and done that. We've bought fancy curling irons and spent hours curling each part in front of the mirror, but our hair still doesn't look ready for the red carpet. But it's easier than you think to get curls that look great, and you probably already have the key in your bathroom. The flat iron is the tool that will give you the natural-looking curls you've always wanted. This method is not only liked by celebrity stylists, but it's also surprisingly easy. No matter what, anyone can get this hairstyle if they work at it.

Start with healthy hair

First things first: hair that is healthy looks nice. If your hair is dry, split, broken, or damaged in some other way, it will be harder to get great results. Fix damage to your hair caused by chemicals, UV rays, or heat as the first step toward getting perfect curls.

Prep with a heat protectant

Do things to keep your hair healthy and strong after it gets better. Hot-style tools, like straighteners, can hurt the surface of your hair very badly, making it look dry and brittle. Does this mean you should never use hot tools? Of course not, but it does mean you need to protect your hair from heat before you start. Heat protectants wrap around the ends of your hair and give each strand a little shield to help it handle the heat.

Start using the iron

The flat iron should now be warm and ready to use, and your hair should be healthy and safe.
You're almost there with your flat iron curls:
1. Split your hair into manageable sections.
2. Take a section of hair and clamp it with your flat iron.
3. Start to move your iron toward the end of the lock.
4. Turn the iron around 180 degrees. One side of the straightener should be wrapped around the hair, but not both. After that, move the iron down your hair one more time. At the very end, your hair will be curled in a beautiful, springy way.
5. Do this again for each little section of hair. Change the direction you twist the iron (towards your face vs. away from your face) with each part if you want your curls to look more natural.
6. You can leave your hair twisted as is, shake it out at the roots, or comb it through for a more natural, laid-back look.
7. Use hairspray. That way, the curls will last all day.

So now you know how to curl your hair with a straightener like a pro. But this is only a general help. Depending on the curls you want, there are different ways to use a straightener to curl your hair. To get S or C-curls, you'll need to use a slightly different method. Clip your hair close to the root for these styles, but not so close that you burn yourself. Pull your hair together in a "S" or "C" form with your free hand. Then, move the iron down your hair, squeezing the strands each time you go down. Let go of the iron a little. With this method, you'll get curls that look more dramatic and Old Hollywood.

Set it with hairspray

One more thing needs to be done to finish making your curls perfect. Spray your curls with hairspray to help them stay put. Try to find a hairspray that soaks up oil so your hair stays clean, shiny, and pretty all day. You're ready to go after setting your curls with hairspray.

Be gentle

Here are some tips to help you get this cute curly look without getting hurt. To begin, don't hold the iron too close to your head. If you want to curl all of your hair, don't start too high. That could burn your skin. Also, it's important to use a good flat iron that won't hurt your hair. It's best to use high-quality tools to make hair straightener curls as safe as possible, even if you use a heat protectant (which you should always do). It's important to have the right straighteners if you want your hair to look its best. Instead of clay or metal plates, we suggest flat irons with titanium or tourmaline plates because they keep heat in better.

A few helpful tips

Anyone can learn how to use a flat iron to curl their hair. To do it, you just need the right goods, the right tools, and some time to practice. **So, here are some more tips and tricks that will help you get good at this style.**

- For different curl looks, use sections of hair that are different sizes. Curlier hair, like coils or ringlets, will come from smaller sections, while curlier hair, like beach waves, will come from wider sections. If you want to get the look you want, keep this in mind as you part your hair.
- The ending curl is affected by both the size of your curl area and your flat iron. If the curls you get from one iron don't work for you, try one that's bigger or smaller and see how the look changes.
- Don't forget that curls aren't just for fancy events; you can style them in any way you like. Choose your favorite hair ornament curl your hair and put it in a ponytail. You can also put half of your hair in a bun. Those waves will make any style look better.

You can try all the pretty hairstyles you thought were only for movie stars now that you know how to curl your hair with a flat iron. Remember that it takes time to get the right curl, so don't be afraid to try again and again.

Using Curling Irons

There is no doubt that the best way to glam up your look is to give your hair volume, shine, and curls. Some people are lucky enough to have naturally curly hair, so using a curling iron or wand to try to make curls come alive can be risky.

Step 1: Select Your Tool
There are a few things you should think about before you buy your favorite curling iron. First, choose whether you want a curling iron with a clamp or a stick. As you might guess, a curling iron with a clamp has a clamp that helps keep your hair in place while you curl it. An iron with a stick does not have a lock. You hold your hair in place while the curl forms by wrapping it around the barrel. Which one you choose depends on your taste and which one is easier for you to use. Next, think about how curly you want your hair to be.

Choose a barrel size of ¾-inch or less if you want to make coils that are tightly wound. If you want big, beachy waves, get a curling iron with a barrel that is at least an inch wide. Should you want to curl your hair, clay or tourmaline tools are always a good choice because they can help smooth out frizz. There's also the work that needs to be done by hand. If twisting your hair around the curling iron barrel doesn't sound like fun, an automatic curling iron might be just what you need.

Step 2: Start Your Look with Freshly Washed Hair
Clean hair is best for getting the most out of your perfectly curled look. Get in the shower and use shampoo and conditioner that is made to control the look of frizz.

Step 3: Blow-Dry Your Hair
After letting your hair air dry about half of the way, use a boar bristle brush to dry it the rest of the way until it's totally dry. Don't forget to use a heat protectant.

Step 4: Test Your Curling Iron's Heat
It's time to use that curling iron or wand now that you've blow-dried your hair. First, make sure the heat setting is right for your hair. Usually, it's best to try the setting with the least amount of heat to see what kind of curl it makes. You can change the heat as needed before you start from there.

Step 5: Section Your Hair
After heating your curling iron, divide your hair into two or three layers that are stacked horizontally. If your hair is thin, divide it into fewer layers, but if it's thick, divide it into more layers. Hold the layers on top out of the way with a lobster clip while you curl the bottom part. You should curl all of your hair, not just the top layers, because more curls make your hair look thicker of course.

Step 6: Curl Your Hair
Now is the time to use your favorite curling tool. What happens next will depend on which one you pick.

Step 7: Shake Out Your Curls
When your hair is all curled, flip it over and give it a good shake to make the curls less tight and give it a more natural look.

Step 8: Set Your Curls
To keep your curls in place, lightly mist your hair with hair spray if you need to.

How to Use a Curling Iron with a Clamp

Here is what you should do if you are using a regular curling iron.

1. **Grab a section of hair.** Cut off a section of hair to curl. How tight the curl is depends on how small the section is. The twist is less tight when the section is bigger.
2. **Position your curling iron.** To use your iron, open the clamp and place it near the root of your hair. Place the hair between the open clamp and the iron. Watch out not to burn yourself.
3. **Close and slide.** To finish, close the clamp just a little and slide it down the hair until it reaches the end. Close the clamp all the way.
4. **Twist, twist, twist.** As you twist your curling iron up toward your roots, wrap the length of the part around it. Give your hair 10 to 15 seconds to heat up.
5. **Open the clamp and release.** Open the clamp slowly and pull the curling iron out of your hair. The curl you just made should now hang loosely. It's not that hard, right?

How to Use a Curling Wand

Here's how to use a curling wand instead if you've chosen to.

1. **Section your hair.** Like when you use a curling tool, you should start by separating the hair you want to twist into a few sections. Don't forget that smaller sections make curls that are tighter and larger sections make looser curls.
2. **Position your wand.** The wand should be held in the hand that is not curling your hair. Then, put it down so that the base is close to the root of your hair section and the barrel points down.
3. **Wrap around.** Wrap the length of your hair around the barrel with your other hand, making your way down until the ends are around the smallest part of the stick.
4. **Wait and release.** After letting your hair heat up for 10 to 15 seconds, take the wand out and pull your hair back to see a beautiful, bouncy curl.

To get a more natural look, curl your hair away from your face. To do this, wind your hair around your curling stick from left to right, going clockwise on the right and counterclockwise on the left.

PART IV
ADVANCED HAIR CUTTING AND PROFESSIONAL DEVELOPMENT

CHAPTER 10
CREATIVE CUTTING AND CUSTOM STYLES

Asymmetrical Cuts

If you want a haircut that is both unique and stylish, you need to forget about the rules. You could say that a classic cut looks good, but it's not new. On the other hand, an uneven style can be very cool and exciting. This cool cut has one side that is longer than the other. It's great for girls who like to stand out. This style is great because it's easy to change to fit your tastes. Everyone can find a style they like, from short cuts to lobs and even long locks.

Asymmetrical Pixie Cut

Cutting your hair short is one of the easiest ways to rock an asymmetrical hairstyle. Because pixies are short, a small difference in length is all you need to make a beautiful asymmetrical look. You could add some layers to lighten up the style so that it doesn't feel too heavy on the longer side.

Asymmetrical Bangs

The sides of your hair don't have to be different lengths all the time for an asymmetrical cut. The only thing you need sometimes to get a great asymmetrical look is some stylishly angled bangs. You will have to wait for your bangs to grow out, though, if you change your mind about this bold style.

Wavy Asymmetrical Bob

Without a doubt, wavy bob haircuts look cute. But when worn with an asymmetrical cut, they can also look classy and grown up. Women of all ages can wear this style, from 20 to 50 years old and up.

Asymmetrical Bob with Bangs

If you chose an asymmetrical bob haircut and want to draw even more attention to the difference in length, you might also want to try front bangs. Because it is straight, a front fringe will make the difference between your hairs on one side stand out right away.

Long Asymmetrical Hair

There aren't many long asymmetrical styles, but there are a lot of short ones. But if you have long hair, that doesn't mean you shouldn't try the cut. By cutting just one side of your hair shorter, you can quickly look stylish and stand out.

Long Asymmetrical Hair with Undercut

A long asymmetrical style with an undercut is the best way to make a really strong difference in length. This look is striking and can't be missed. One side is long and flowy, and the other side is shaved short.

Asymmetrical Shag

Many haircuts can look good with an asymmetrical cut, even shag. To get the look, get a mid-length cut that isn't straight and add lots of choppy layers. The layers should begin at the top and end at the front with bangs.

Asymmetrical Undercut

Getting an undercut is a fun way to follow the asymmetrical trend. Have your stylist cut off one side of your hair and leave the other side long. You can keep your look girly by choosing a deep side part and leaving a lot of hair on top.

Unique Asymmetrical Haircut

There are many ways to change the look of an asymmetrical haircut to fit your style. Hence, if you want a soft look, you can choose a small change in length. You can make a stronger statement with a significant difference in length and asymmetrical bangs, though, if you like that look.

Asymmetrical Layered Bob

A stylish and young-looking look can be achieved with an asymmetrical layered bob haircut. You can also get the look by adding texture with a sea salt spray. This will give your hair a slightly messy look, giving you a beautiful laid-back look.

Avant-Garde Hair

Avant-garde hair is large, fun, one-of-a-kind, and very artistic. You have come to the right place if you want to learn how to do real avant-garde hairstyles for fun or your next picture.

What Is Avant-Garde Hair?

Avant-garde hair is any style of hair that is very stylized and looks weird in some way. Since you've probably heard the word "avant-garde" before, most likely in the context of fashion or the arts, you probably have a good idea of what it means. That being said, the exact meaning of avant-garde in the dictionary is "new or experimental ideas" and the people who come up with them. The translation from French refers to the front line of an army, also called the advance guard or vanguard. These days, we mostly use it to talk about a style of art. The point of avant-garde styles is that they aren't meant to be worn every day. Bold, over-the-top styles that are part of a collection or an artistic statement are called avant-garde. You won't see these trends very often outside of fashion shows and magazine shoots.

The Rules for Crafting an Avant-Garde Hairstyle

There are no rules for avant-garde hair, which is fun. But avant-garde hair can look bad very quickly. You want your hairpiece to look good, not like it was put together by someone with too many ideas. Here are some tips to help you get that avant-garde look for your next art project, movie, or picture, or just to stand out when you're out and about. A lot of the time, big, trendy wigs aren't made of real hair. When you're making a hairpiece for an avant-garde style, there are some useful things to keep in mind.

Weight

Your hairstyle is going to be worn by you or another person. It shouldn't be too heavy for them to break their neck. While you're coming up with ideas for your look, you might keep adding hairpieces, clips, jewelry, and other things to keep the shape of the style. To get the look you want, you might need to add more fake hair. That will get heavy when it's all put together. Make sure to use structure parts and things that are light.

Structure

Let's talk about hair form while we're on the subject of weight. Should the piece you're making depend on height, you should think about how it will be put together inside. To put your piece on again, you need something light. You can use straws or pipe cleaners, or you can use foam, wires, or rollers. You can make it stand out, but it shouldn't be too heavy. Also, it has to stay hidden under the hair so that the result doesn't look sloppy.

Balance

Balance is very important, even for a short picture take. You will need to check your piece's balance if you are making a big sculptured haircut. If you style a hairpiece on a dummy head, it doesn't mean that your style won't fall off of the model or you. A piece that isn't balanced will fall off with one wrong tilt of the head if your model is walking, talking, or moving. As you style your hair, make sure you test it.

Simple Avant-Garde Looks to Style Yourself

"Simple" and "avant-garde" don't belong together. But there are ways to style your hair that aren't too hard to do but will still give you an avant-garde look. When putting together your look, there are a few things to keep in mind so it looks great on camera. Most of the time, you don't need to make a big artistic wig or hairpiece to style these. You can just put them on your model. To keep a haircut cutting edge, it doesn't need to be hard to do; just keep it interesting to look at. Most of the time, you can do this by shaping. A modern hairdo is often artistic, and even the most basic ones have their shape. Here are some tips on how to style your hair like a pro even if you're not one.

Over-Teasing

A clear style doesn't always mean big objects or sharp lines. If you over-tease your hair, you can get an avant-garde look with a simple style. You can choose to add more style elements to the dramatic outline you'll get or leave it alone. A huge pile of curled, cloudy hair makes a statement on its own and will make you or your model look like they are from another world. You can add as much information as you want. You can tease the back of your hair but leave the front neat to frame your face. You only need a brush and some hairspray to make it go along with your ideas.

A Wet Finish

Any look will stand out if you give it a high gloss finish. A lot of people don't have shiny hair that looks like its dripping. Another simple way to style something at home is to do this. Use finishing oil on your hair to make it look too wet to handle without ruining your style. This idea is great for a look for a picture shoot. If the light is right, the gloss will shine.

Bold Faux Bangs

With bobby pins and your model's real hair, you can make big, beautiful, and dramatic fake bangs to frame their face. It will look best on a figure whose hair is long. Like you would for a side part, sweep your real hair to the side. You can shape your hair with bobby pins, but this will depend on the look you want. You can make shapes and textures that are more extreme by pinning them in different ways or by clipping short extensions into just the bangs. To keep it looking like a real haircut, make sure you hide the clips. You can also use hair oil on this style to make it shine or keep it natural and wild. It all depends on how you feel about art.

Exaggerated Victory Rolls

It looks hard to do the 1940s victory roll hairdo yourself, but it's not. That's why it's great for building a look around for a more experimental one. If you know the basics of the classic look, you can use them to make an avant-garde haircut with more shape. It's up to you if you want to make big, swooping rolls or use one roll with other avant-garde features. Try out different pair-ups.

Big Updo

You can make a bunch of hair on top of your head look cool in a lot of different ways. The famous "bird's nest" style is a big bun with curled hair around the edges. You can see this style a lot on runway models. You can make it as big and crazy as you like. Feel free to use any 80s-style outfit. You should use a lot of perfume. Pretty much any style can be turned into a star. You can make a big fauxhawk or add fun knots, ties, bands, or anything else that fits your style. This is fun because you can't go wrong; just make something that people will love.

Avant-Garde Inspired Haircuts

Any of the ideas above can be toned down to make an everyday look that stands out. Since avant-garde is all about being creative and pushing the limits, the only rule for an avant-garde haircut is that it has to do at least one strange thing.

Short Hair Ideas

Use strong shapes, like short hair with sharp lines. Get a short, sharp fringe or a geometric cut like an asymmetrical bob. Pick out the best things for your face. With a pixie cut with a lot of layers, you can get a bold shape with lots of volume, and you'll never have hair in your eyes.

Color

Straight hair that hasn't been styled can be given a unique look with bright color choices like color-blocked hair or money pieces. Your bright hair coloring will make a statement once it's done, so you won't have to do any more styling. Depending on your taste, this could be colorful hair, bright colors that stand out, a bold spot of color (like dying just your bangs), or anything else you like. It's better if the color is bright and not very realistic.

Upgrade Your Updo

Do you only want a trim? Long hair can be styled in fun ways when you get tired of leaving it open. Find any big hairstyle ideas you like and make them simple. For a simple but stylish hairdo, put your hair in a big messy bun, a bunch of buns, or a French braid that's too big. With the right colorful accessories, you can take a simple haircut and make it look very stylish.

The Psychology of Hair: Understanding Client Preferences

To be successful, you need to know more than just how to do your job. You also need to know how your clients think and what hairstyles they like. It's important to remember that customers want more than just a haircut or color change if you want to build long relationships and give great service.

We're going to talk about the psychology of hair and how knowing what your clients want can help you get better at what you do.

1. **The Power of Consultation**: A detailed consultation is the first thing you should do to meet your client's psychological needs. This isn't just a procedure; it's a very important chance to get to know each other better. You should pay close attention as your clients talk about their hair problems, wants, and hopes. Take notes and ask deep questions to find out what drives them and what they expect from you. This not only helps people trust you, but it also lets you make good suggestions.
2. **Body Language and Non-Verbal Cues**: During the meeting, pay close attention to your client's voice and body language. Body language, stance, and facial reactions can tell you a lot about how someone is feeling and how comfortable they are with you. If a client seems unsure or hesitant, take the time to listen to their worries and reassure them. The person is more likely to be happy with the result if they are calm and sure of themselves.
3. **Empathy and Emotional Connection**: Getting to know your clients on an emotional level is one of the best ways to learn about their hair tastes. Understand how they feel and what they're going through with their hair. Recognize their complaints and enjoy their wins, whether it's getting a new look or beating hair problems. By truly understanding your client's feelings, you build a safe and trusted space where they can feel heard and appreciated.
4. **Cultural and Societal Influences**: Hair has a lot of cultural and social meaning. Pay attention to how your clients' cultural past and social norms may affect the hairstyles they choose. Hair has different meanings in different cultures. Knowing these differences can help you serve people in a way that is sensitive to and respectful of their culture. Spend some time learning about these things so that you can better help a wide range of clients.
5. **Psychological Impact of Hair**: Hair has a big effect on how someone feels about themselves and their self-esteem. Know that a client's hair choices may come from a desire to feel better about themselves or show who they are. You should be ready to offer

support, positive words, and advice to help your clients make hair choices that are in line with their own goals and dreams.
6. **Managing Expectations**: An important part of the hairstylist-client interaction is managing the client's standards. Tell them the truth about what they can do with their hair type, health, and style choice. Clear and honest conversations about what's possible and what's not allowing clients to set reasonable goals and be happy with the result.
7. **The Role of Trust**: Trust is the most important thing in any hairstylist-client interaction. Your clients need to trust not only your basic skills but also that you know what they want and need from their hair. It takes time, stability, and a real desire to make them happy to build trust in you.

Building a Solid Client Base: Hairstylist's Definitive Guide

In the fast-paced world of hairstyling, skill is only one part of the equation for success. Hairstylists need to build a strong client group of loyal customers to do well in their jobs. As a hairstylist, you can get new clients by making your shop feel warm and welcoming, tailoring experiences to each client, using social media to show off your work, and always providing excellent quality and service. Use your scissors like magic wands to make every client feel like a star.

Craft an Inviting Salon Atmosphere

Making the shop feel friendly is important for getting new clients and keeping the ones you already have. First impressions are very important. The mood you've created in your business sets the tone for your clients when they walk in. A clean, stylish room with nice chairs and well-lit mirrors makes the experience good right away. Your clients will feel like they've entered a place that fits your personality if you add a personal touch to the decor and work your style into it. Think of it as setting the stage for an event you'll never forget. The environment you make shows that you care about their happiness and comfort. It's not just about how it looks; it's about making them feel important and understood. By making a welcoming space a priority, you'll not only build a loyal customer base, but you'll also make a place where people can't wait to return for the great service and relaxed setting you've carefully created.

Master the Art of Communication

Communication is key to building good ties with clients. It's all about getting and giving knowledge. Start by paying attention to what your clients have to say about their likes, concerns, and thoughts. Ask them open-ended questions to find out more about what they need. Whether it's a quick trim or a full change, letting your clients know that you're listening and understanding builds trust and loyalty. Think of conversation as the link between you and your clients. A strong link is made when they know you're truly interested in what they want. It's not just words; it's about knowing what they want and making them feel like they're important. By getting good at talking to people, you're not only shaping great hair, but you're also making it clear to your clients that you care about making them happy.

Deliver Consistent Quality

If a hairstylist wants to stand out, they need to be consistent. People keep coming back not only because you're good at what you do, but also because they know they'll get good results. To give constant, high-quality service, you need to know about the newest goods, methods, and trends. Over time, this level of dependability builds trust, which keeps customers coming back and even telling their friends about your business. Being consistent is the most important thing you can do for your hairstyling journey. It's like building a strong base that your business can depend on. Imagine that a customer is happy no matter what service they get and still leaves happy. By always doing a good job, you're not only styling hair, you're also building an image for being dependable. This image attracts clients who are looking for hairstylists they can trust. Remember that it's not just about the hairstyles you do; it's about the lasting impact you make with your constant greatness.

Personalize the Experience

It's important to recognize that each client is unique, and tailoring your services to meet those needs can have a big effect. Know their names; remember how they used to dress and pay close attention to the specific things they ask for. Giving them specific advice based on their hair type and way of life shows off your skills and creates a memorable memory. Think of each customer as a separate piece of art that is waiting for your artistic touch. You can add unique touches that fit their tastes by making the experience more personal. This dress or suit fits just right, like a custom-made outfit. This level of attention to detail not only shows how knowledgeable you are, but also how much you care about making them happy. It turns into more than just getting a haircut; it becomes a link between you and the person. By personalizing, you make the trip unique, where they aren't just customers but also people you want to service in their special way.

Leverage Social Media

In this day and age of technology, social media is a great way to reach a lot of people. You can show off your work, show clients before and after changes, and interact with clients online by using sites like Instagram and Facebook. Sharing interesting content regularly keeps your work noticeable and lets potential clients know about your skills. Think of social media as a stage where you can show off your skills. With each post, you show what you know and what you're passionate about. It's kind of like an open-air gallery where your work is always on show and anyone interested in your skill can see it. You're not just a hairdresser in a studio when you use social media. You're also a digital artist whose work can move and inspire people far away. When you use this digital channel, you're reaching people outside of your business and letting people all over the world admire your skills.

Offer Promotions and Loyalty Programs

By using the idea of value, you can make things work out well for everyone with deals and reward schemes. A lot is something everyone can enjoy. Offer special deals to people who are buying from you for the first time, or group services for important events. Creating reward programs that thank customers for their ongoing support helps people feel like they belong. Think of discounts as a nice treat that makes customers happy. During their journey to change their hair, it's like finding a secret gem. Everyone is interested in deals or sets of services that grab people's attention and bring in possible customers. Also, reward schemes are a nice way to show your customers that you value the trust they put in you. Think of what you have to offer as a bridge that ties original interest with long-term commitment. Clients are more likely to stay in touch as they use your services and enjoy the extras. It's not just about making sales; it's also about getting to know clients and making sure they feel valued throughout their hairstyling path. By using these tips, you're not only getting and keeping customers, but you're also building a group of people who love the experiences you offer.

Attend Networking Events

Going to networking events can be very helpful in many areas, not just the business world. Participating in hair shows, training classes, and industry events gives you the chance to meet other hairstylists, business owners, and potential clients. Building relationships with other professionals and important people in your field can help your client base grow naturally. Think of networking events as places where people meet and make real links. The links between them are like puzzle pieces that, when put together, make a bigger picture of your hairstyling journey. You're not only sharing information when you talk to each other and share your thoughts, but you're also growing your business network. These connections are more than just phone numbers; they're chances that are just ready to be taken advantage of. Think of these events as places where partnerships can grow. Every time you talk to someone, you plant a seed that could grow into partnerships and leads. As you move through networking, you're building a road map that will lead you to a bigger audience and a better hairstyle experience. By actively taking part, you build a network that makes your position known and increases your reach in ways that standard marketing can't.

Stay in Touch through Email Marketing

Mailing your customers through email marketing is an easy way to stay in touch with them. When you send out emails regularly, you can talk about new services, give style advice, and offer special deals. By communicating with them regularly, you keep your company in their minds and gently remind them to make their next meeting. Think of these newsletters as friendly updates sent straight to their email address. It's like getting a digital note every day that keeps them interested and up to date. By giving them useful information, you show that you want to improve their hairstyling experience outside of the studio chair. If you think of this way of talking as a bridge between meetings, it works just fine. You're not just sharing information with each email; you're also making people feel like they're connected. When your clients feel like you care about their well-being and happiness, they are more likely to come back. By using email marketing, you can build a connection with your customers that go beyond hair care. You can create loyal customers who value your knowledge and appreciate your efforts to keep them updated and looked for.

Invest in Continued Education

The area of hairstyling is always changing, with new styles and techniques coming out all the time. The way it flows is like a river that never stops. You can keep your skills sharp and up-to-date by spending money on ongoing education. It's like getting your tools sharpened so you can handle new tasks well. Think of continuing your education as a path that helps you stay on track. It's not enough to just learn things; you also have to be open to change and new ideas. You're showing that you want to be a leader in your field by being open to new information. Think of each learning chance as a piece of a puzzle that fits together to make your knowledge full. You're speaking the language of progress when you keep up with the latest developments. Many clients want hairstylists who can easily learn and use new methods. By continuing your education, you do more than just improve your skills; you also build your professional brand and make sure your clients have the best experience possible.

Ask for Referrals and Reviews

Customers who are happy with your business can be your biggest fans. After giving great service, you might want to ask for reviews and recommendations. It's like setting seeds of good ideas and comments that can grow into something great. Thanks from happy customers and great reviews on websites like Yelp and Google can help your image and bring in new clients who are looking for reliable hairstylists. Referrals and reviews are like a wave that spreads because of how great your work is. When happy clients tell others about their good experiences, it's like dropping a stone into a pond: the effect goes into the water and spreads outward. These words have meaning and build trust. They show possible clients what kind of service they can expect. Think of these things as building blocks that will help you learn how to style your hair. Every review and recommendation you get boosts your reputation and power in the field. You're not just getting feedback when you actively seek them out; you're also building a group of happy customers who will become your brand champions, creating a cycle of trust and growth.

CHAPTER 11
COLOR INTEGRATION

Basic Steps for Coloring Your Hair at Home

Do you want to change the color of your hair? Good job! The good news is that you can dye your hair if you want to. The bad news is that it's not always simple. Coloring your hair is a big deal, and it's even bigger of a deal if you do it yourself. Know what you're doing before you draw. You can learn more about how to do it, or you can let your stylist choose for you both! In the second case, if you decide to get a professional to dye your hair, be honest about how your hair looks during the meeting. You D.I.Y fans, on the other hand, can do your dye job at home with this step-by-step guide. Here's what you need to know before you begin. Find out everything you need to know about hair dye below:

Hair Dye Basics

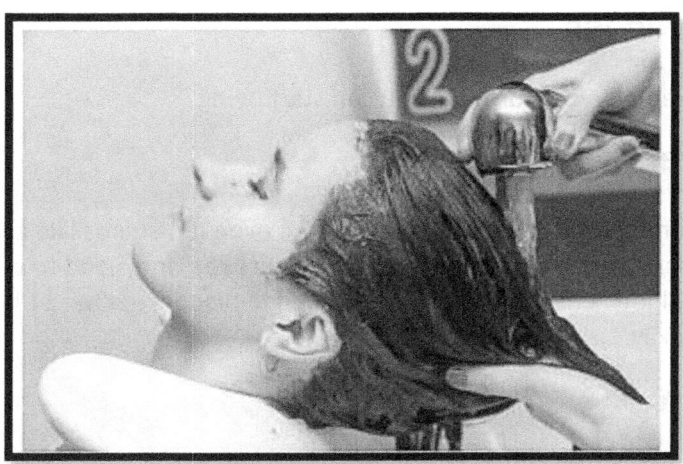

Hair dye comes in a range of formulas, from semi-permanent to permanent. There are three main types of formulas: semi-permanent, demi-permanent, and permanent. Each formula can change the length of your hair in different ways and give you different results. When you color your hair, the hair shaft swells up, which can make thin hair look stronger? In addition, it can improve the hair's natural shine and health as a whole. You can buy dyes in a lot of different colors or mix them to get the shade and finish you want.

Hair Dyeing Tutorial: From Formula to Finish

Figure out which formula is ideal for you.

Semi-Permanent

Semi-permanent colorants are gentler than permanent formulas because they contain ammonia or hydrogen peroxide. The color stays on the hair until it is washed out totally. This is a good choice for people who aren't sure what color they want or who only want a new shade for a short time.

Demi-Permanent

Demi-permanent hair color is a mix of a semi-permanent and a permanent colorant. It has a small amount of hydrogen peroxide but no ammonia. This type of hair color stays in the hair for about 20 washes and puts more color into the hair shaft than semis.

Permanent

Hydrogen peroxide and ammonia are mixed to make these colorants. It's impossible to wash out the color because the chemicals get into the hair shaft and leave it there. This way of dyeing your hair is great for people who are ready to go all the way.

Hair Dyeing Process

Now that you've picked out your formula, you can start dying.

Check for Irritants

You should do the skin test that comes in the dye box, even if it seems like a waste of time. After all, a fresh color job isn't worth a bad new skin job either! You only need to put a little dye on the inside bend of your elbow. Check for any kind of allergic response after 24 hours. You can go on now if everything is okay.

Prep Your Skin

Use a lubricant like Vaseline to prepare your skin, especially the head, so you don't have to rub it raw to get the dye off. Additionally, don't forget to wear those safety gloves throughout the whole process.

Strand Test

The strand test is a step that is very important to the process but is often missed. In this way, you can find out how quickly your hair will adjust and change color. It will also tell you how long it takes to get the color you want. As soon as you know roughly how long it will take, keep that in mind during the whole process of applying the dye.

Dye Application Process

1. **Begin with Dirty Hair**

Because shampooing touches the skin, you are more likely to get a rash on your head after washing your hair. The natural oils in hair also keep the head from getting stung when peroxides or bleach are used on it.

2. **Section Hair**

Split your hair into four manageable sections and use duckbill clips or hair claws to hold them in place.

3. **Dye Application**

After following the directions on the box to mix the dye, use an application brush to spread it out evenly. Start applying at the bottom and work your way up, section by section. Pay close attention to the time window and make sure you follow the steps. Going over or under the time can change the whole shade!

4. **Wash, Condition, and Style**

Use the shampoo and conditioner that come with the kit to take out the dye, or make your own if your hair is already dyed. Then, condition the hair. When you see a lot of color bleed, don't worry. This is mostly the color that stuck to your hair. It might take a few washes, but the water should be clear when it's done, which means that all the dye is gone. You should also set aside extra time to deep condition your hair. Your hair will need extra care and wetness after being dyed. Finally, style your hair however you like, and then go out into the world with your brand-new hairstyle.

Techniques for Integrating Cut and Color

Cutting and coloring hair at the same time takes imagination, technical skill, and a deep understanding of how hair works. This mix can completely change a client's look, bringing out their best features and giving them a unique style.

Here are some advanced techniques for integrating cut and color so that the results are stunning.

1. **Pre-Cut Consultation and Analysis**
- **Client Consultation:** Start by having a full conversation with the client to learn about their hair background, tastes, and way of life. Talk about the look they want, how much upkeep they can handle, and any pictures that inspire them.
- **Hair Analysis:** Look at the client's hair's natural color, structure, density, and chemical treatments that have been done on it before. This helps the stylist plan the best cut and color for the result.

2. **Strategic Sectioning**
- **Sectioning for Color Placement:** Split the hair into parts based on where you want to put color methods like highlights, lowlights, or other hues. Think about how the hair will fall naturally and how it will look in the end.
- **Custom Sectioning for Cut:** Plan your cut so that it goes with where the colors are placed. For instance, when you add layers, think about how the color will change the depth and flow of the layers.

3. **Balayage and Layered Cuts**

- **Balayage Technique:** This method of hand-painting hair gives it a natural, sun-kissed look that goes well with layered cuts. The color should be put on the levels of the surface where the sun would naturally shine on them, making the layers stand out.
- **Layered Cutting:** Keep the balayage placement in mind when you do a layered cut. To get a smooth look, make sure the layers begin where the balayage starts to get lighter.

4. **Face-Framing Highlights and Graduated Cuts**
- **Face-Framing Highlights:** These are put around the face to make it look brighter and draw attention to the client's features. They work well with graded cuts where the length gets longer as you move toward the back.
- **Graduated Cut:** When you do a graduated cut, the hair is shorter in the back and gets longer as it moves toward the front. This cut draws attention to the front parts of the hair, which goes well with highlights that frame the face.

5. **Dimensional Color with Textured Cuts**
- **Dimensional Color:** Use different shades of color to give your hair more depth and structure. This method works especially well with cuts that have a lot of texture, like broken bobs or shaggy styles.
- **Textured Cutting Techniques:** To make texture, use cutting methods like point cutting, slide cutting, or razoring. The general result is better when different shades of color with different lengths and textures work together.

6. **Root Shadowing and Blunt Cuts**
- **Root Shadowing:** In this method, the roots are made a little darker than the rest of the hair. It makes the change from the natural color to the lighter ends look natural, which works especially well with short cuts.
- **Blunt Cut:** Root shadowing makes a striking difference and adds complexity to a blunt cut that goes straight across. The shadow at the roots makes the bluntness stand out and gives the hair a glossy look.

7. **Peek-a-Boo Highlights and Asymmetrical Cuts**
- **Peek-a-Boo Highlights:** These are highlights that are hidden by putting them under the hair's top layers. They slowly show up through movement or certain hairstyles, which adds a sense of depth and surprise.
- **Asymmetrical Cuts:** If you have an asymmetrical cut, where one side is longer than the other, you can make it stand out with peek-a-boo highlights. Every time you turn your head, the color shows through, making the cut even more special.

8. **Combining Ombre with Long Layers**
- **Ombre Technique:** A gradient effect in which the hair goes from dark roots to lighter ends. With long, fluid layers, this method works great because the color change makes the hair move and flow more.
- **Long-Layered Cuts:** Make sure the layers start where the ombre starts to get lighter when you cut long layers. This will make the cut and color go well together, drawing attention to the length and volume.

9. **Maintenance and Aftercare**

- **Color Preservation:** To keep the color bright, suggest shampoos and conditioners that protect color. Tell your guests how to keep their hair from getting damaged by the sun and heat.
- **Regular Trims:** Get your hair trimmed regularly to keep it looking new and to avoid split ends, which can ruin the look.
- **Touch-Up Appointments:** Make sure you have touch-up appointments for both the cut and the color. This makes sure that the style stays consistent and well-done over time.

Maintaining Hair Health with Color Services

1. **USE AN ANTIOXIDANT SHAMPOO**

What is the best way to fight shade fade? A shampoo with lots of antioxidants. Color Motion+ Color Protection Shampoo has Free Radicals Protection Technology and a lot of vitamins to protect your client's color. Free radicals are what cause colors to fade. This powerful technology stops them from forming by protecting metals from water. For the color-protecting effects to last between salon visits, you need to use the right shampoo. This will leave your hair smooth and shiny.

2. **APPLY A WEEKLY HAIR MASK**

Taking care of your hair and keeping it healthy is the first step to keeping your color even and beautiful. Like getting a facial once a week, your client needs to use hair masks and conditioners every week to keep their hair healthy and full of color. Color Motion+ Moisturizing Color Reflection Conditioner should be worked through the mid-lengths to the ends of their hair after washing with their favorite color-locking shampoo to bring back the color and shine. Once a week, give your hair a deeper conditioning treatment by putting Color Motion+ Structure Mask on ends that are feeling stressed and sensitive. This will help to deeply strengthen and smooth your hair.

3. **WASH HAIR LESS OFTEN**

As simple as it may seem, the more your client washes their hair, the faster the color molecules will fade. Each strand of hair swells up and a little color pigment leaks out when it gets wet. To keep their hair looking new, they have to extend the washing cycle. Tell them to wash their hair less often and add dry shampoo to their kit. Dry shampoo is a mist that keeps hair clean and looking clean between washes.

4. **PROTECT FROM ROOT TO TIP**

Did you know? The sun can do more than just tan your skin. It can also fade and lighten your hair. This will keep your color safe in the sun. Spray INVIGO UV Hair Color Protection Spray on wet or dry hair. The shade-saving recipe has vitamin B5 in it to keep hair strong and healthy and to keep the sun from bleaching the color. It's great for taking on vacation or spraying hair during the hot summer months.

5. **GIVE REGULAR TRIMS**

During their color visits, make sure your client gets regular trims as well. This will help the color look even and healthy. When you dye your hair, split ends make the base dry and sensitive, which means the color might not soak in properly or go deep enough. Keep the ends of their hair cut short for a better base for their current color.

6. BE GENTLE WITH HEAT

Be careful with heat on your hair. Heat can make hair sensitive, which can make it dry and hard to style. This can happen when you blow dry, curl, or smooth your hair. This can make your signature shade of hair color look flat and dull since the color looks best on hair that is shiny and healthy. A heat protectant spray will keep hair safe from heat and smooth the skin in two steps: first, it will protect, and then it will feed. You can also get your client to love their natural texture by not using heat on their hair and letting it dry naturally. To add body to a natural wave, scrunch Spritz through the mid-lengths to the ends.

7. PREP FOR COLOR

Are they all set for their next meeting? Before getting their hair colored, have your client use a clarifying shampoo a few days ahead of time to get rid of any buildup. We tell our clients not to wash their hair before their visit because the natural sebum oils in their hair will help protect the head while the color is being applied.

8. USE A PRE-COLOR TREATMENT

A lot of the time, clients' hair has uneven porosity, which makes the product uneven after coloring. For these clients, spray Color Motion+ Pre-coloration Treatment on the dry parts of their hair that are the most damaged and fragile. After that, blow dry your hair to seal the treatment. Then, color it as normal. The result? Your hair will feel smooth and shiny, and it will be ready to color without any problems.

9. OPT FOR WELLAPLEX

If your client's hair is sensitive, you should use Wellaplex, especially if you're going to lighten it. It will give any hair type a finish that looks healthy. By strengthening the hair ties from the inside, the smart recipe helps to repair damage and make each strand stronger. Wellaplex is suggested for all lightning services to keep harm to a minimum. You can also use Wellaplex mixed with hair dye if your client's hair is damaged from previous coloring visits.

CHAPTER 12
CONSULTATION AND CLIENT MANAGEMENT

Effective Client Consultations

A good meeting with the client is the key to providing excellent hairstyle services. It makes it easier to understand what the client wants, keep their demands in check, and build trust.

Here is a full guide on how to have good consultations with clients so that they are happy and stay loyal.

1. **Preparation**
   - **Create a Welcoming Environment:** Make sure the area around your shop or meeting is clean, comfy, and friendly. A calm environment makes clients feel at ease, which makes them more likely to talk about their wants and worries.
   - **Have Tools Ready:** Get a consultation form, a mirror, hair shades, style books, and digital devices that can connect to online galleries. These tools make it easier to see and talk about possible styles.

2. **Initial Interaction**
   - **Greet Warmly:** To get to know someone, start by saying hello. A friendly and sincere welcome sets a good mood for the consultation.
   - **Listen Actively:** Pay close attention to what the client says and thinks at first. Show that you value what they have to say by doing things like nodding and making eye contact.

3. **Comprehensive Client Assessment**
   - **Hair History:** Find out about the client's hair history, such as any chemical treatments, color changes, or problems they've had in the past. This knowledge is very important for figuring out how their hair is right now.
   - **Lifestyle and Maintenance:** Talk to them about their daily routine, how they like to live, and how much time they are willing to spend on hair care. This makes it easier to offer styles and treatments that work with their way of life.
   - **Health and Allergies:** Ask if they have any skin problems, allergies, or sensitivities to make sure the treatments and items you offer will not hurt them.

4. **Exploring Preferences and Goals**
   - **Visual Aids:** Show pictures, hairstyles, and digital files to help the client describe the look they want. It can also be very helpful to tell them to bring pictures that inspire them.
   - **Detail-Oriented Questions:** Ask them what they like and don't like about their present haircut, what styles they like, and what length and color they'd like their hair to be.
   - **Realistic Expectations:** Tell them what they can expect based on their hair type, health, and past treatments. Don't let failure happen by having unrealistic standards.

5. **Personalized Recommendations**
   - **Style Suggestions:** Based on the meeting, suggest haircuts that look good on their face shape, hair type, and way of life. Show with pictures what these styles might look like.

- **Color Options:** Talk about color choices that go with their style and skin tone. Use color swatches and computer tools to help people picture what might happen.
- **Treatment Plans:** Suggest any treatments that are needed to get or keep the look you want, like cuts, color changes, or conditioning treatments.

6. **Professional Insight and Advice**
- **Expert Opinions:** Tell us what you know about why some colors or styles might work better than others. Use your knowledge to help the client make the best choice.
- **Hair Care Advice:** Tell them how to keep their hairstyle and color looking good at home. Give suggestions for good items and show how they can help.

7. **Agreement and Documentation**
- **Confirm Details:** Write down a summary of the agreed-upon plan that includes the style, color, and any treatments that were selected. Make sure the client knows what the plan is and agrees with it.
- **Document Everything:** Use a form or a computer system to write down the facts of the consultation. That way, you'll have a record of future visits and can keep things consistent.

8. **Building Trust and Relationship**
- **Follow-Up Appointments:** Make follow-up dates for repairs and upkeep. Care that is given regularly strengthens the bond between two people and keeps the style fresh.
- **Check-In Communication:** Send a message or call the client to see if they are happy with the service. This shows you care about what they do and how it turns out.

Building and Maintaining Client Relationships

To be successful in haircutting for a long time, you need to build and keep good ties with your clients. Loyal customers not only come back, but they also bring you new customers, which helps your shop grow. **Here is a complete guide on how to make and keep these important connections.**

1. **First Impressions Matter**
- **Professional Atmosphere:** Make sure your salon is clean, well-kept, and friendly. Setting the mood for the client's experience is important.
- **Warm Welcome:** Welcome every customer with a smile and a good mood. When customers walk in, a friendly welcome makes them feel at ease and important.

2. **Effective Communication**
- **Active Listening:** Pay close attention to what the client says so you can understand their wants and needs. Say what you heard again to make sure you understand.
- **Clear Explanations:** Be clear about your methods, processes, and the results you want to see. This openness builds trust and makes sure that standards are reasonable.

3. **Personalized Service**
- **Customization:** Make sure your services are tailored to the specific wants of each client. Make unique suggestions based on the information you get from meetings.

- **Attention to Detail:** Don't forget the little things that can make the customer's experience better, like remembering their favorite goods or mags or even offering their favorite drink.

4. **Consistency**
- **Deliver Consistent Quality:** Make sure that every customer gets good service every time they come in. Service that is always the same builds trust and dependability.
- **Regular Check-Ins:** Make sure clients are happy with the service by calling them after their meeting. Taking the initiative to do this shows that you care about their experience.

5. **Professionalism**
- **Punctuality:** Show up for your meetings on time. A big part of being responsible is respecting your client's time.
- **Ongoing Education:** Learn about the newest hairstyles, tools, and methods. Continuing your schooling shows that you want to give the best service possible.

6. **Building Trust**
- **Honesty:** Tell the person the truth about what you can do for them based on their hair type, health, and past treatments. By having reasonable standards, you can avoid being let down.
- **Transparency:** Make it clear how much the services and any extra treatments or goods cost. Clear pricing builds trust.

7. **Creating a Memorable Experience**
- **Comfort and Relaxation:** Make sure your clients have a calm place to rest. Give away things for free, like a head rub or a cup of tea or coffee.
- **Engagement:** Have talks that matter. Clients can feel valued and respected when you remember personal things about them, like their last trip or family events.

8. **Loyalty Programs**
- **Incentives:** Run loyalty programs that give customers rewards for coming back, telling their friends, or buying your goods. Offering discounts, free services, or special deals can help you keep clients.
- **Referral Bonuses:** Give customer's rewards for bringing you new customers. Referrals from other people are very strong and can help you get a lot more customers.

9. **Feedback and Improvement**
- **Seek Feedback:** Every so often, ask your customers for feedback to find out what they like best about your service and what you could do better. This can be done with polls, idea boxes, or face-to-face talks.
- **Implement Changes:** Listen to what people say and act on it. Clients will feel more valued if you show that you care about their views and are ready to make things better.

10. **Digital Engagement**
- **Social Media Presence:** Keep in touch with your clients through social media. You can interact with your audience through comments and messages, share tips, and show off your work.
- **Email Newsletters:** Let people know about new services, sales, and hair care tips through emails. Talking to your clients regularly keeps them updated and interested.

11. **Handling Complaints Gracefully**

- **Listen and Apologize:** If a customer has a problem, don't talk over them; just listen. Sincerely apologize for any trouble this may have caused.
- **Offer Solutions:** Give ways to fix the problem. Make sure the customer is happy before they leave, whether it's a free service, a deal, or a second chance.

12. Personal Touch

- **Handwritten Notes:** Send clients birthday cards or thank-you notes written by hand. This particular touch can change the way people feel about your business in a big way.
- **Remember Preferences:** Keep detailed records of what styles, colors, and goods your clients have liked in the past. Clients will know you care about their wants if you bring up these details in future meetings.

CHAPTER 13
BUSINESS AND CAREER DEVELOPMENT
Setting Up a Salon or Home Studio

If you open a hair shop business from home, you can set your hours and work from the comfort of your own home while making money. Even when the economy was bad in the US, hair shops did well, so they are a safe business to start up as long as you do it right. But just because you're running your hair shop out of your house doesn't mean it will be easier to set up than a store. There are still a lot of things that need to be done for an at-home hair shop business to be successful.

Step 1: Make a Business Plan
You should have a plan before you start any business. If you want your business to grow from an idea in your head to the one you've always dreamt of, you don't need a detailed plan. All you need is a general outline. If someone wants to start a hair shop at home, they will need to think of a name for it. A catchy name helps get the word out about a business, but it's still important that people can tell from the name that it's a hair shop. So, when coming up with the business name, it's important not to go too far. The name will be needed on formal papers, so picking a name as soon as possible will help the process go more quickly. Because setting up a hair shop at home will take some time, try to make a reasonable schedule as you plan. It could take a few months before you can start running your business. This depends on the paperwork you need to file with the government, any home improvements that need to be made, getting the tools you need and getting some loyal customers.

Step 2: Set a Budget
Starting any business can cost a lot of money. A home-based hair shop is no different. A hair shop that you can run from home costs about $62,000 to get started. This money pays for things like licenses, permits, workshop materials, and other small, occasional costs. If the business needs high-end tools and finishing, this price could go as high as $500,000. If someone needs money to start their own home hair service business, they can get some types of credit and loans. **These ways to get money are:**
- Small Business Administration (SBA) Loan
- Microloans
- Alternative Lenders
- Equipment Financing

Step 3: Figuring Out the Legal Requirements
Laws may be different in each state, and neighborhood, and for each type of home insurance. You should check with all of these to make sure the rules are being followed correctly. If someone doesn't follow the rules and laws that are in place, they could get fined a lot or even lose their beauty license. You must be able to open a salon business from home in your state. Talk to your state about it to see if you need any permission to do that. The Small Business Administration office in your area is a good place to learn about licenses, permits, and other legal requirements. **In some places, you need the following licenses and permits:**

- A Cosmetology License
- Business Permit
- Sales Tax Permit
- Zoning Permit

There may be state laws against running a hair shop out of your home. If you live in a Homeowners Association (HOA), the HOA may also have rules about what is allowed in your neighborhood. Some neighborhoods do not allow people to run companies out of their homes. Running a business out of your home may be against the rules of some homeowner's insurance companies and plans. Some home insurance companies won't work with these kinds of businesses. In contrast, some house insurance companies might raise rates or ask for an extra policy to be added.

Step 4: Designate a Space, Design it, and furnish it

After you've checked with the government, you can get ready to open a hair shop in your home. There should be a clear area for it, like a den or extra bedroom. It's the rule in some places that you have a certain room. Putting up walls and having a public bathroom are also required in some places. This is still what most clients' want, even though the business is in a person's house. Organize the room and put all the goods where they belong so they are easy to find. For those just starting, it might be hard to buy the best gear, but it's still important to avoid going too cheap and instead focus on the products' quality. The following things are needed to set up an at-home hair salon:

- **Salon Chairs**

Salon chairs should be cozy for both you and your client. Seating with cushions and a height that can be changed is important. It's not a good idea to just put the client in a regular kitchen chair because they might still want to feel like they're in a salon and won't be as comfy sitting in a hard kitchen chair for a long time.

- **Hooded Hair Dryer**

This is important for some haircuts and colors, and it will make the client feel like they are in a shop. If you want to save money, a small hair dryer with a hood might be a better choice. The dryer can be moved around more easily and costs less than dryers that stay in one place.

- **Hair Washing Sinks or Shampooing bowls**

Again, this doesn't have to be the most expensive bowl you can find, but you shouldn't use a bathroom sink or kitchen sink to wash the customer's hair. It won't be as easy for you or the client, and it will feel more like a home service than a hair shop.

- **Hair Dyes and Other Styling Products**

If you want to offer services like perms and dying and styling hair, you should make sure you have the right tools. Make sure you have a lot of colors and ways to mix them so you can give the customer what they want.

- Other random items might include a curling iron, a blow dryer, and mirrors, shelves for store items, shampoo, conditioner, hairspray, and hair gel.

For those who want to have a store, try using the same items you sell when you do clients' hair. The client can try the product while you style their hair and let you know what they think.

Step 5: Advertising

Unluckily, it can be harder to advertise an in-home hair service business than it is to advertise a store. Stores usually have big signs and are in places with a lot of foot traffic. People who run home hair shops have trouble advertising because of the rules set by the Homeowners Association. Most Home Owners Associations (HOAs) in the area don't let you put any signs on your house, and some don't let you put any signs in your yard either. The best ways to get people to know about a home-based business are through word of mouth and social media. Tell your clients and friends about your business. Print out business cards to give out, and have your clients give them to their friends and family. Set up a social media page for your business and ask customers and friends to follow it. This will bring more people to your website. Hashtags can also help get people to visit your social media pages. Also, make sure that the business hours, services, and contact information are easy to find on your social media account or an extra link to your official website. You can make reservations at a lot of hair shops online. It is now easy for clients to see what dates are available and make them. It also lets you do other things besides checking your calendar and answering the phone.

Step 6: Set Prices
If you want to open your hair shop in your home, you should know that the prices may be cheaper than those charged by hairdressers in studios. This is very important when you first start. People will buy more if the prices are lower and more competitive. You should not set prices too low so that you don't lose money on the business, but if prices are too high, people may go somewhere else to get what they need. Customers tend to stick with brands and people they know and trust. If your new business has lower prices, customers may be more likely to switch from their current place and stylist to yours.

Step 7: Keep a Record of Spending and Profits
Any business should keep track of both the money it makes and the money it spends. You have to pay federal income tax on any hair shop business you run, whether it's from home or a gym. Some states may have state taxes, and some states tax some goods and services through sales tax. Items that are offered in stores may also be subject to sales tax, so it's important to keep track of those too. **You should write down how much money you made so that you can save money on taxes. You might be able to get a tax break for the money you spent on:**
- Training
- Continuing Education
- Business Conferences or Seminars
- Cosmetology Books and Magazines

Step 8: Continue to Grow the Business
You can still grow your business after the shop is set up and people start coming in regularly. A great way to get new customers is to have referral programs. Offering rewards to regular customers can also help hair salons keep customers and get them to keep coming back, which is important for any business. There are many ways to advertise your business online and off, even after it's opened. This will help it grow and get more customers. People who have been to your at-home hair shop should be encouraged to tell their friends and family about it. If things go well with the business, you might be able to hire more cosmetologists to help. You shouldn't hire too many new trainers at once. For a small group of customers, a reservation might work until you're

sure the business will keep growing. You will lose money if you hire too many stylists and don't have enough people. You may even have to fire some designers. You have to put a lot of work and money into starting a business. It can be scary. It costs a lot to open a home hair studio, but the beauty business is growing quickly and has done well even when the US economy has been bad. While working from home gives you more freedom with your schedule, it takes a lot of work to make this kind of job work.

Approximately how much money do hair salon owners make in a year?

People who own hair salons make around $14,500 to $385,000 a year. This is a big number that depends on where the business is located and how well it is doing. Most hair shop owners make between $70,000 and $175,000 a year.

How long does it take to complete cosmetology school?

The schooling for hairdressing lasts for about nine months. Plus, they get extra training to do other things like nail and skin treatments.

Continuing Education and Certification

Continuing education and certification are vital components of a successful career in hair styling. The beauty industry is dynamic, with trends, techniques, and technologies continually evolving. To stay competitive and provide the best services to clients, hair stylists must commit to lifelong learning and professional development. Here's a comprehensive guide on the importance and benefits of continuing education and certification in hair styling.

1. Importance of Continuing Education
- **Staying Current with Trends:** The fashion and beauty industry is ever-changing. New trends in haircuts, coloring techniques, and styling methods emerge regularly. Continuing education ensures that stylists are up-to-date with the latest trends and can offer contemporary styles to their clients.
- **Enhancing Skills:** Ongoing education provides opportunities to refine existing skills and learn new ones. Advanced training in areas like precision cutting, creative coloring, and updos can set a stylist apart from their peers.
- **Improving Client Satisfaction:** Clients seek stylists who are knowledgeable and skilled in the latest techniques. Continuous learning enables stylists to deliver superior results, leading to higher client satisfaction and loyalty.
- **Expanding Service Offerings:** By learning new techniques and services, such as keratin treatments, hair extensions, or scalp treatments, stylists can broaden their service menu and attract a wider clientele.
- **Professional Growth:** Education fosters professional growth by boosting confidence, inspiring creativity, and providing a sense of accomplishment. It can also open doors to new career opportunities within the industry.

2. Benefits of Certification

- **Credibility and Trust:** Certifications from recognized institutions or industry bodies enhance a stylist's credibility. Clients are more likely to trust a certified professional who has demonstrated a commitment to their craft.
- **Competitive Edge:** In a competitive market, having certifications can give stylists an edge. It distinguishes them as dedicated and skilled professionals who have met specific standards of excellence.
- **Higher Earning Potential:** Certified stylists often command higher prices for their services. Clients are willing to pay a premium for expertise and quality assurance that comes with certification.
- **Networking Opportunities:** Certification programs often provide opportunities to network with industry professionals, instructors, and peers. These connections can lead to mentorship, collaborations, and new job opportunities.
- **Industry Recognition:** Earning certifications can lead to recognition within the industry, including awards, features in trade publications, and invitations to participate in prestigious events and competitions.

3. Types of Continuing Education Programs

- **Workshops and Seminars:** Short-term programs that focus on specific techniques or trends. These can be hands-on or lecture-based and are often conducted by industry experts or product companies.
- **Advanced Courses:** Comprehensive courses that delve deeply into advanced techniques in cutting, coloring, styling, and other specialized areas. These are typically offered by beauty schools or professional training institutes.
- **Online Learning:** Online courses and webinars offer flexibility for stylists to learn at their own pace. These programs can cover a wide range of topics and often include video demonstrations and interactive elements.
- **Trade Shows and Conferences:** Attending industry events provides exposure to the latest products, tools, and techniques. These events often include educational sessions, workshops, and live demonstrations.
- **Apprenticeships and Mentorships:** Learning directly from seasoned professionals through apprenticeships or mentorship programs provides invaluable hands-on experience and personalized guidance.

4. Pursuing Certification

- **Research Accredited Programs:** Look for certification programs accredited by reputable industry organizations, such as the National Accrediting Commission of Cosmetology Arts and Sciences (NACCAS) or other recognized bodies.
- **Choose Relevant Certifications:** Depending on your career goals, select certifications that align with your area of interest. For example, certifications in advanced coloring techniques, hair extensions, or trichology (the study of the scalp and hair health).
- **Commit to the Process:** Certification programs often require a significant investment of time and resources. Be prepared to commit fully to the coursework, practical exams, and any continuing education requirements to maintain the certification.

- **Leverage Employer Support:** Some salons and employers may offer financial support or time off for employees pursuing further education and certifications. Check with your employer about available resources.

5. Maintaining Certifications

- **Continuing Education Units (CEUs):** Many certifications require ongoing education to maintain validity. Participate in CEU programs to stay current with industry standards and retain your certification.
- **Stay Informed:** Keep up-to-date with changes in certification requirements and industry standards. Regularly review the guidelines set by certifying bodies to ensure compliance.
- **Renewal Processes:** Be aware of the renewal processes and deadlines for your certifications. Timely renewal ensures that your qualifications remain current and recognized.

6. Maximizing the Benefits of Continuing Education and Certification

- **Apply New Skills:** Immediately apply new techniques and knowledge gained from continuing education in your practice. This not only reinforces learning but also demonstrates value to your clients.
- **Market Your Qualifications:** Promote your certifications and continued education achievements to clients and potential employers. Display certificates in your salon, update your professional profiles and highlight your qualifications in marketing materials.
- **Seek Feedback:** After implementing new skills and techniques, seek feedback from clients and colleagues. Constructive feedback helps in refining your skills further.
- **Stay Inspired:** Use the knowledge and inspiration gained from continuing education to experiment and innovate in your work. This keeps your passion for hair styling alive and encourages creativity.

CHAPTER 14
TROUBLESHOOTING AND CORRECTION

Common Cutting Mistakes and Fixes

A haircut is one of the most important things we can do to improve our looks. A good haircut can make us look better, feel better about ourselves, and like a million bucks. But if it's not done right, it can make us angry, let down, and stuck in a way that doesn't work for us.

Ignoring Face Shape and Hair Type

People often make the mistake of not taking into account their face shape and hair type when getting a haircut. How your hair looks and feels is very important in figuring out what hairstyles will look best on you.

Understanding Face Shapes

- **Oval Face:** You can wear a lot of different haircuts with an oval face shape, which makes it the most flexible.
- **Round Face:** If you have a round face, choose haircuts that make your face look taller and longer, like long layers or a side-swept bang.
- **Square Face:** Styles with soft, rounded ends, like a layered bob or a side-parted pixie cut, can make a square face look rounder.
- **Heart Face:** For a heart-shaped face, a chin-length bob or a haircut that makes the cheekbones wider will look good.
- **Diamond Face:** If you have a diamond face shape, try a rough pixie cut or a flowing bob to make your cheekbones stand out.

Working with Hair Types

- Straight Hair: You can wear smooth, straight cuts or stacked styles that show off your hair's structure.
- Wavy Hair: If you have wavy hair, add to your natural waves with a layered haircut or go for a beachy, messy look.
- Curly Hair: Love your curls? Get a haircut that brings out their shape and keeps frizz under control, like a layered curly bob or long layers.
- Thick Hair: Layered haircuts will make thick hair look less bulky and livelier.
- Thin Hair: Women with thin hair can add body and texture to their hair with stacked cuts or a short, textured bob.

Lack of Communication with Your Stylist

To avoid problems with your haircut, you need to be able to talk to your hairstylist. A lot of people make the mistake of not being clear about what haircut they want or not giving enough information about their hair. **Here are some things you can do to make sure you and your stylist agree:**

1. Bring visual references: To help your stylist understand the look you want, bring pictures of hairstyles you like.
2. Be clear about the length and style you want: Say exactly what length you want and give specifics about the style, like layers, bangs, or any specific coloring methods.
3. Discuss lifestyle and maintenance: Tell your stylist what you do every day and how long you're willing to spend styling your hair. Giving them this information will help them give you a haircut that fits your lifestyle.

Remember that your hairdresser is there to help you get the look you want, but they need to hear from you to understand what you want.

Not Considering Hair Maintenance

It's important to think about how much upkeep a haircut needs before getting it. Some styles may look great in the salon, but they can be hard to keep up every day. Before you decide on a haircut, you should think about how much time and work you are willing to put into styling and taking care of it.

For example:
- Short Pixie Cut: As for the short pixie cut, it might need to be trimmed and styled often to keep its shape and look finished.
- Long Layers: Long layers can be worn in many ways and don't need much care if you want a more natural, messy look. You may need to spend more time styling with heat tools, though, if you want smooth, defined layers.
- Bangs: Bangs can make any haircut look better, but they need to be trimmed regularly so they don't get too long and get in the way of your vision.
- Layered Bob: A layered bob is flexible and easy to style, but you may need to use products and tools to keep its shape.

When picking out a haircut that fits your upkeep needs, think about your daily habits, lifestyle, and styling tastes.

Skipping Consultations and Research

People also often make the mistake of not getting enough information or consulting with a stylist before getting a haircut. During consultations, you and your stylist can talk about your thoughts, worries, and goals, making sure that you both understand what you want.

During a consultation, consider:
- Bringing inspirational photos: This will help you and your stylist talk about what you want and make sure you both have the same idea.
- Asking for their professional opinion: Your stylist has a lot of experience and knowledge, so don't be afraid to ask for their advice based on your hair type, face shape, and the look you want.
- Discuss any concerns or limitations: If you have specific worries or restrictions, like hair loss, skin problems, or allergens, make sure to bring them up during the meeting.

Also, take the time to learn about hairstyles, trends, and methods that interest you. This will help you explain your needs clearly and give you a better idea of what you're looking for.

Being Influenced by Trends Alone

For ideas, trends can be very helpful, but keep in mind that not all trends are good for everyone. Because everyone is different and has their style tastes, mindlessly following trends without thinking about what works best for you can make you unhappy with your haircut.

Instead of depending only on trends, think about these things:
- Adapt trends to suit your features: If you love a trend but aren't sure if it will look good on you, ask your stylist how it can be changed to fit your face shape, hair type, and personal style.
- Take inspiration from celebrities with similar features: Find famous people or public figures whose face shapes or hair types are like yours and look at how they style their hair. This can help you figure out what will work best for you.
- Trust your instincts: Go with your gut; you know yourself best in the end. If you don't like a trend or think it fits with your style, don't follow it. Instead, pick a haircut that makes you feel good about yourself.

Going for Drastic Changes without Preparation

The thought of trying out new hairstyles is fun, but making big changes without thinking them through can be disappointing. Before getting a very short haircut, think about the following:
- Gradual transitions: If you're used to having long hair and want to try a short style, you might want to cut your hair shorter over time. This will help you adjust to the change and make sure you don't feel bad about it later.
- Research maintenance and styling techniques: When you make big changes, you often need to learn new ways to maintain and style your hair. You should be ready to put in the time and effort to learn how to style and take care of your new haircut.
- Consult with your stylist: Your hairdresser can help you get used to your new style. They can tell you how to style and take care of your new hairstyle and help you set reasonable goals for the results.

You'll be more likely to love and accept your new haircut if you mentally and physically get ready for a big change.

Neglecting Regular Trims and Maintenance

To keep your haircut healthy and in good shape, you need to fix it and take care of it regularly. A lot of people make the mistake of skipping these meetings, which can lead to split ends, odd lengths, and an overall messy look.

To keep your haircut looking neat and new:
- Schedule regular trims: Aim for a trim every 6 to 8 weeks, depending on how fast your hair grows, to keep it in shape and avoid split ends.
- Follow a hair care routine: Use shampoos, creams, and style products that are right for your hair type and that your stylist suggests. You might also want to add heat protectants and deep conditioning treatments to your routine to keep your hair healthy and safe.
- Embrace regular styling: Even if you like your hair to look more natural, styling it for a few minutes can make a big difference in how it looks overall. Find quick and easy ways to style your hair that fit your life and hair type.

Don't forget that regular cuts and care are the best ways to keep your haircut looking great.

DIY Haircuts and Over-Reliance on Online Tutorials

It can be tempting to cut your hair these days when there are so many online instructions and do-it-yourself projects. Do-it-yourself haircuts, on the other hand, can often go wrong if you don't have professional training and experience.

Here's why you shouldn't cut your hair:
- Lack of expertise: Hairstylists go through a lot of training to learn the skills and methods they need to give great haircuts. You could make mistakes that are hard to fix if you don't get the right training.
- Precision and symmetry: To get precision and symmetry in a haircut, you need to know what you're doing and have done it many times. These are important things that most do-it-yourself haircuts lack, which leads to an uneven and unattractive result.
- Limited visibility: It can be hard to cut your hair because you can't see well and the angles aren't right. This can cause lengths and levels that aren't even, which is hard to fix.

Finding a trained barber is always the best way to make sure you get the best results.

Overlooking Haircare Products and Tools

Having the right hair care items and tools can change how your haircut turns out. A lot of people forget how important it is to use good products and tools, which can change how your hair looks and how healthy it is. **Consider the following:**
- Invest in quality tools: For example, buy hairdryers, straighteners, and curling irons that are made for professionals. These tools are made to do less damage and give you better style results.
- Use the right products: Pick hair care items that are right for your hair type and problems. Shampoos, conditioners, hair tools, and treatments are all in this group. If you want specific advice, talk to your stylist.

- Protect your hair: Always use a heat protectant spray on your hair before styling it with heat tools to keep damage to a minimum. Also, to keep your hair from breaking and getting tangled, use a wide-toothed comb or a brush made just for your hair type.

You can keep your haircut looking good and healthy by buying good items and tools and using them the right way.

Not Embracing Professional Advice and Expertise

Last but not least, one of the biggest mistakes people make is not fully utilizing skilled help and advice. There are trained professionals called hairstylists who can help you choose the best haircut for your face shape and way of life.

When you go to the hairdresser,
- Be open to suggestions: Be willing to listen to what your stylist has to say. They may suggest a haircut or style that you haven't thought of. Listen to what they have to say and trust their knowledge.
- Ask questions: Don't be afraid to ask questions if you don't understand something or want more information. Your stylist's job is to give you advice and make sure you're happy with the choices being made.
- Establish a long-term relationship: If you get to know your stylist well, they will be able to understand your hair better over time. Based on your changing wants and tastes, they can make unique suggestions and changes.

You can get a haircut that looks great on you if you listen to and follow the advice of professionals.

Addressing Client Concerns and Feedback

1. **Listen**

Every client and issue is different, so pay close attention to what the client is saying and don't speak up. Show that you care about them and that you value what they have to say.

2. **Figure Out What the Client Wants**

Simply ask "what," "when," "where," and "how" to find out what happened and what the client wants. What would make them happy? How much do they want back, or just a fix? How can I keep the customer?

3. **Keep Calm**

You should never swear at a person or raise your voice. Don't get angry or guarded, and don't let things hurt you. If the client is making a scene, take them to your office or a spare room where you can talk about it without other clients being around. You don't want to ruin their therapy.

4. **Apologize**

Saying "I'm sorry" can help calm things down, and admitting you were wrong shows that you are an adult. If you want to say sorry, say "I'm sorry you feel that way" instead of "I'm sorry about the situation." This shows that you understand and don't take responsibility.

5. **Make Amends**

Always do what you can to fix the problem right away. This will show the customer how important customer service is to you, and it should keep them from going on social media to complain about your business. Fix any mistakes for free, and think about giving them a discount on their next service. A little act of kindness can mean a lot. For instance, fixing a client's broken gel paint and giving them a bottle of cuticle oil or nail polish for free.

6. **Follow Up**

Check with the client by phone a few days later to see if the money has gone into their account or if they were happy with the free or cheap service. This will let you know if you were able to solve their problem.

7. **Be Positive About Future Encounters**

Don't let one bad customer make you doubt yourself. Figure out what went wrong and move on. Do not let a bad experience with a client ruin their future meetings, even if you don't think you did anything wrong. Do not fear seeing them again. Treat them like any other client and start over. Always make sure you have detailed meetings with clients to make sure they are happy with the service you will provide, how much it will cost, and how long it will take. A thorough meeting also shows the client that you care about what they want and what they expect from you.

8. **Know When to Say Goodbye**

As a hair or beauty professional, you will have to deal with issues from time to time. However, you are not there to be abused or scared. If a customer bothers you too much, thank them for their business and suggest another service that should be able to handle their needs.

9. **Stop It Happening Again**

You should learn from your mistakes and use customer feedback to find places where your business is weak. For instance, wait times and treatment instructions were not clear. Do what you can to make sure these issues don't happen again. Set up a way for people to make comments, and make sure everyone on staff knows about it. You can also use role play to help.

10. **A Handy Tool to Remember - L.E.A.R.N**
    - Listen
    - Empathize
    - Apologize
    - React
    - Now

Maintaining Cutting Tools and Equipment

For high-quality hairstyle services, it's important to keep cutting tools and other equipment in good shape. Tools that are well taken care of make sure that stylists and clients can be precise, and work quickly, and safely.

Here is a complete guide on how to keep your cutting tools and equipment in good shape.

1. **Regular Cleaning and Sanitization**

- **Daily Cleaning:** Clean your scissors, combs, clippers, and other tools every day in the evening. To get rid of hair, product buildup, and other dirt, use a soft cloth and the right cleaning solution.
- **Sanitization:** To stop the spread of germs and other pathogens, clean tools after each use. Follow the manufacturer's guidelines for the right way to clean hair tools with a cleaning solution.
- **Barbicide:** Soak combs, brushes, and other non-electrical tools for the suggested amount of time in Barbicide or a similar cleaning solution. Before the next use, rinse well and let dry.
- **Clipper Blades:** Use a small brush to get rid of hair from the clipper blades. After each use, spray the blades with something that kills germs.

2. **Proper Storage**
- **Dry Storage:** To keep tools from rusting or corroding, make sure they are completely dry before putting them away. Dry the tools well with a clean, soft towel.
- **Protective Cases:** To keep scissors and clippers from getting broken, store them in protection cases. Cases are another way to keep tools clean and in order.
- **Blade Guards:** When you're not using clippers or shears, make sure they are safe by putting blade guards on them to protect the cutting points from damage.

3. **Sharpening and Adjustments**
- **Regular Sharpening:** Get the blades of your scissors and clippers sharpened by a professional every so often. Bad blades can damage hair and make cuts that aren't even.
- **DIY Sharpening:** Use a sharpening stone or tool made for shop scissors for small touch-ups. Do what the maker says to keep the blades from getting damaged.
- **Adjust Tension:** Make sure you regularly check and fix the tension of your scissors. The right force makes the cutting go smoothly and keeps your hands from getting tired. To get the best tightness, use the adjusting screw.

4. **Lubrication**
- **Clipper Blades:** If you want to keep your clipper blades working easily, oil them before and after each use. For a few seconds, turn on the clippers to spread the oil out equally.
- **Scissor Joints:** Put a drop of scissor oil on the pivot point of your scissors every so often. This stops wear on the blades and keeps them running smoothly.

5. **Inspection and Maintenance of Electrical Equipment**
- **Regular Inspection:** Look for signs of wear, broken cords, and missing parts on electrical tools like scissors and hair dryers. Take care of any problems right away to avoid crashes.
- **Cleaning Vents:** To keep hair dryers and clippers from getting too hot, clean the vents on them. Clean the vents and filters with a small brush to get rid of dust and other small things.
- **Battery Maintenance:** For electric tools, charge and take care of the batteries according to the manufacturer's instructions. Don't charge batteries too much, and keep them somewhere cool and dry.

6. **Tool-Specific Care**

- **Scissors:** If you drop your scissors, the blades could become out of line or less sharp. For the scissors to stay sharp, only cut hair with them.
- **Combs and Brushes:** Regularly clean combs and brushes by taking out the hair and putting them in a solution that kills germs. Before you use them again, make sure you rinse and dry them well.
- **Razor Blades:** Make sure to change your razor blades often to get a clean cut. Razors should be kept in a dry place so they don't rust.

7. **Preventive Measures**
- **Avoid Moisture:** To keep tools from rusting and corrosion, keep them away from water when they're not in use. Keep tools somewhere dry and cool.
- **Use Quality Tools:** Spend money on good tools and equipment because they last longer and work better. High-quality tools also need to be fixed and replaced less often.
- **Handle with Care:** Be careful when using tools so you don't drop them or handle them wrong. When you handle your tools properly, it lasts longer.

8. **Training and Awareness**
- **Staff Training:** Make sure that everyone on your staff knows how to take care of and maintain tools properly. Review safety rules and repair methods regularly.
- **Stay Informed:** Know about the newest goods and ways to do upkeep. To learn the best ways to take care of tools, go to classes or training events.

PART V
MASTERY AND BEYOND

CHAPTER 15
STAYING CURRENT

Trends and Innovations in Hair Cutting

Hair cutting, a fundamental aspect of personal grooming and fashion, has evolved significantly over the years. From traditional barbering techniques to advanced styling methods, the industry has continuously adapted to changing trends and technological advancements. Here is an extensive look at the current trends and innovations in haircutting, reflecting the dynamic nature of this field.

Current Trends in Hair Cutting

1. **Textured Cuts:** One of the most prominent trends in recent years is the emphasis on textured haircuts. This style involves creating layers and movement within the hair, giving it a more natural and effortless looks. Textured cuts are versatile and can be adapted to various hair types and lengths, making them a popular choice for both men and women.
2. **Blunt Bobs:** The blunt bob has made a significant comeback, characterized by its sharp, straight-across ends. This haircut exudes sophistication and can be tailored to suit different face shapes and hair textures. Variations like the asymmetrical bob and the long bob (lob) add a modern twist to this classic style.
3. **Curtain Bangs:** Curtain bangs, inspired by the 1970s, are making resurgence. These bangs are parted down the middle and swept to the sides, framing the face softly. They are low-maintenance and can seamlessly grow out into the rest of the hair, making them a favored choice for those seeking a change without a drastic cut.
4. **Shaggy Layers:** The shag haircut, another nod to the 1970s, is characterized by its choppy layers and tousled finish. This style works well with natural curls and waves, adding volume and texture. The modern shag is often combined with curtain bangs for a cohesive look.
5. **Undercuts and Fade Styles:** For men, undercuts and fade styles remain popular. These cuts involve gradually tapering the hair from short to long, creating a sleek and clean appearance. Variations include skin fades, high fades, and low fades, each offering a distinct look.
6. **Pixie Cuts:** Pixie cuts continue to be a bold and stylish choice for women. This short haircut is easy to maintain and can be customized with different lengths, textures, and colors to suit individual preferences. Modern pixie cuts often incorporate longer bangs or asymmetrical elements for added flair.

Innovations in Hair Cutting

1. **Digital Consultation Tools:** Technology has transformed the way clients and hairstylists communicate and plan haircuts. Digital consultation tools, such as virtual try-on apps,

allow clients to visualize different hairstyles and colors before committing to a cut. These tools use augmented reality (AR) to superimpose hairstyles onto the client's image, enhancing the decision-making process.
2. **Advanced Haircutting Tools:** Innovations in haircutting tools have improved precision and efficiency. Laser-guided scissors and clippers, for example, help stylists achieve perfectly straight lines and consistent lengths. These tools are particularly useful for intricate cuts and styles that require meticulous attention to detail.
3. **Sustainable Practices:** The push for sustainability has influenced the hair-cutting industry as well. Many salons are adopting eco-friendly practices, such as using biodegradable capes, recycling hair clippings, and employing energy-efficient equipment. Additionally, there is a growing demand for cruelty-free and vegan hair products.
4. **Education and Training:** The rise of online education platforms has made advanced haircutting techniques more accessible to stylists worldwide. Virtual workshops, webinars, and video tutorials offer ongoing education, enabling stylists to stay updated with the latest trends and innovations. This continuous learning ensures that professionals can offer the best services to their clients.
5. **Customizable Haircutting Experiences:** Salons are increasingly focusing on personalized customer experiences. This includes tailored consultations, bespoke haircuts, and customized aftercare routines. By understanding individual client needs and preferences, stylists can deliver highly personalized services that enhance client satisfaction and loyalty.
6. **Integration of AI and Robotics:** Artificial intelligence (AI) and robotics are beginning to make their way into the hair-cutting industry. AI-powered software can analyze hair type, face shape, and personal style preferences to recommend the best cuts and styles. Robotic haircutting systems, while still in the experimental stage, promise to offer highly precise and efficient cuts in the future.

Advanced Workshops and Courses

Advanced workshops and courses in hair cutting are essential for hairstylists looking to enhance their skills, stay updated with the latest trends, and offer superior services to their clients. These educational opportunities cover a wide range of topics, from mastering specific techniques to understanding the latest innovations in the industry.

Types of Advanced Workshops and Courses

1. **Mastering Cutting Techniques:** These workshops focus on honing advanced cutting techniques that go beyond the basics. Stylists learn precision cutting, texturizing methods, and how to create various styles such as layered cuts, bobs, and pixie cuts. Emphasis is placed on understanding hair structure, growth patterns, and how to work with different hair types.
2. **Creative Haircutting:** Creative haircutting courses are designed to inspire stylists to push the boundaries of traditional haircuts. These workshops encourage experimentation with

unconventional shapes, asymmetrical cuts, and unique texturizing techniques. Stylists learn to think outside the box and develop their artistic expression in hair cutting.
3. **Men's Haircutting and Barbering:** Specialized courses in men's haircutting and barbering focus on techniques specific to male clients. These include mastering fades, undercuts, and classic styles like the pompadour and crew cut. Workshops often cover beard grooming and maintenance, ensuring a comprehensive understanding of male grooming.
4. **Curly and Textured Hair Cutting:** Cutting curly and textured hair requires specialized knowledge and techniques. Workshops in this area teach stylists how to work with natural curls, coils, and waves. Topics include understanding curl patterns, reducing bulk without losing shape, and creating styles that enhance natural texture.
5. **Precision and Advanced Techniques:** These courses focus on achieving the highest level of precision in hair cutting. Stylists learn advanced techniques such as point cutting, slide cutting, and scissor-over comb. The goal is to perfect the execution of cuts and achieve a flawless finish.
6. **Digital and Technological Integration:** With the rise of digital tools and technology in hair cutting, workshops are now available that focus on integrating these innovations into daily practice. Stylists learn to use digital consultation tools, augmented reality for style visualization, and advanced haircutting equipment like laser-guided scissors.

Key Elements of Advanced Workshops and Courses

1. **Hands-On Training:** Practical experience is a critical component of advanced workshops. Stylists engage in hands-on training sessions where they practice new techniques on mannequins or live models. This allows for immediate feedback and refinement of skills.
2. **Expert Instructors:** Courses are typically led by industry experts and renowned hairstylists. These instructors bring a wealth of knowledge and experience, providing valuable insights and demonstrating cutting techniques. Learning from accomplished professional's helps stylists gain confidence and proficiency.
3. **Small Class Sizes:** To ensure personalized attention and effective learning, many advanced workshops maintain small class sizes. This allows instructors to provide individualized guidance and support, ensuring that each participant can master the techniques being taught.
4. **Comprehensive Curriculum:** Advanced courses offer a well-rounded curriculum that covers both theory and practice. Participants learn about the latest trends, tools, and products in the industry. Courses may also include modules on client consultation, safety, and hygiene practices.
5. **Certification:** Upon completion of an advanced workshop or course, participants often receive a certification. This credential can enhance a stylist's professional reputation and open up new career opportunities. Certifications are also a testament to the stylist's commitment to ongoing education and excellence in their craft.

Notable Advanced Workshops and Courses

1. **Vidal Sassoon Academy:** The Vidal Sassoon Academy is renowned for its cutting-edge education in hair cutting. Advanced courses here focus on precision cutting techniques and innovative styling methods. The academy's approach emphasizes creativity and technical excellence.
2. **Toni & Guy Academy:** Toni & Guy offer advanced workshops that cover a wide range of hair-cutting techniques. Their courses are designed to inspire creativity and enhance technical skills. Stylists learn the latest trends and how to adapt them to suit individual clients.
3. **Paul Mitchell Advanced Academy:** Paul Mitchell's advanced courses offer in-depth training in cutting techniques, color theory, and styling. The academy's programs are designed to elevate stylists' skills and keep them updated with the latest industry innovations.
4. **Sassoon Advanced Academy:** Sassoon's advanced courses focus on perfecting precision cutting techniques. Stylists learn the signature Sassoon methodology, which emphasizes clean lines and geometric shapes. The academy also offers specialized courses in creative cutting and color.
5. **Redken Exchange:** Redken Exchange provides advanced education in hair cutting, coloring, and styling. Their workshops focus on the latest trends and techniques, with an emphasis on innovation and creativity. Stylists learn to deliver personalized and cutting-edge services to their clients.

Networking and Professional Associations

Networking and professional associations play a pivotal role in the career development and success of hair-cutting professionals. These platforms provide opportunities for education, collaboration, and growth within the industry. Engaging with peers, attending events, and joining associations can significantly enhance a stylist's knowledge, skills, and professional network.

Importance of Networking and Professional Associations

Networking and participating in professional associations offer numerous benefits, including:

1. **Access to Education and Training:** Professional associations often provide access to advanced education and training opportunities. These can include workshops, seminars, webinars, and certification programs that help stylists stay updated with the latest techniques, trends, and innovations.
2. **Career Advancement:** Networking with other professionals and industry leaders can lead to new career opportunities, including job openings, collaborations, and mentorships. Being part of a professional association can enhance a stylist's reputation and credibility within the industry.

3. **Knowledge Sharing:** Networking events and association meetings provide platforms for sharing knowledge and experiences. Stylists can learn from their peers, discuss challenges, and exchange ideas on best practices and emerging trends.
4. **Industry Recognition:** Membership in a reputable professional association can provide recognition and validation of a stylist's skills and commitment to their profession. This can be beneficial for attracting new clients and building a loyal clientele.
5. **Support and Resources:** Professional associations often offer resources and support services, such as legal advice, business development tools, and marketing assistance. These resources can help stylists manage and grow their businesses effectively.
6. **Community and Camaraderie:** Being part of a professional community fosters a sense of belonging and camaraderie. Stylists can build meaningful relationships with their peers, share their passion for the industry, and collaborate on projects and initiatives.

Notable Professional Associations for Hair Cutting Professionals

1. **Professional Beauty Association (PBA):** The PBA is one of the largest and most influential associations in the beauty industry. It offers a wide range of educational programs, networking events, and resources for hair stylists, including the prestigious North American Hairstyling Awards (NAHA).
2. **National Cosmetology Association (NCA):** The NCA provides education, advocacy, and support for cosmetology professionals. Membership benefits include access to industry news, educational resources, and networking opportunities at national and regional events.
3. **Intercoiffure America/Canada:** Intercoiffure is a prestigious organization that brings together top salon owners and stylists from around the world. Membership is by invitation only and offers access to exclusive events, advanced education, and a network of elite professionals.
4. **American Association of Cosmetology Schools (AACS):** AACS represents beauty and cosmetology schools in the United States. While primarily focused on education, the association also provides networking opportunities and resources for beauty professionals looking to further their careers.
5. **International SalonSpa Business Network (ISBN):** ISBN connects salon and spa owners and managers to share business strategies and best practices. The association offers events, webinars, and resources focused on business development and growth in the beauty industry.
6. **National Hairdressers' Federation (NHF) / National Beauty Federation (NBF):** Based in the UK, NHF/NBF provides support, advice, and resources for salon owners and beauty professionals. Membership includes access to legal and business support, training, and networking events.

Strategies for Effective Networking

1. **Attend Industry Events:** Participating in industry events such as trade shows, conferences, and workshops is an excellent way to meet other professionals, learn about new products and techniques, and stay updated with industry trends.
2. **Join Professional Associations:** Becoming a member of a professional association offers access to a wide range of benefits, including education, networking, and resources. Active participation in association activities can enhance visibility and credibility within the industry.
3. **Engage on Social Media:** Social media platforms like Instagram, Facebook, and LinkedIn are powerful tools for networking and building an online presence. Engaging with other professionals, sharing work, and participating in online discussions can expand a stylist's network and attract new opportunities.
4. **Collaborate with Peers:** Collaboration with other stylists and professionals can lead to new learning experiences and creative projects. Joint ventures, such as co-hosting workshops or creating content together, can strengthen relationships and enhance professional growth.
5. **Seek Mentorship:** Finding a mentor in the industry can provide valuable guidance and support. Mentors can offer insights into career development, technical skills, and business strategies, helping stylists navigate their professional journey more effectively.
6. **Participate in Local Community Events:** Engaging with the local community through events, charity work, or educational programs can help build a loyal client base and establish a positive reputation. Networking within the community can also lead to referrals and new business opportunities.

CHAPTER 16
MASTERING YOUR CRAFT

Refining Techniques

Refining techniques in hair cutting are essential for achieving a high level of precision, creativity, and efficiency. Advanced skills and meticulous attention to detail allow stylists to create customized looks that meet their client's unique needs and preferences.

Understanding Hair Anatomy and Growth Patterns

To refine hair-cutting techniques, it is crucial to have a deep understanding of hair anatomy and growth patterns. Hair grows in various directions, and each person's hair has unique characteristics such as texture, density, and elasticity. By studying these aspects, stylists can make informed decisions on how to approach a haircut.

Mastering Basic Techniques

1. **Scissor over Comb:** This fundamental technique is essential for achieving smooth transitions and blending different lengths of hair. Practice and precision are key to mastering this method. By using the comb as a guide, stylists can ensure uniformity and control while cutting.
2. **Point Cutting:** Point cutting involves using the tips of the scissors to create texture and remove bulk without altering the overall length. This technique adds movement and softness to the hair, making it a versatile tool for refining various styles.
3. **Slide Cutting:** Slide cutting is used to create subtle layers and remove weight from the hair. By sliding the scissors along the hair shaft, stylists can achieve a natural, feathered effect. This technique is especially useful for blending layers and creating a seamless look.
4. **Blunt Cutting:** Blunt cutting involves cutting the hair straight across, resulting in a clean, sharp edge. This technique is often used for bobs and other geometric styles. Precision is critical, as any unevenness will be noticeable in the final result.

Advanced Techniques and Tools

1. **Razor Cutting:** Razor cutting is an advanced technique that creates soft, textured edges and adds movement to the hair. The razor can be used to remove bulk, create layers, and achieve a more natural finish. It requires a steady hand and a good understanding of how hair behaves.
2. **Texturizing Shears:** Texturizing shears have notched blades that remove varying amounts of hair with each cut. They are used to thin out thick hair, add texture, and blend layers. Proper use of texturizing shears can enhance the overall look and feel of a haircut.

3. **Clipper Cutting:** Clippers are essential for achieving precise, short haircuts and fades. Mastering the use of clippers, including understanding the different guard lengths and techniques such as fading and tapering, is crucial for creating clean, professional results.
4. **Precision Cutting:** Precision cutting involves meticulous attention to detail and exactness. This technique is often used for creating sharp lines and defined shapes. Stylists must have a steady hand and a keen eye for symmetry and proportion.

Refining Techniques for Different Hair Types

1. **Straight Hair:** Cutting straight hair requires precision, as any unevenness will be easily visible. Techniques such as blunt cutting and point cutting are effective for creating clean lines and adding subtle texture. Attention to detail is crucial to avoid creating harsh lines.
2. **Curly Hair:** Curly hair has a unique structure that requires specialized techniques. Dry cutting is often recommended to see the natural curl pattern and ensure that the hair falls correctly. Techniques such as twist cutting and slide cutting can help enhance the natural curl and remove bulk.
3. **Wavy Hair:** Wavy hair benefits from techniques that enhance its natural texture without adding excessive volume. Layering and texturizing are effective for creating movement and reducing weight. Point cutting and slide cutting can help blend layers and create a seamless look.
4. **Fine Hair:** Fine hair requires careful handling to avoid making it appear thin or lifeless. Techniques that add volume and texture, such as layering and texturizing, are beneficial. Blunt cutting can also be used to create the illusion of thickness and structure.

Incorporating Technology and Tools

1. **Digital Consultation Tools:** Using digital consultation tools, such as virtual try-on apps, can help stylists and clients visualize different hairstyles before committing to a cut. These tools use augmented reality (AR) to superimpose styles onto the client's image, enhancing the consultation process.
2. **Laser-Guided Scissors:** Laser-guided scissors are an innovative tool that helps stylists achieves precise cuts. The laser projects a straight line onto the hair, serving as a guide for cutting. This tool is especially useful for creating straight lines and ensuring symmetry.
3. **Advanced Clipper Technology:** Modern clippers come with various attachments and features that enhance precision and versatility. Adjustable blades, digital controls, and cordless options provide stylists with greater control and ease of use.

Refining hair

Getting better at refining hair is something you learn as you work. It's a creative skill that takes time to learn and get good at, but it can be hard to do well on hair of different textures and types. As hairstylists, we use this skill all the time, and it's something we should talk about more!

THE TOOLS YOU NEED!

When you're refining your hair, it's important to have the right tools on hand. You want to be able to use them easily and know that they will help you get the look you want. For me, I have different pairs of scissors for different types and kinds of hair because I feel more comfortable using certain pairs on certain types. To make things better, I always use soft-cut scissors—they're amazing!

THE PREP

It is very important not to use items that will weigh down the hair when you are prepping it because you will be taking weight out of it. The JOICO K-PAK Reconstructing Shampoo and Conditioner is something I would suggest because it protects, feeds, and makes hair soft and easy to work with. Yes, if it were necessary, I would use a color protection shampoo like JOICO K-Pak Color Therapy, which is also very light and my favorite.

THE SOFT-CUT APPROACH

Working on a graded bob is the best way for me to explain this skill. Take a piece of hair from the back of the head and start cutting it with soft-cut scissors. Holding the piece at a right angle, you want to cut deeply into the hair straight down. The cut is the most beautiful, soft, and light. It helps you lose weight and add beautiful layers at the same time. After that, the hair falls out normally, leaving no lines.

VERTICAL GRADUATION

Vertical graduation is a great way to lose weight and make your body look better at the same time. Over-direct the sections by slightly tilting them down and using the straight blade on the bottom of your soft-cut scissors. As you finish the cut, close the shears to make a faint graduation. This makes a shape that looks great on everyone and a style that is easy to wear.

SIMPLE THINNING

Of course, one of the best ways to get rid of weight in the hair is still to remove weight. Many clients have been put off by thinning because of the bad reputation it had a few years ago. But if you teach them and show them you're the real deal, you can easily lose weight and give them the haircut and look of their dreams.

Developing a Signature Style

Step 1: Find Your Inspiration
You need to find ideas for your unique haircut before you can make it. Look at different trends, magazines, social media sites, and even the way celebrities dress to get ideas of what you like and what looks good on your hair and face. Save pictures or make a mood board that you can show your barber later. Before making any changes to your haircut, you should have a clear idea of what you want.

Step 2: Research Barber Services and Supplies
Now that you know what style you want, it's time to learn more about barbers and the services they offer. For the haircut you want, look for barbershops that do that thing well. Read reviews and look at their work to cut down your choices. You should also learn about the basic hair tools you will need to get the style you want. This information will help you talk to your barber clearly and make sure they have all the tools they need.

Step 3: Consultation with Your Barber
Setting up a meeting with the barber of your choice is very important when making a unique haircut. Talk about your ideas, show them the pictures that gave you ideas, and describe your lifestyle, daily routine, and upkeep tastes during this meeting. A good barber will listen carefully, make ideas based on their knowledge, and then work with you to build and improve your idea. Trust their skilled opinion and be open to what they have to say.

Step 4: Trust the Process

That's it! You've found a barber you can trust and agreed on a plan. Now just sit back and let them do their thing. Trust the process and keep in mind that it takes time to make a signature haircut. To get the result you want, your barber may have to make a few changes, try out some new techniques, or play around with different barber tools. Don't give up if it doesn't look exactly how you wanted it at first; changes can always be made at later meetings.

Step 5: Maintain Your Signature Look

Once you have your unique haircut, it's important to take good care of it. Listen to what your barber says about what products to use, how to style your hair, and when to go for care visits. Buy professional-grade clippers, knives, and cleaning tools that are made for barbers to keep your haircut looking clean and sharp. Remember that a signature look needs care and attention all the time.

Step 6: Be Bold and Confident

Lastly, be proud of your signature haircut, and don't be afraid to show off your style. Your style should show who you are and make you feel strong and happy. Try putting it together in different ways, with new items or decorations, and don't be afraid to be different. When you own your unique look, you need to be sure of yourself.

Step 7: Experiment with Barber Supplies

You can play around with barber tools now that you have your unique haircut and are feeling good about yourself. With the right tools, you can keep up your style and even try something new.

Step 8: Share Your Signature Look

Now that you have your unique haircut and all the tools you need as a barber, it's time to show off your new look. Post a picture of your unique style on Instagram, Facebook, or Twitter. You can also give other people ideas by joining online groups or sites that talk about hairstyles and personal care. You never know, you might even start a pattern!

Step 9: Adapt and Evolve

You may change your style and tastes over time. Don't be afraid to change your unique look. Your hairdo should show who you are and what's in style right now. Keep up with the newest hairstyles, cleaning tips, and barbershop supplies. Be willing to try new things and play around with your style.

Step 10: Enjoy the Journey

The process of making a unique haircut should be fun and satisfying. Enjoy the process, have fun trying out new looks, and be proud of the result. Remember that a unique haircut is more than just a hairstyle; it's a way to show who you are and how you like to dress. Find ideas, talk to your barber, trust the process, keep up with your style, be brave and sure of yourself, try out different barber tools, show off your unique look, change and adapt, and most of all, enjoy the trip!

Teaching and Mentoring Others

Mentoring upcoming hairstylists is a duty that comes with the power to change jobs and the next generation of hairdressing stars. As a mentor, you play a very important role, whether you're an experienced stylist who wants to give back or a teacher in a beauty school.

As a mentor, here are ten tips for showing future hair stylists how to do their job well.

1. **Establish Clear Goals**

Start by giving your mentees clear goals that they can reach. Having clear goals will help them stay on track and keep them motivated, whether it's learning basic cutting skills in a month, advanced drawing skills in a semester, or creating their unique style over a year. SMART goals are clear, measurable, attainable, relevant, and have a due date.

2. **Create a Safe Learning Environment**

A safe, nonjudgmental place makes it easier to try new things and learn. Set up an environment where mistakes are seen as opportunities to learn and not as failures. Mentees can get out of their comfort zones, ask questions, and eventually grow in this setting.

3. **Demonstrate and Explain Techniques Thoroughly**

Show new techniques slowly and clearly explain each step when you first start using them. To help students who learn in different ways, use training methods that involve sight, sound, and touch. For instance, after showing them how to do something, let them try it while you talk them through it and give them physical cues when needed.

4. **Personalize Your Teaching Approach**

There are different learning styles and speeds for each mentor. Some people may be great at artistic styling but terrible at making precise cuts. Change the way you teach to meet the needs of each student. This one-on-one method helps mentees feel more confident and lets them grow at their own pace.

5. **Encourage Practice and Persistence**

You need to practice a lot to get good at anything. Encourage your mentees to practice often, both during mentoring meetings and on their own time. Remind them that they need to be persistent and that everyone starts at the beginning. To keep them going, celebrate their growth, no matter how small it is.

6. **Provide Constructive Feedback**

When given properly, feedback is a great way to get better. Before you tell them how to improve, you should focus on what they did well. When you give comments, be specific and always do it in a way that helps the person grow, not one that makes them feel bad.

7. **Stay Updated on Industry Trends**

There are always new styles, methods, and items coming out in the world of hair styling. Your mentees will be ahead of the curve and ready for a great job in the field if you stay up to date on these changes and use them in your lessons.

8. **Teach Business Skills**

Being a good stylist requires more than just technical skills. You also need to know how to run a business. Teach your mentees how to deal with customers, sell themselves as dressers, handle money, and do other important business tasks. These lessons will help them a lot as they start their jobs.

9. **Foster Professionalism**

From the start, teach your mentees how to be efficient. Being on time, what to wear, personal cleanliness, and good conversation skills are all part of this. Being professional is important for both getting and keeping clients and making a good name for yourself in the business.

10. **Be a Role Model**

Setting a good example might be the most powerful way to teach. Your work should show that you care and are dedicated, creative, and strong. Let the way you act as a mentor motivates your students to do their best, keep learning, and be honest in their work.

CHAPTER 17
PORTFOLIO DEVELOPMENT

Creating a Professional Portfolio

1. **Define Your Goals:** You should set your goals before you start putting together your resume. Are you trying to get new clients, get a job at a top spa, or show off your work to people who might want to work with you? Knowing what you want to achieve will help you make your resume fit your needs.
2. **Identify Your Audience:** Think about the people who will be looking at your portfolio. If you want to reach high-end salon owners, your resume should show that you are sophisticated and use advanced methods. Display your flexibility by offering a range of styles and cuts if you want to attract a wider range of clients.

Compiling Your Best Work

1. **Select High-Quality Images:** Pick professional, high-resolution pictures that show off your work in the best way. Do not use pictures that are hazy or badly lit. Buy a good camera or, if you need to, pay for an expert shooter.
2. **Showcase a Variety of Styles:** Make sure your resume has a wide range of haircuts and styles. Focus on various cutting styles, like short cuts, layered cuts, pixie cuts, bobs, and unique haircuts. A bigger range of people will be interested in your abilities if you show them.
3. **Include Before and After Shots:** "Before and after" pictures are a great way to show how your skills can change things. To make the differences stand out, make sure the pictures are taken from the same angle and in the same lighting.
4. **Highlight Specialty Work:** If you're good at certain things, like styling wavy hair, men's grooming, or wedding hair, make sure to include examples of your work in these areas. You can stand out from other stylists by focusing on what you do best.
5. **Use Testimonials:** Write comments from happy customers. Getting good feedback on your resume can help you build trust with possible bosses or clients.

Organizing Your Portfolio

1. **Create a Cohesive Layout:** Put your resume together in a way that looks clean and professional. Make it easy to find your way around by using the same plan and design throughout. Put styles that are similar together to make a smooth flow.
2. **Write Descriptive Captions:** For each picture or set of photos, write a short description that explains the methods used, what the client asked for, and the result. This gives the picture some background and shows that you know how to use different cutting techniques.

3. **Include an About Section:** In this part, you should write an interesting introduction that talks about your past, schooling, experience, and work mindset. People will feel more connected to you if you add a human touch.
4. **Add Contact Information:** Make sure that your contact information is easy for people to find. Add your email address, phone number, and links to your business social media accounts. If you have a spa or workshop, give the address and information on how to book.

Choosing the Format

1. **Digital Portfolio:** A digital portfolio can be used in many ways and is easy to get to. To show off your work, you can make a business website or use sites like Behance, Instagram, or LinkedIn. Digital galleries let you show your work to more people and make it easy to keep up to date with new work.
2. **Printed Portfolio:** You can use a printed portfolio for meetings, clients, and in-person interviews. If you want your pictures to look professional, choose a good binder or book style and print them on shiny paper. In-person talks and a physical resume can make an impact that lasts.
3. **Hybrid Approach:** To reach as many people as possible, think about using both digital and paper forms. A digital portfolio can get people to look at it online, while a paper copy can be used for talks and one-on-one conversations.

Enhancing Your Portfolio

1. **Keep It Updated:** Add new work to your portfolio regularly to keep it fresh and up-to-date. Get rid of old styles and add new ones that are in line with current trends and show how your skills are growing.
2. **Seek Professional Feedback:** Have coworkers, teachers, or professionals in the field look over your resume and give you feedback. A fresh look from someone else can help you figure out what you need to work on and make sure your portfolio looks clean and professional.
3. **Showcase Your Personality:** Your resume should show off your unique style and attitude. Let your uniqueness show through in the work you choose, the way it's designed, or the stories you tell.
4. **Network and Share:** Get the word out about your resume at professional groups, networking events, and on social media. Share your work with people who are influential in your field, possible clients, and people you want to work with to get more attention and chances.

Photographing Haircuts

Preparation

1. **Clean and Style the Hair:** Make sure the haircut is clean and looks great. To give your hair a finished look, use the right items to add shine and reduce frizz. This step is very important because it brings out the details of the haircut and makes it look better.
2. **Choose the Right Background:** A plain background is best because it puts the attention on the haircut. A white, black, or gray background is best, but you can also use a background that goes with the color of the hair. Backgrounds that are too busy or crowded might take attention away from the subject.
3. **Set up Proper Lighting:** When you're taking pictures, you need good lighting. Light from the sun is best, but if you can't get it, use a softbox or ring lights instead. Place the lights so that there are no sharp shadows and the hair is properly lit. Try different lighting settings to find the best way to show off the features of the haircut.

Camera Settings

1. **Use a Quality Camera:** Smartphone cameras are getting better, but a DSLR or digital camera gives you more power over the settings and better pictures. To get clear pictures, make sure the camera's quality is good.
2. **Adjust Aperture and Focus:** A smaller aperture (f/2.8 to f/5.6) makes the depth of field wide, which blurs the background and keeps the focus on the haircut. Make sure the hair is sharp and in focus by focusing by hand.
3. **Set the ISO:** To avoid blurry pictures, keep the ISO as low as you can. An ISO of 100 to 200 works best in well-lit places. If you need to raise the ISO because there isn't much light, be careful to keep the quality of the picture.

Composition

1. **Capture Multiple Angles:** Take pictures of the haircut from the front, the side, the back, and the top. Every point shows a different part of the haircut and gives a full picture. Make sure the hair is shaped the same way from every angle and pay attention to balance.
2. **Focus on Details:** Draw your attention to small details like layers, fades, and textures. Close-ups show off the skill and give your collection more depth. If you can, use a closeup lens to get clear pictures of small features.
3. **Include Contextual Shots:** To add context, include some wide shots of the client's face or shoulders. These pictures show how the haircut makes the person look better generally.

Conclusion

To sum up, becoming a great haircutter takes a mix of professional skill, imagination, and attention to detail. This guide has gone over the basic haircutting methods, tools, and tips that can help you get better at it. Remember that practice is the best way to get better at what you do, no matter how skilled you are as a stylist. You can give your customers great haircuts that boost their confidence and style if you know how to discuss with them, learn basic and advanced cutting methods, and keep up with the latest trends in the industry. Accept that you are always learning, look for ideas in a variety of places, and keep your love for making beautiful haircuts alive. In the end, haircutting is more than just cutting hair. It's also about changing how people look, making them feel better about themselves, and making connections with clients that last. You can do well in this exciting and satisfying field if you work hard and strive for greatness. Good luck on your way to becoming a skilled hairstylist that people want to hire!

INDEX

"

"Before and after" pictures, 151
"layering" is the most common method used., 61

1

180 degrees of elevation, 25, 26

3

3 Methods, 21

8

80s-style outfit, 107

A

A beauty stand or a simple table, 8
A big part of the art of hair cutting, 2
A bigger range of people will be interested in your abilities, 151
a change in your hair type, 35
A comb has a shaft with teeth, 7
A Cosmetology License, 124
A cowlick is a small spot, 66
A crew cut with a side part is added for a more polished look, 69
A digital portfolio can be used in many ways, 152
A digital portfolio can get people to look at it online, 152
A few helpful tips, 95
A fresh look from someone else, 152
A girl's haircut that looks fun and a little retro, 86
A guideline is a clear, sharp line that is drawn between hairs of different lengths, 58
A haircut is more than just cutting hair short, 2
A haircut is one of the most important things, 129
A hairdresser needs to know about the latest fashions, 2
A Handy Tool to Remember - L.E.A.R.N, 134
A high and tight fade crew cut, 69
A leave-in conditioner should be used most days of the week, 37
A long-layered "shag" haircut is made, 26
a paper copy can be used for talks and one-on-one conversations., 152
A pixie cut is usually very short, 82
A plain background is best, 153
A Rebellious Mohawk to Make a Statement, 81
A square face has sharp angles, 15
A styling razor, 5
A stylish and young-looking look can be achieved with an asymmetrical layered bob haircut, 103
A stylist needs to know more, 2
A Wet Finish, 106
Accept that you are always learning, 154
Access to Education, 141
accuracy, 3, 20, 53
accuracy and health,, 3
achieving smooth transitions, 144
Active Listening, 120
Adapt and Evolve, 148
add body by running some gel, 79
Add Contact Information, 152
add context, 153
add depth, 17, 54
Add new work to your portfolio, 152
add the diffuser, 38
Add your email address, 152
adding barrettes, 84
adding careful decorations and personal touches to your desk, 9
adding depth and less bulk, 2
adding layers or cutting the hair, 87
Adding texture to hair can make a haircut look great, 54
Addressing Client Concerns, 133
Addressing Client Concerns and Feedback, 133
Adjust Aperture and Focus, 153
Adjust Tension, 135
adopting eco-friendly practices, 139
Advanced Clipper Technology, 145
Advanced Courses, 127
advanced education, 141, 142
Advanced Techniques and Tools, 144
Advanced training in areas like precision cutting, 126
Advanced workshops and courses, 139
Advanced Workshops and Courses, 139, 140, 141

Advantages, 36, 37, 38, 40
Advantages vs. drawbacks, 38
Advantages vs. the drawbacks of straight hair, 36
Advantages vs. wavy hair disadvantages, 37
Advertising, 125
Afro hairstyles with kinky hair, 40
Afro-style, 50
afro-textured hair, 39
Agreement and Documentation, 120
alive and encourages creativity., 128
allergies, 10, 119
Alternative Lenders, 123
amazing mane, 38
American Association of Cosmetology Schools, 142
An area where hair is cut often has electrical tools, 11
an asymmetrical haircut, 103
an extra link to your official website, 125
An ISO of 100 to 200 works best in well-lit places, 153
An office that is well-designed, 7
an S-shaped design, 33
Angle is another part of haircutting, 25
Angles, 24, 25
Angles and Elevation, 24
Anti-Fatigue Mats, 11
antiseptic wipes, 11
Apologize, 133, 134
Application of hair products like conditioner, 19
APPLY A WEEKLY HAIR MASK, 117
Apply New Skills, 128
Apply styling products throughout your hair, 90
Approximately how much money do hair salon owners make in a year?, 126
Are you trying to get new clients, 151
arrange your tools and goods, 8
arrector pili, 13
art, style, and fashion, 2
Artificial intelligence (AI) and robotics, 139
ask customers and friends, 125
Ask for Referrals and Reviews, 112
ask questions, 133, 149
asymmetrical bangs, 103
Asymmetrical Bangs, 99
asymmetrical bob, 100, 107, 138
Asymmetrical Bob with Bangs, 100
asymmetrical cut, 99, 100, 102, 116
Asymmetrical Cuts, 99, 116
Asymmetrical Layered Bob, 103
Asymmetrical Pixie Cut, 99
Asymmetrical Shag, 102
asymmetrical style, 101
asymmetrical styles, 101

Asymmetrical Undercut, 102
attainable, 149
Attend Industry Events, 143
Attend Networking Events, 111
attending events, 141
Attention to Detail, 121
Attire, 10
attract a wider clientele, 126
attract a wider range of clients., 151
avant-garde, 104, 105, 106, 107
avant-garde hair, 105
Avant-Garde Hair, 104
Avant-garde hair is any style of hair, 104
Avant-garde hair is large, 104
Avant-Garde Inspired Haircuts, 107
Avant-Garde Looks to Style, 105
average person, 14
avoid blurry pictures, 153
avoid getting an electric shock, 11
Avoid hair care products that are drying, 92
avoid mistakes and bad reactions, 11
Avoid Moisture, 136
Avoid Overloading, 11
awesome profile, 38

B

Balance, 105
Balayage and Layered Cuts, 116
bald faux hawk, 76
Bandages, 11
Bangs, 44, 85, 130, 138
Bangs can make any haircut look better, 130
barbers can work close to the hairline, 7
Barbicide, 10, 135
basic cuts to styles that set trends., 78
Basic Layer Cut, 62
Basic Steps for Coloring Your Hair at Home, 113
BASIC TECHNIQUES, 17
BASICS OF HAIR CUTTING, 12
bathroom sink, 124
Battery Maintenance, 136
Be a Role Model, 150
Be aware of the renewal processes, 128
Be Bold and Confident, 148
be careful to keep the quality of the picture., 153
Be clear about your methods, 120
Be gentle, 95
BE GENTLE WITH HEAT, 118
Be Positive About Future Encounters, 134
beachy hair, 29

beachy waves, 96
beating hair problems, 108
beautiful curls cleaned out, 30
Beautiful Halo of Hair, 86
beautiful laid-back look., 103
beautiful shapes in villages, 7
beautiful ways, 92
Become Your Hair Expert, 46
becoming a great haircutter takes a mix of professional skill, 154
becoming a skilled hairstylist, 154
Begin with Dirty Hair, 115
Being a good stylist requires more than just technical skills, 149
being able to show yourself, 2
Being able to wear straight hair is the best, 27
Being Influenced by Trends Alone, 131
Being professional is important, 150
bespoke haircuts, 139
best tightness, 135
big fauxhawk, 107
big of sections, 20
Big Updo, 107
bigger face, 15
biggest and loosest curls, 31
Bind Your Hair In A Ponytail, 47
binder or book style, 152
Bitching shears are similar to blending/thinning, 55
Blade Guards, 135
blankets on hand, 8
Blend all the hair forward, 45
Blend and Layer, 53
BLEND FADE LINES, 59
Blending, 55, 56
blending different lengths of hair, 144
blends artistic vision with science accuracy, 3
Blow Dry Your Hair, 88
Blow-Dry And Final Adjustments, 50
Blow-dry the right way, 92
blow-dry your hair, 34, 90, 91, 92
Blow-Dry Your Hair, 96
blow-dry your hair over a circle brush, 34
Blow-Drying Hair Straight, 91
Blunt Bobs, 138
blunt cut, 17, 116
Blunt Cut, 116
boar bristle brush, 91, 96
Boar-bristle, 90
Bob without Bangs for Your Mature Mini-Me, 85
bobs, 6, 15, 16, 17, 116, 140, 144, 151
Body Language and Non-Verbal Cues, 108
Bold Faux Bangs, 106

boosting confidence, 127
Bowl Haircut for Kids That Can't Sit Still, 82
Breaks, 11
Bring Back the Long Locks, 80
Bring visual references, 130
Brush the hair, 44
Brush the hair well to get rid of any knots or snarls, 44
Brushed Back Top Cut, 79
brushes, 8, 9, 89, 90, 91, 135, 136
brushing out all the knots, 42
build trust with possible bosses or clients., 151
build your professional brand, 112
building a road map, 111
Building a Solid Client Base, 109
building an image for being dependable, 110
building an online presence, 143
Building and Maintaining Client Relationships, 120
Building Trust, 120, 121
Building Trust and Relationship, 120
bunch of boxes or bins, 9
bursitis, 4
BUSINESS AND CAREER DEVELOPMENT, 123
Business Conferences or Seminars, 125
business hours, 125
Business Permit, 124
Buy a good camera, 151
Buzz Cut Styles, 68
Buzz for Boys, 79
buzz-cut hair is defined by its sharp lines, 68

C

Caesar haircut, 80
Camera Settings, 153
Capes and Towels, 10
Capture Multiple Angles, 153
Career Advancement, 142
career goals, 127
career opportunities, 127, 141, 142
carefully sectioned and cut at certain angles, 3
carpal tunnel syndrome, 4
Ceramic brush, 89
ceramic-coated barrel brush, 90
Ceramic-coated barrel brush, 90
certain haircut might make a square chin look more defined, 2
Certification, 126, 127, 128, 141
certification in hair styling, 126
certification programs, 127, 141
Certifications from recognized institutions, 127
Certified stylists, 127

Chairs and Armrests, 10
change how the cut turns out., 25
change the color of your hair, 113
change the direction of your cuts, 63
change the length of your hair in different ways, 113
change your mind, 99
changes are puberty, 35
Changing the cutting angle and slope, 26
changing the length, 17
Check and re-evaluate your parts, 20
Check each corner to make sure the angle is the same, 45
Check for Irritants, 114
check that the line you cut is straight across from the hair, 43
Check The Length And Shape After The Cut, 48
Check with your employer about available resources., 128
Check-In Communication, 120
chemical treatments, 35, 115, 119
chemicals, 92, 94, 114
Children's Haircuts, 78
child's hair is naturally curly or wavy, 80
Chin-Length Bob, 83
chin-length bob or a haircut, 129
Chin-Length Bob with Bangs, 83
Chin-Length Bob with Bangs Is As Sweet As Can Be, 83
Chip Into the Ends to Soften the Line., 44
choice of drinks, 9
Choose a barrel size, 96
choose LED lights, 8
Choose Relevant Certifications, 127
Choose The Length, 48
Choose the Right Background, 153
choosing a deep side part, 102
Choosing the Format, 152
Choosing the Right Location, 8
choppy layers, 102, 138
chose an asymmetrical bob haircut, 100
Chunking, 55
Classic, 69, 81, 82, 85
classic and traditional, 72
classic taper haircut, 72
classy hairstyles, 27
clean and oil the blades regularly, 8
Clean and Style the Hair, 153
Clean hair is best, 96
cleaning, 8, 42, 135, 148
Cleaning, 9, 135
Clear Explanations, 120
Clear pricing builds trust, 121
clear style, 106

client are safe, 7
Client Comfort and Amenities, 9
Client Position, 19
Client Protection, 10
Client safety is very important, 10
Clients are more likely to trust a certified professional, 127
client's hair is sensitive, 118
client's image, 139, 145
Clients seek stylists, 126
client's skin, 10
Clipper attachments, 64
Clipper Attachments, 64
Clipper Attachments (Rakes), 64
Clipper Blades, 135
Clipper closed cuts to 0mm., 56
Clipper Cuts, 64, 67
CLIPPER CUTS, 64
Clipper open cuts to 1.5mm, 56
Clippers, 6, 7, 18, 145
clippers are a must, 3
Clippers are mostly used to cut men's hair, 6
Clippers are often used to make very short haircuts like fades, 6
clippers, and thinning shears, 3
Clipping hair is more like slicing hair with the clippers, 64
Close and slide, 97
Close Cropped Sides, 79
closeup lens to get clear pictures, 153
Close-ups show off the skill and give your collection more depth, 153
cloudy hair, 106
coarse and kinky hair, 24
coiled hair, 38, 39, 40
Coiled Hair, 38
Coiled hair can make coils in the first two inches of growth, 38
Coiled hair that has been cared for properly, 38
Coiled hairstyles, 39
coiled or kinky hair, 37
coil-like shapes, 38
coily hair, 32, 33
Coily hair, 32
Coily Hair, 19, 32
coily hair comes in three different styles, 32
coin-sized amount of pomade, 75
Collaborate with Peers, 143
collaboration, 141
collaborations, 127, 142
collection or an artistic statement, 104
Color, 107, 115, 116, 117, 118, 120, 146

color change, 108, 116
color in the same way every time, 19
COLOR INTEGRATION, 113
color looking good, 120
color without any problems, 118
color-blocked hair, 107
coloring, 107, 115, 118, 126, 127, 130, 141
coloring hair, 115
Comb the hair away from the ears, 45
Comb your hair back and tie it in a low ponytail. You need to make sure that your hair is smooth and that an elastic band holds all of it in place., 47
Comb Your Hair Thoroughly, 47
Combining Ombre with Long Layers, 116
combs, 5, 6, 8, 9, 36, 55, 135, 136
Combs, 7, 18, 136
Combs have been used since ancient times, 7
Comfort and Relaxation, 121
comfort zones, 149
comfortable, 7, 8, 9, 10, 11, 19, 108, 146
Commit to the Process, 128
Common rakes, 65
common tools, 8
Communication is key to building good ties with clients, 109
Community and Camaraderie, 142
Compare a ½-inch hair strand, 49
Competitive Edge, 127
competitive market, 127
Compiling Your Best Work, 151
complete guide, 120, 135
completely change a client's look, 115
Completely Shaved Style for a Fresh Feel, 80
Composition, 153
Comprehensive Client Assessment, 119
Comprehensive Curriculum, 140
comprehensive guide, 126
Conclusion, 154
conditioners, 32, 117, 133
conditioning treatment, 93, 117
Conditioning your hair is very important, 51
Confirm Details, 120
confusing hairstyle, 72
Consider Hair Type and Thickness, 53
Consistency, 121
Constructive feedback helps in refining your skills further., 128
Consult with your stylist, 131
Consultation, 10, 108, 115, 139, 145, 147
CONSULTATION, 119
CONSULTATION AND CLIENT MANAGEMENT, 119
contact information, 125, 152

Continue to Grow the Business, 125
continued education achievements, 128
Continuing Education, 125, 126, 127, 128
Continuing education and certification, 126
continuing education requirements, 128
continuing your education, 112
Continuous learning enables stylists, 126
control the volume, 79
Controlling Hair, 7
Cosmetology Books and Magazines, 125
Cosmopolitan magazine of your lady, 39
counterclockwise, 97
coursework, 128
Cowlicks, 14
Craft an Inviting Salon Atmosphere, 109
Create a Cohesive Layout, 151
Create a Safe Learning Environment, 149
Create a Welcoming Environment, 119
Create the patron saint, 65
Create Volume, 5
Creating a Memorable Experience, 121
Creating a Professional Portfolio, 151
Creating reward programs, 111
creating styles that enhance natural texture, 140
Creating the nape-sectioned hair, 22
creative, 107, 126, 141, 143, 145, 150
creative coloring, 126
CREATIVE CUTTING AND CUSTOM STYLES, 99
creative projects, 143
Credibility, 127
Credibility and Trust, 127
Crew Cut Styles, 68
Crew Cut to Beat the Heat, 81
critical component of advanced workshops, 140
cultural and social meaning, 108
Cultural and Societal Influences, 108
curl kinky hair that the curls, 39
Curl Your Hair, 93, 96
curl your hair away from your face, 97
Curl Your Hair with a Flat Iron, 93
curled hair, 29, 32, 38, 107
curled look, 17, 96
curliest of the three hair types, 39
curling iron or a perm, 27
curling irons, 11, 35, 92, 93, 132
Curling Irons vs. Flat Irons, 92
Curls Type 3c hair, 31
Curls Type 3c hair has a mix of loose and tight corkscrew curls, 31
curly guys, 39
Curly Hair, 18, 30, 46, 129, 145
Curly hair has more "real" curves than wavy hair., 30

Curly hair is dryer than straight hair, 30
curly hair type 3b, 31
Curly-haired women, 30
current trends, 138, 152
Current Trends, 138
Custom Sectioning for Cut, 116
customers walk in, 120
Customers who are happy with your business can be
    your biggest fans, 112
Customization, 120
customized aftercare routines, 139
custom-made outfit, 110
cut any hair in the middle, 6
cut at a 45-degree angle, 26
Cut backward from the front of the head, 45
cut curly or natural hair, 79
cut horizontally., 26
cut men's hair, 6
cut straight through hair, 4
Cut the hair with scissors, 51
Cut the Length., 44
Cut the patron's hair out of their left ear very small,
    45
Cut the sides and back of the hair, 67
Cut tiny V-shapes across the ends, 44
cut to the same length, 58
Cut with Flipped Ends for a Vintage Look, 86
Cut Your Hair, 48
Cut your hair while it's still dry, 19
cutting any hair in the passageway between them, 6
cutting hair, 2, 4, 7, 8, 42, 54, 62
cutting layers for shorter haircuts, 61
cutting leaves, 58
cutting method, 5
cutting off some length on top, 79
cutting off the cut, 7
cutting straight hair, 3, 46
CUTTING TECHNIQUES, 41, 53
cutting the hair a little longer, 14
cutting wavy hair, 2
Cutting, Trimming, and Perfecting Hairstyles, 4

D

daily routine, 119, 147
Damage avoidance and better hair control., 19
Dampen Your Hair, 49
Dampen Your Hair (Don't Soak), 49
dates are available, 125
David Bisbal, 38
deadlines for your certifications, 128

Decide The Length, 48
decorations that show off your style and brand, 9
deep conditioner, 39, 40
deeper meaning, 39
define the wave design and get rid of bulk., 18
Define Your Goals, 151
Defining the sectioned hair portions, 23
degrees of elevation, 25, 26
degrees of elevation stay the same, 25
Deliver Consistent Quality, 110, 121
deliver superior results, 126
demi-permanent, 113
Demi-Permanent, 114
Demonstrate and Explain Techniques Thoroughly,
    149
density, and elasticity, 144
depending on your preference, 72
Designate a Space, Design it, and furnish it, 124
Detail-Oriented Questions, 119
Detangle your hair, 47
Developing a Signature Style, 147
development tools, 142
Diamond Face, 16, 129
diamond face shape, 16, 129
Diamond Face Shape, 16
different colors or mix, 113
different combs and brushes, 8
different curl looks, 95
different cutting methods, 4
different face shapes, 2, 138
different meanings in different cultures, 108
different pair-ups., 106
different parting, 15
different results, 113
different roles work together, 25
different shapes, 5, 36
different sizes, 64, 95
different styles that depend on how thick and big the
    curls are, 30
different types of hair, 27, 80
different types of rakes, 64
Different types of shears can do different things, 5
Digital and Technological Integration, 140
digital files, 119
Digital galleries let you show your work to more
    people, 152
digital portfolio, 152
Digital Portfolio, 152
Dimensional, 116
Discuss lifestyle and maintenance, 130
disinfect all tools between clients, 8
Disinfection, 10

Display your flexibility by offering a range of styles and cuts, 151
Divide hair into small sections, 89
divide the hair into three sections, 22
divide your hair into sections, 22
Dividing the right and left crown of the hair, 21
DIY Haircuts and Over-Reliance on Online Tutorials, 132
DIY Sharpening, 135
do a full review, 10
Do not bend your arms, 19
Do not cut too much hair at once, 18
Do not thin your hair too much, 19
Do not use pictures that are hazy or badly lit, 151
do patch tests on new clients, 11
Document Everything, 120
doing other jobs that could come into touch with body fluids, 10
Doing the same things over and over or standing for long periods, 3
Don't cut or style your hair quickly, 20
Don't make uneven sections, 20
Don't rush hairstyling, 20
Don't Soak, 49
Don't spend hours brushing your hair, 34
Don't use too many plugs at once, 11
Draw your attention to small details like layers, 153
drawer organizers, 8
drawing attention, 2, 16, 117
Dry each section by pulling it with a brush, 89
dry hair, 19, 47, 88, 117
Dry your fringe with a hair dryer and style, 44
DSLR or digital camera, 153
Dye Application, 115
Dye Application Process, 115

E

Each style and cutout is just a different take on the theme, 26
ear-to-ear sections, 19
Easy handling while cutting or styling hair., 19
EASY REGULATION STYLE CUT, 65
Eating right and working out regularly, 35
edgy cut that stands out, 2
Edgy Stacked Bob with No Bangs, 87
Education and Training, 139, 141
Education fosters professional growth, 127
educational resources, 142
Effective Client Consultations, 119
Effective Communication, 120

electric motor moves the blades, 6
electrical equipment, 8
Electrical Safety, 11
Elevation, 24
email address, 111
Email Newsletters, 121
emergencies, 11
Emergency Contacts, 11
Emergency Preparedness, 11
Empathize, 134
Empathy and Emotional Connection, 108
emphasis on innovation and creativity, 141
employing energy-efficient equipment, 139
Encourage Practice and Persistence, 149
Engage on Social Media, 143
Engagement, 121
Engaging with peers, 141
enhance client satisfaction and loyalty, 139
Enhancing Skills, 126
enhancing the consultation process, 145
Enhancing Your Portfolio, 152
enjoy some awesome hair volume, 39
Enjoy the Journey, 148
entire scalp, 51
equation for success, 109
Equipment Financing, 123
ergonomics and body mechanics, 3
Ergonomics and Personal Comfort, 9
Ergonomics and Physical Safety, 11
Ergonomics and Posture, 19
Establish Clear Goals, 149
Evaluate The Hair Length, 49
Evaluate The Length And Shape, 49
Ever-classic styles, 84
every angle and pay attention to balance, 153
Every point shows a different part of the haircut, 153
everyday conditioner, 40
exact and accurate work, 7
Exaggerated Victory Rolls, 106
exclusive events, 142
expand a stylist's network and attract new opportunities., 143
Expanding Service, 126
Expanding Service Offerings, 126
experiment and innovate in your work, 128
Experiment with Barber Supplies, 148
Expert Instructors, 140
Expert Opinions, 120
Exploring Preferences and Goals, 119
Extra hair spray, 67
extra layer of cleanliness, 10
extra towels on shelves or closets, 9

F

face shape and hair type, 129
Face Shapes, 15, 129
Face the skipper, 44, 45
face types, 3
Face-Framing Highlights, 116
Face-Framing Highlights and Graduated Cuts, 116
Face-Framing Layers, 84
face-to-face talks, 121
facial reactions, 108
Fade, 40, 56, 69, 70, 77, 138
Fade blade clipper, 56
fades, and textures, 153
fake hawk hairdo, 76
fast-paced world of hairstyling, 109
Faux Hawk Haircut Style, 76
favorite curling tool, 96
favorite goods, 121
feathering, 5, 61
feathery edges, 18
features in trade publications, 127
Feedback and Improvement, 121
few big hair clips, 43
Figure Out What the Client Wants, 133
figure out what you need to work on, 152
Figure out which formula is ideal for you., 113
Figuring Out the Legal Requirements, 123
financial support, 128
Find any big hairstyle ideas, 108
Find Someone Who Gets *Your* Hair, 46
find the guideline, 63, 64
Find Your Inspiration, 147
Finding a good place to cut hair, 8
finding a secret gem, 111
Finding a trained barber, 132
fine details, 3
Fine Hair, 34, 79, 145
fine teeth to cut and smooth hair precisely, 18
Finishing, 55
Fire Safety, 11
First Aid Kit, 11
first half-inch of hair, 40
First Impressions Matter, 120
first three inches of curls, 38
First, Dry and Style Your Bangs, 43
fit clients of different heights, 8
fit the client's attitude and way of life, 3
flat surface should be part of your workspace, 8
Floors, 10
fluorescent lights, 8

Focus on Details, 153
focus on precision cutting, 141
Focus on various cutting styles, 151
Follow a hair care routine, 132
follow the directions on how to use them, 11
Follow Up, 134
Follow with a general blow-dry, until the hair is about 50% dry, 88
following the directions on the box, 115
following the hair's normal growth pattern, 18
Follow-Up Appointments, 120
forehead and jaw are narrow, 16
four hairstyles for curly hair, 39
Framing or hair trimming is similar to paper pattern cutting, 64
French Crop Haircut Style, 76
French crop is a standard haircut for guys, 76
fresh and up-to-date, 152
fresh color job, 114
frizzy and uneven, 19
Frizzy Hair, 55
From Formula to Finish, 113
from semi-permanent to permanent., 113
from smooth and polished to rough and full, 3
front fringe, 100
front of your hairline, 76
Full, 73
full-length mirror, 8
full-man bun, 73
Furniture and Layout, 8
Further sectioning the sectioned hair, 22

G

general outline, 123
Gentleman, 69
gentleman's cut, 69
geometry, 3
get a crew cut, 69
get a good idea of the hair's color, 8
get a job at a top spa, 151
get a mid-length cut, 102
Get an anti-fatigue mat, 9
get clean cuts and keep hair from getting damaged, 8
get clear pictures, 153
get rid of any residue, 9
get rid of any smudges,, 10
Get rid of old styles and add new ones, 152
Get rid of the hair around your ears, 45
get the length and mix you want, 18

Get the patron ready by setting up the chair cloth drape, 42
Get the word out about your resume, 152
Get Your Bangs Ready., 44
getting a facial once a week, 117
Getting an undercut is a fun way to follow the asymmetrical trend, 102
getting and keeping clients, 150
getting feedback, 112
getting good at using different cutting tools and techniques, 3
Getting good feedback on your resume, 151
getting tendonitis, 4
Girls' basic pixie cuts are cute, 82
Girls can style it with hair items, 86
girls' haircut that ends just above the shoulders, 86
Give each client a clean cape and towel, 10
GIVE REGULAR TRIMS, 118
give the address and information on how to book, 152
give the ends some texture, 4
give your hair a finished look, 153
giving birth, 35
Gloves, 10
Going for Drastic Changes, 131
Going to a stylist, 79
good experiences, 112
Good luck on your way to becoming a skilled hairstylist that people want to hire!, 179
good personal cleanliness, 10
Grab a section of hair, 97
Gradual transitions, 131
graduated bob, 3
Graduated Cut, 116
Grasp the section of hair, 62
great asymmetrical look, 99
great candidates, 87
great haircuts, 132, 154
great way to show how your skills can change things, 151
Greet Warmly, 119
growth patterns, 20, 140, 144
Growth Patterns, 14, 144
Growth Patterns and Face Shapes, 14
guard setting, 72
Guidelines, 58

H

Hair (Defined), 61
Hair Analysis, 115
Hair Anatomy, 13, 144
hair around your curling stick, 97
hair bulb, 13, 14
Hair Care Advice, 120
hair changes that you can't explain, 35
Hair Clipper, 6, 55
Hair Clipper Tools, 6
Hair clippers and hair trimmers, 6
Hair clippers are often the most well-known tool, 6
Hair Comb, 7
hair combings are so popular, 7
HAIR CUT STYLES, 42
HAIR CUTTING, 46, 98
HAIR CUTTING FOR DIFFERENT TEXTURES, 46
hair cutting is a complex skill, 3
Hair cutting is a complicated mix of art and science, 2
Hair Cutting Scissors, 4
hair different forms, 7
Hair Don't Care With This Pixie Haircut, 82
hair dryers, 11, 135
Hair Dye Basics, 113
Hair dye comes in a range of formulas, 113
Hair Dyeing Process, 114
Hair Dyeing Tutorial, 113
Hair Dyes and Other Styling Products, 124
hair extensions, 126, 127
hair from different sections can mix, 20
hair growth cycle, 14
Hair growth cycle, 14
Hair growth patterns, 14
Hair Growth Patterns, 14
Hair History, 119
Hair Ideas, 107
Hair items for wavy hair, 37
hair papilla, 13
hair product like flexible pomade, 80
hair products, 11, 19, 34, 89, 139
Hair products, 36, 40
hair products and chemicals, 11
Hair products for straight hair, 36
hair shops online, 125
Hair should be cut straight across, 43
hair should be pulled back and neatly shaped, 10
hair style volume and layers, 5
Hair styling products, 39
Hair stylists, 4
hair texturizing can be bad for your hair, 54
hair tools, 133, 135, 147
hair type and problems, 133
hair types and hairlines, 69
Hair Washing Sinks or Shampooing bowls, 124
Hair Whorls, 14
haircut shortens, 72

Haircut Styles, 70, 71, 77
Haircutting, 4, 21, 50, 139, 140
haircutting is more than just cutting hair, 154
hair-cutting shears, 4
Haircutting Shears, 4
haircutting systems, 139
hair-cutting workspace, 7, 8
hairdresser, 2, 110, 130, 131, 133
hairdryer's tip, 38
Hairline Patterns, 15
Hairlines can be round, 15
hairlines, and necklines, 7
hair's natural movement, 14
hair's natural shine, 113
hairstyle is a clean, 72
Hairstyles for kids, 78
Hairstyles for straight hair, 36
Hairstyles for wavy hair, 37
hairstyling journey, 110, 111
hairstylist, 30, 109, 110, 130
Hairstylist's Definitive Guide, 109
hairstylists must keep their bodies in the right position, 3
hairstylists started as newbies, 93
half-bun with a trim fade, 73
Hand and Arm Position, 19
Hand Washing, 10
hand-held mirror, 8
Handle with Care, 136
Handling Chemicals and Products, 11
Handling Complaints Gracefully, 122
Hands-On Training, 140
Handwritten Notes, 122
Hashtags can also help get people to visit your social media, 125
Have coworkers, 152
Have Tools Ready, 119
Have your stylist cut off, 102
having certifications can give stylists an edge, 127
Having good storage options, 9
Having sharp razor shears,, 45
Health and Allergies, 119
healthy hair day, 29
Heart Face, 16, 129
Heart Face Shape, 16
heart-shaped face, 16, 129
heat setting, 91, 93, 96
height for both cutting and styling., 19
hiding any flaws, 2
high hairstyles, 40
higher client satisfaction and loyalty., 126
Higher Earning Potential, 127

Highlight Specialty Work, 151
highlight your qualifications in marketing materials., 128
high-resolution pictures, 151
High-Top Fade, 40
HOA, 124
hold on to the scissors, 17
Holding and Positioning Tools, 17
Holding Clippers, 18
Holding Razors, 18
Holding Scissors, 17
Holding the Comb, 18
home or a gym, 125
home-based business, 125
Homeowners Association, 124, 125
home-styling razor comb, 7
Hooded Hair Dryer, 124
Horizontal rear trim, 43
hormonal birth control, 35
Hormonal Changes, 35
how different cuts affect the hair's natural flow and fall, 2
How do I get the perfect salon-quality blowout?, 89
How does hair grow?, 13
How long does it take to complete cosmetology school?, 126
How much are the teeth separated, 5
how much curl and volume you want., 89
how skilled you are as a stylist, 154
how the haircut makes the person look better generally., 153
HOW TO CUT YOUR HAIR, 51
how to deal with customers, 149
How to Do a Buzz-Cut with a Rake, 65
How to Do a Standard Flat Top, 67
How to Frame Short Hair, 44
How to Frame Short Hair (Off the Ears), 44
How to Frame Sides of Long Hair, 44
HOW TO HOLD THE SHEARS, 43
How to Trim Bangs, 43
How to Trim Long Hair, 42
How to Use a Curling Iron with a Clamp, 97
How to Use a Curling Wand, 97
HOW TO USE THINNING SHEARS, 63
how your clients think, 108
how your skills are growing, 152
Hybrid Approach, 152
Hydrogen peroxide, 114

I

I added a length mark 3 inches, 36
Identify Your Audience, 151
Ignoring Face Shape, 129
Ignoring Face Shape and Hair Type, 129
imagination, 2, 115, 154
Imagine a magnet pulling the hair straight out of the head, 61
Implement Changes, 121
implementing new skills, 128
importance and benefits of continuing education, 126
Importance of Networking, 141
important parts of the science of hair cutting, 3
Improving Client Satisfaction, 126
Inadequate Clipping, 20
Include an About Section, 152
Include Before and After Shots, 151
Include Contextual Shots, 153
include some wide shots of the client's face or shoulders, 153
include understanding curl patterns, 140
includes mastering various design, 2
includes tailored consultations, 139
including awards, 127
including job openings, 142
Inconsistent Tension, 20
Incorporating Technology, 145
Incorporating Technology and Tools, 145
increasing speed and accuracy, 3
index and middle fingers, 74, 76, 77
industry, 111, 126, 127, 128, 138, 139, 140, 141, 142, 143
industry bodies enhance a stylist's credibility., 127
Industry Recognition, 127, 142
informed decisions on how to approach a haircut, 144
Initial Interaction, 119
in-person interviews, 152
In-person talks and a physical resume can make an impact that lasts, 152
Inspection and Maintenance of Electrical Equipment, 135
inspiring creativity, 127
Instagram, 110, 143, 148, 152
Integration of AI and Robotics, 139
Intercoiffure America/Canada, 142
interesting introduction, 152
Internal, 54
International SalonSpa Business Network, 142
INTRODUCTION, 1, 2
INTRODUCTION TO HAIR CUTTING, 1

Invest in a high-quality blow dryer, 90
Invest in Continued Education, 112
Invest in quality tools, 132
ISBN, 142
It can be hard to handle and style the hair correctly, 20
It's also about changing how people look, 154
It's better to use your arms and shoulders, 19
it's important to keep learning and practicing, 3
It's the edge of the hair around your forehead, 15

J

job interview or the office, 76
Join Professional Associations, 143
joining associations, 141
Joint ventures, 143
Justin Bieber, 36
jutting forward motion, 76

K

Karen movement stole the bob haircut, 83
Keep a first aid kit that is well-stocked, 11
Keep a Record of Spending and Profits, 125
keep a stock of throwaway neck strips, 8
Keep Calm, 133
keep clippers and trimmers in good shape, 8
keep cowlicks in mind, 14
keep damage to a minimum, 92, 133
keep electrical wires neatly arranged, 8
keep good ties with your clients, 120
keep harm to a minimum, 118
Keep hazardous chemicals, 11
Keep hazardous chemicals in a different room with good airflow, 11
Keep in mind that hair typically grows forward on the face and neck., 65
Keep It Updated, 152
keep learning, 3, 150
Keep On Sectioning, 50
Keep Sectioning, 50
keep sections separate and in order, 20
keep the blades straight, 17
keep the customer, 133
keep the ISO as low as you can, 153
Keep the length and angles, 18
Keep the Natural Curls Carefully Sculpted, 78
keep the scissors and comb in the hand you prefer, 62
Keep the tension even while sectioning, 20
keep the whole workspace organized and clean, 10

keep things clean, 8, 9
keep track of many gadgets, 11
keep up to date with new work, 152
keep up with the latest trends in the industry, 154
keep your back straight and bend your knees if you need to., 19
keep your company, 111
keep your curls in place, 96
keep your hair healthy and shiny, 35
keep your haircut healthy, 132
keep your haircut looking neat and new, 132
keep your hands from getting cut, 5
keep your love for making beautiful haircuts alive, 154
keep yourself from getting hurt or strained., 9
keeping the guard number going down, 72
keeping things clean, 10
Keeping used tools, 8
Keeping used tools in a closed bin and clean, 8
keeping your office clean and well-organized, 9
Keratin, 2
keratin treatments, 126
Key Elements of Advanced Workshops, 140
Key growth patterns, 14
kinda, 38
King Louis XV's mistress, 74
kinky hair, 32, 37, 39, 40
Kinky hair, 39, 40
Kinky Hair, 39
kinky hair is easy to spot, 40
kinky hair looks great, 40
kitchen sink, 124
know a lot about the hair's nature, 53
know how to use different cutting techniques, 151
Know When to Say Goodbye, 134
Knowing what you want to achieve will help you make your resume fit your needs., 151
Knowledge Sharing, 142

L

Labeling, 9, 11
Labeling storage bins can help you save time, 9
Lack of Communication with Your Stylist, 130
Lack of expertise, 132
lateral framing, 44
latest trends, 139, 140, 141, 154
LAYER CUTS, 61
Layered Bob, 130
layered cut and color, 27
layered cuts, 15, 28, 116, 140, 151
Layering, 17, 18, 50, 61, 145

layering principle, 64
Learn about the different types of hair that women have, 27
learn basic and advanced cutting methods, 154
learn new ones, 3, 126
learning about fashion trends, 3
learning to type or play an instrument, 64
Leave the hair on the bottom of the head free, 49
leave-in conditioners, 32
leaving a lot of hair on top., 102
left-handed people, 62
less damage from heat, 90
Let your uniqueness show through in the work you choose, 152
Leverage Employer Support, 128
Leverage Social Media, 110
Lifestyle and Maintenance, 119
Lifestyle Nutrition, 35
Lift and hold parts of hair with the comb, 18
LIFTING HAIR, 62
LIFTING HAIR WITH THE COMB, 62
Light from the sun is best,, 153
lightly mist your hair with hair spray if you need to., 96
Limited visibility, 132
lines, and shapes used in the cutting process, 3
LinkedIn, 143, 152
links to your business social media accounts, 152
Listen, 119, 121, 122, 133, 134, 148
Listen Actively, 119
Listen and Apologize, 122
lock of hair and straightening, 23
Long Asymmetrical Hair, 101
Long haircuts look good with a shaggy cut, 61
Long Layered Cut for a Soft Look, 85
Long Layers, 130
long relationships, 108
Long, Face-Framing Layers for the Kids Next Door, 84
Long-Layered Cuts, 117
long-term commitment, 111
look for ideas in a variety of places, 154
Look for signs of wear and tear on cords, 11
look over your resume, 152
looking at or "seeing through" the hair from the previous rule, 63
love of Bambi, 39
Low, 70, 73
lower layers of the skin, 13
lower your risk of getting injuries, 11
low-maintenance, 138
Loyalty Programs, 121
Lubrication, 135

M

Madame de Pompadour, 74
magazine shoots, 104
magnetic strips, 8
Mailing your customers through email marketing, 111
main types of formulas, 113
maintain the certification, 128
maintain tools properly, 136
Maintain Your Signature Look, 148
Maintaining Certifications, 128
Maintaining Hair Health, 117
Maintenance and Aftercare, 117
make a bigger picture of your hairstyling, 111
Make a Business Plan, 123
Make A Hair Bun, 49
make a simple haircut look interesting and dynamic, 2
Make Amends, 134
make changes to get the look you want, 53
make different styles look good, 2
make every client feel like a star, 109
make exact moves, 17
make flat tops, 67
make hair more interesting, 55
make hair thinner when combs are used., 5
make haircuts, 3
Make it clear how much the services and any extra treatments or goods cost, 121
Make left and right ponytails, 22
make rolling your hair easier, 22
Make sure that each section is properly held in place with hair ties or clips, 20
Make sure that every customer gets good service every time they come in, 121
Make sure that every surface is fully covered, 10
Make sure that your contact information is easy for people to find, 152
make sure the camera's quality is good, 153
Make sure the client's head is in the right place, 19
Make sure the cut is right, 43
Make sure the hair is shaped the same way, 153
Make sure the hair is sharp and in focus by focusing by hand, 153
Make sure the hair is smooth, 45
Make sure the haircut is clean, 153
Make sure the haircut is clean and looks great., 153
make sure the pictures are taken from the same angle and in the same lighting, 151
make sure to include examples of your work, 151
make sure tools are unplugged, 11
make sure you keep a good stance, 11

Make sure your hair is blended, 72
make sure your portfolio looks clean and professional, 152
Make sure your resume has a wide range of haircuts and styles, 151
Make sure your tools are close at hand, 9
make the differences stand out, 151
make the endpoint down, 24
make the room feel warm and inviting, 9
make your haircut or style look bad, 20
making a good name for yourself in the business., 150
Making a place where clients feel welcome, 9
making connections with clients, 154
making eye contact, 119
making sure that each one is cut an even length., 74
Making sure that tools and equipment are clean, 9
making the jaw area bigger and the face wider, 16
Man Bun Hairstyles, 73
Manage multiple tools that need electricity with power strips, 8
Managing Expectations, 109
mannequins or live models, 140
Many different styles exist, 76
Many nerves end at the hair follicle, 13
many variations, 70, 71
Market Your Qualifications, 128
marketing assistance, 142
Mask on ends, 117
Master the Art of Communication, 109
Mastering Basic Techniques, 144
MASTERING YOUR CRAFT, 144
MASTERY AND BEYOND, 137
meaningful relationships, 142
measurable, 149
Measuring The Upper Layer With The Bottom One, 50
mechanics, 3
medium heat and wind works best, 91
Medium-Length Cut, 84
Medium-Length Cut with Subtle Layers to Embrace the Mane, 84
medium-length hair, 39
medium-length or longer, 38
Meet the 0 guideline, 60
Membership benefits include access, 142
Membership is by invitation only, 142
Men with straight hair look best with short hairstyles, 36
MEN'S HAIR TYPES, 36
Men's Haircut Style, 72
Men's Haircuts, 68
menopause, 35

men's grooming, 151
Men's hair comes in 4 different styles, 36
mentor motivates your students, 150
Mentoring upcoming hairstylists, 149
mentorship, 127
messy hairstyles, 37
metals from water, 117
Method, 17
Mia Farrow did in Rosemary's Baby, 82
Microloans, 123
middle fingers on the shank, 17
Mid-fade, 70
milkshake taking all the boys to the yard, 38
millennial generation, 87
Mirrors and Surfaces, 10
Mistakes and Fixes, 129
Mistakes to Avoid When Blow-Drying Hair Straight Like a Pro, 91
Mitchell's advanced courses, 141
mix hair of different lengths and layers, 53
mix layers smoothly, 3
mix of the pompadour, 75
mixing angles and elevation, 26
mixing teeth that are shaped like combs, 4
models or celebs, 2
modern and trendy, 74
modern hairdo, 106
mohawk fade is a haircut with buzzed, 77
Mohawk Haircut, 77
mohawk haircut comes in two main styles, 77
mohawk haircut for guys, 77
mohawk haircut is similar to the fake hawk haircut, 77
mohawk is a great haircut for kids who like to make a statement, 81
mohawks, 67
Mohawks to military cuts governing, 64
Moisturizing Color Reflection Conditioner, 117
more dramatic and Old Hollywood, 94
more oval shape, 15
more oval-shaped, 14
more shape and straightness, 23
more z-shaped curls, 33
most common cuts barbers, 7
most common sizes, 64
most expensive bowl, 124
most guys with curly hair., 39
most important parts of cleanliness in a hair salon, 9
most obvious reasons for changes in hormones, 35
most standard haircuts, 80
most styles, 74
Motion+ Color Protection Shampoo, 117
Motion+ Moisturizing Color Reflection, 117
move down a guideline, 58
Move the comb a little further back into a segment, 63
Moving too quickly, 92
multiple tools, 8

N

NACCAS, 127
NAHA, 142
National Accrediting Commission of Cosmetology Arts and Sciences, 127
National Beauty Federation, 142
National Cosmetology Association, 142
National Hairdressers' Federation, 142
Native American Mohawk group, 77
natural balance, 15
natural butter are better choices, 40
Natural Curls, 78, 86
natural hair color, 26
natural home treatments, 34
natural light, 8
natural look, 17, 96, 97
Natural Partings, 15
natural patterns, 15
natural shape, 2
NBF, 142
Neck Strips, 10
needs and preferences, 139, 144
Network and Share, 152
Networking and participating, 141
Networking and participating in professional associations offer numerous benefits, 141
Networking and Professional Associations, 141
networking events, 111, 142, 143, 152
networking opportunities, 142
Networking Opportunities, 127
new career opportunities within the industry, 127
new clients, 109, 112, 142
new flat irons, 93
new information, 112
new job opportunities., 127
new styles and techniques, 112
New trends in haircuts, 126
NHF, 142
NHF/NBF provides support, 142
nice-looking coils, 38
nonjudgmental place, 149
normal conditioner, 39
normal haircut, 5
Not Considering Hair Maintenance, 130

Not cutting too much., 45
Not Embracing Professional Advice and Expertise, 133
Not working from root to tip, 92
Notable Advanced Workshops, 141
Notable Professional Associations, 142
nylon bristle brush., 91

O

Off the Ears, 44
offer contemporary styles, 126
Offer Promotions, 111
Offer Promotions and Loyalty Programs, 111
Offer Solutions, 122
old styles, 152
Ombre Technique, 116
ongoing education, 112, 128, 139, 141
Ongoing Education, 121
Ongoing education provides opportunities, 126
ongoing support, 111
Online Learning, 127
Open the clamp and release, 97
OPT FOR WELLAPLEX, 118
Organize the room, 124
Organizers for drawers can help you keep small things like tools,, 9
Organizing Your Portfolio, 151
original interest, 111
Other Causes, 35
other hair treatments for guys, 36
other simple emergency items, 11
other styles, 6, 36
Oval Face, 15, 129
Oval Face Shape, 15
Over-Graduating, 54
Overlooking Haircare Products and Tools, 132
Over-Teasing, 106
over-the-top styles, 104

P

pair of metal scissors, 43
Part Down Your Hair From The Middle, 48
part of the head, 23, 62, 65
Part your hair down the middle and brush it all backward, 42
Participate in Local Community Events, 143
participate in prestigious events, 127
participate in prestigious events and competitions, 127
participating in online discussions, 143
participating in professional associations, 141
past treatments, 119, 121
Pat hair dry with a towel, 88
Patch Tests, 11
Patients should also be able to sit in the chair, 8
Paul Mitchell Advanced Academy, 141
pay federal income tax, 125
pay for an expert shooter., 151
peek-a-boo highlights, 116
Peek-a-Boo Highlights, 116
people of other races and ethnicities can also have kinky hair, 39
People often make the mistake, 129
People think of the shorter style as the standard one, 77
people who might want to work with you, 151
People will feel more connected to you if you add a human touch., 152
People with oval faces can wear their hair, 15
people you want to work with to get more attention and chances, 152
Perfecting the Final Hairstyle, 6
permanent, 113, 114
Permanent, 114
permanent colorant, 114
personal expression, 3
Personal Hygiene, 10
personal style preferences, 139
Personal Touch, 122
Personal Touches and Decor, 9
personality and tastes, 78
Personalize the Experience, 110
Personalize Your Teaching Approach, 149
personalized customer experiences, 139
Personalized Recommendations, 119
Personalized Service, 120
phone number,, 152
Photographing Haircuts, 153
Pick out a brush based on your hair type and the results you want, 89
Pick professional, 151
picking how much to cut, 42
picture some background, 151
picture the patron hanging upside down., 62
Pinch The Hair Between Fingers, 49
pivot zone of the hair-cutting shear, 4
Pixie Cut, 130
Pixie Cuts, 138
pixie cuts,, 151
pixies are short, 99
Place clients in chairs, 11
Place the scissors so that the blade goes easily, 17

Placement, 115
Plants, art, and comfy chairs, 9
Playing soft music, 9
please be careful not to cut off too much hair, 55
Point cutting and texturizing, 19
Point cutting gives hair volume, 17
Point-cutting can make natural waves look better, 18
pointing downwards, 89
pompadour, 68, 73, 74, 75, 76, 140
pompadour fade is a popular variation, 74
Pompadour hair comes in many styles, 74
pompadour haircut, 75
Pompadour Haircut Style, 74
pompadour hairstyle, 74
pompadour style, 74
pompadour style that adds a side fades, 74
popular hairstyle for men called the "military cut,", 68
PORTFOLIO DEVELOPMENT, 151
Position your curling iron, 97
Position your wand, 97
Positioning Clippers, 18
Positioning Razors, 18
Positioning Scissors, 17
Positioning the Comb, 18
possible clients, 112, 152
powerful products, 93
powerful tools for networking, 143
practical exams, 128
practice and learn, 3
practice is the best way to get better at what you do, 154
Practice Makes Perfect, 93
precise cuts, 3, 145, 149
Precision and Advanced Techniques, 140
precision and control, 3
Precision and symmetry, 132
Preferential frame, 62
pregnancy, 35
PREP FOR COLOR, 118
Prep with a heat protectant, 94
Prep Your Skin, 114
Preparation, 119, 131, 153
prestigious North American Hairstyling Awards, 142
prevent pain, 19
Preventive Measures, 136
previous coloring visits, 118
primarily focused on education, 142
Printed Portfolio, 152
Problems to Avoid, 54
PROCEDURE, 61
process of applying the dye, 114
product residue, 10

Products should not be mixed unless told to do so., 11
professional association, 142, 143
Professional Atmosphere, 120
Professional Beauty Association, 142
professional community fosters, 142
professional community fosters a sense of belonging and camaraderie, 142
PROFESSIONAL DEVELOPMENT, 98
professional groups, 152
Professional Growth, 127
Professional Insight and Advice, 120
professional network., 141
professional setting, 8
professional skills, 3
Professionalism, 121, 150
professionals in the field, 152
Proper Posture, 11
PROTECT FROM ROOT TO TIP, 117
protect hair from damage by cutting down, 90
protect the stylist's health, 11
protect your client's color, 117
Protect your hair, 133
Protection is Key, 92
protection spray, 92
Protection Spray, 117
Protection Technology, 117
Protective Cases, 135
Provide Constructive Feedback, 149
provide individualized guidance and support, 140
provide opportunities for education, 141
providing a sense of accomplishment, 127
providing excellent quality and service, 109
Psychological Impact of Hair, 108
Pull all of your hair down to the middle, 61
pull of gravity, 25
pull techniques, 62
Pull the hair away from the head after rolling, 22
Punctuality, 121
pursuing further education and certifications, 128
push the comb into the hair and lift it,, 62
Put anti-fatigue mats on the floor, 11
Put clean, dry tools away in a clean, dry case, 10
put down the comb and pick up the shears, 52
Put in smoke alarms and always have a fire extinguisher, 11
Put on clean, business-like clothes, 10
Put on your finishing touches, 89
Put styles that are similar together to make a smooth flow., 151
Put up a list of emergency contacts, 11
Put your resume together in a way that looks clean and professional., 151

Putting a rubber band around your hair, 48
Putting on a beard with any kind of man's hair., 74
putting up the perfect hair-cutting workspace,, 8

Q

quality and regularity of the final haircut., 20
quiff haircut came out in the 1950s, 75
Quiff Style, 75

R

raise the ISO, 153
Rakes, 64
rat-tail comb, 19, 49, 50
Razor Blades, 136
Razor combs, 5
razor may still be able to make an exact cut, 5
razors, 3, 5, 8, 9, 17
Razors, 18, 136
razors can make edges, 3
reach as many people as possible, 152
reach high-end salon owners, 151
React, 134
real curly hair, 30
Realistic Expectations, 119
Reasons for Hair Type Changes, 35
reasons why hair changes, 35
recycling hair clippings, 139
Redken Exchange, 141
Redken Exchange provides advanced education, 141
reduce the hair, 7
Referral Bonuses, 121
refine existing skills, 126
Refining hair, 145
Refining Techniques, 144, 145
refining your hair, 146
Regular Check-Ins, 121
regular conditioner, 37
Regular Inspection, 11, 135
regular kitchen scissors, 4
Regular Sharpening, 135
Regular Trims, 117, 132
regularly strengthens, 120
Remember Preferences, 122
Renewal Processes, 128
Repeat The Process On The Other Side, 49
repeated strain, 11
replace any broken tools., 11
replace the previous guard, 58
reputation and power in the field, 112

Research Accredited Programs, 127
Research Barber Services and Supplies, 147
Research maintenance, 131
resources for salon owners, 142
rest your index and middle fingers, 17
retro 1950s, 74
review and recommendation, 112
right moisturizer, 31
ring finger, 17, 43
ring lights, 153
rock-and-roll musicians, 75
Root Shadowing, 116
Root Shadowing and Blunt Cuts, 116
Round brush, 89
Round Face, 15, 129
round face look, 2
Round Face Shape, 15
round hair bulb, 13
Run a blade along the hair section, 54
Rushing, 20

S

Safe Usage, 11
Safety and Hygiene Practices, 9
Sales Tax Permit, 124
Salon Chairs, 124
same conditioner, 40
Sanitation and Safety, 8
Sanitation of Tools, 9
Sanitization, 135
sanitized tools in a different area, 8
Sassoon Advanced Academy, 141
scalp and hair health, 127
scalp treatments, 126
Schedule regular trims, 132
schooling, 121, 126, 152
science of hair structure, 3
Scissor Cut with Fringe for a no-fuss Style, 83
Scissor Joints, 135
Scissor over Comb, 144
scissor-over comb, 140
Scissors, 3, 17, 53, 136, 145
scissors and shears should be sharpened often., 8
scissors are used to make straight cuts, 3
scissors' chops, 63
scorching heat can't damage or break your valuable strands, 92
sea salt spray, 103
sebaceous gland, 13
Section Hair, 115

section the front of the hair, 21
Section the Hair, 53
Section your hair, 97
Section Your Hair, 96
Section, Section, Section, 93
sectioning based on how you want to style it, 19
sectioning clips, 8
Sectioning For Hair Straightening, 23
sectioning hair, 19, 20
Sectioning Hair, 19, 20
Sectioning hair is an important part of hairstyling, 19
Sectioning into 3 layers, 23
Sectioning into three parts, 22
Sectioning Of the Hair for Hair Rollers, 22
Sectioning the front, 21
sectioning the hair, 21
Sectioning the Hair, 21
Sectioning the remaining hair, 22
Sectioning the sides of the hair, 23
Sectioning to the size of the hair roller, 22
Sectioning Wet Hair Incorrectly, 20
sections of hair, 21, 23, 53, 74, 95
Seek Feedback, 121, 128
seek feedback from clients and colleagues., 128
Seek Mentorship, 143
Seek Professional Feedback, 152
select certifications, 127
Select High-Quality Images, 151
Select Your Tool, 96
Semi, 73, 114
seminars, 3, 141
semi-permanent, 113, 114
Send clients birthday cards, 122
sensitivities, 119
Separate the hair on each side, 44
Separate the hair on top of the head, 21
serum for frizzy hair, 90
Set it with hairspray, 95
Set Prices, 125
Set the ISO, 153
Set up a social media page for your business, 125
Set up Proper Lighting, 153
Set Your Curls, 96
Setting a good example might be the most powerful way to teach, 150
Setting Up a Salon or Home Studio, 123
Setting up your hair-cutting workspace is very important, 7
Setting Up Your Workspace, 7
shaggy fake hawk, 76
Shaggy Layers, 138
Shake Out Your Curls, 96

shampoo, 34, 42, 47, 92, 96, 115, 117, 118, 124, 146
shampooing touches the skin, 115
Shampoos, 133
Shape the Final Hairstyle, 4
Share Your Signature Look, 148
Share your work with people who are influential in your field, 152
sharing work, 143
sharp blades that look like comb teeth, 7
sharp blades that move back and forth, 6
Sharp scissors are best for making clean cuts., 19
sharp shadows, 153
Sharpening and Adjustments, 135
Shavers don't cut hair in straight lines, 5
Shears, 4, 8, 55
Shears are an important tool that is often used to cut hair, 4
shiny coils give off a very sexual vibe, 38
shop scissors for small touch-ups, 135
Short, 39, 44, 77, 79, 82, 83, 86, 107, 127, 130
short cuts, 7, 28, 44, 99, 116, 151
short fade or trim and a long fringe on top, 76
short haircut, 36, 131, 138
short hairstyles with layers, 5
Short military haircuts and shake, 39
short mohawk, 76
short mohawk fade, 76
short pixie cuts, 15
Shorter & Cleaner Haircuts, 6
shorter hair, 7, 81
show off the features of the haircut, 153
show off your work, 109, 110, 121, 151, 152
Show pictures, 119
Show up for your meetings on time, 121
Showcase a Variety of Styles, 151
Showcase Your Personality, 152
Side Part, 69, 72
side parts, 15, 16, 19, 37
Side Swept Bangs, 87
sideburns, 7, 45, 51, 64, 65, 66, 67
Sideshow Bob, 38
side-swept bangs, 15, 87
sign of rebellion and confidence, 75
significant difference in length, 103
significant investment of time and resources, 128
significantly enhance a stylist's knowledge, 141
Simple Avant-Garde Looks to Style Yourself, 105
Simple Long Hair "Shaggy Cut", 61
simple ponytail look amazing, 30
SIMPLE THINNING, 147
Single Layer Cut, 87

Single Layer Cut with Side Swept Bangs Taking Center Stage, 87
single-layer cut bluntly just above the chin, 86
skin and fibrous tissue, 13
skin fade, 82
skin problems, 10, 119, 131
Skipping Consultations, 130
Skipping Consultations and Research, 130
Skipping styling products, 91
Skipping styling products or not applying them evenly, 91
sleek and clean appearance, 138
slicked-back look, 27
Slide, 54, 67, 144
slight shortening, 15
slightly messy look, 103
slow layers of hair, 6
Small Business Administration, 123
Small Business Administration (SBA) Loan, 123
Small Class Sizes, 140
small curving, 36
small difference in length, 99
smaller aperture, 153
smaller pieces that are easier to work with are usually better., 20
Smartphone cameras are getting better, 153
smooth out the line, 5
smooth out the lines, 4
smooth the edges of beards, 7
Soak tools in a disinfectant solution, 10
social media, 87, 109, 110, 121, 125, 134, 147, 152
social media page, 125
Social media platforms, 143
Social Media Presence, 121
Softness, 53
Some clients might want a bold, 2
Some extra length should be left on top of a standard haircut for kids, 79
some hair texturizers, 55
some hair types, 24
Some hair types, 42
some of the best haircuts for kids of all types,, 78
Some of the things that affect the result, 5
sorta, 38
spa or workshop, 152
specialized areas, 127
SPECIALIZED HAIRCUTS, 68
specific standards of excellence, 127
speeds up the drying process, 90
Split your hair into manageable sections., 94
spraying a little hairspray, 73
spraying hair during the hot summer months., 117

Square Face, 15, 129
Square Face Shape, 15
Staff Training, 136
stand for long periods, 11
standard bowl haircut, 82
Standing Position, 19
Start cutting, 43, 77
start putting together your resume, 151
Start to move your iron toward the end of the lock., 94
Start using the iron, 94
Start with healthy hair, 94
Start Your Look with Freshly Washed Hair, 96
Stay away from short, blunt bangs, 16
Stay away from style items with plastics, 92
stay competitive, 126
Stay in Touch through Email Marketing, 111
Stay Informed, 128, 136
Stay Inspired, 128
Stay Updated on Industry Trends, 149
STAYING CURRENT, 138
Staying Current with Trends, 126
Step Back and Assess, 53
Step forward and back so that your feet are shoulder-width apart, 19
step haircuts, 67
STEP-BY-STEP AFRO-CUT, 51
STEP-BY-STEP TAPER, 66
STEPS FOR BUZZ / BUTCH, 65
Steps for Simple Marine Style Cut, 66
steps to keep electricity safety in check, 11
Stick to Dry Hair Trims, 46
Stop It Happening Again, 134
stop the spread of germs, 10, 135
Storage, 9, 10, 135
Storage Solutions, 9
store bigger things, 9
straight blowout, 91
Straight Hair, 18, 27, 36, 47, 49, 129, 145
straight hair is hair that comes straight out of the scalp, 36
Straight hair that hasn't been styled, 107
straight lines, 18, 139, 145
straight razor, 5
Straight Razors, 5
straight, wavy, or twisted hair., 40
Straight-Edge Razor, 55
straight-edge razor is great, 55
straighten your hair, 23
Straightening the hair, 23
Straight-haired women are more likely to have "oily" hair, 27

strand of straight hair, 27
Strand Test, 114
Strategic Sectioning, 115
Strategies for Effective Networking, 143
strengthen relationships, 143
Stress is another common reason why hair health goes down, 35
stressful time, 35
strict military buzz cut, 75
strong chin, 15
strong difference in length., 101
Structure, 105, 117
Style Suggestions, 119
style tools, 9, 20, 94
styles like undercuts and buzz cuts, 6
Styles that end at the chin, 15
STYLING AND FINISHING TECHNIQUES, 88
styling wavy hair, 151
styling your curly hair, 39
stylishly angled bangs, 99
stylist's commitment, 141
stylists are taught methods that reduce physical stress, 3
stylists are up-to-date with the latest trends, 126
stylists can broaden their service menu, 126
Stylists can improve their skills and learn new ones by going to classes, 3
Stylists can make a lot of different styles, 3
Stylists engage in hands-on training sessions, 140
Stylists learn to deliver personalized and cutting-edge, 141
stylists make cuts, 2
stylists need to stay up to date, 3
subtle layers, 144
Subtle Layers, 84
successful in haircutting, 120
suggest starting on a lower guard, 70
Support and Resources, 142
Supportive Footwear, 11
Sustainable Practices, 139
sweep or clean the floor to get rid of hair, 10
sweeping hair up, 74
switch the hair clipper guard, 72

T

Tail Comb, 55
Take a section of hair and clamp it with your flat iron., 94
Take breaks often to stretch and rest, 11
Take off the band and let the hair fall, 62
Take pictures of the haircut from the front, 153
taking into account natural splits such as the center part, 19
taking pictures, 153
Taking the initiative, 121
talking as a bridge between meetings, 111
Taper Haircut Style, 72
tapered haircut shortens, 72
Teach Business Skills, 149
teach your mentees how to be efficient, 150
teachers, 152
Teaching and Mentoring Others, 149
technical skill, 3, 115
technique adds movement, 144
technique elements, 2
techniques, 3, 11, 115, 126, 127, 128, 131, 138, 139, 140, 141, 143, 144, 145, 148, 149
Techniques for Different Hair Types, 18, 145
Techniques for Integrating Cut, 115
technologies continually evolving, 126
Tell your clients and friends about your business, 125
Temperature Control, 93
temples, 15, 89
ten tips for showing future hair stylists, 149
tension of your scissors, 135
terms of science, 2
Test Your Curling Iron's Heat, 96
Textured, 116, 138, 140
Textured Cuts, 116, 138
Texturing, 2
Texturing and layering are two important techniques, 2
Texturize Curls and Waves, 53
Texturizing, 4, 5, 17, 53, 54, 55, 144
texturizing and feathering razor, 5
texturizing can give your hair movement, 18
texturizing cut, 54
texturizing methods, 54, 55, 140
texturizing shears, 17, 54, 144
Texturizing Shears, 4, 5, 54, 144
Texturizing shears have two-finger blades, 4
The 3 layer sectioning method, 23
The anagen phase, 14
The area of hairstyling is always changing, 112
the artistic and science sides of hair cutting, 3
the background, 9, 153
the base of the "empty" hair shaft, 14
the basic haircutting methods, 154
The Basics, 92
The beauty industry is dynamic, 126
the best things to use for your form are hair wax, 36
The blow dryer comes with a flat tip piece, 90

The bob's line is what draws people in, 54
The chairs and armrests should be cleaned with disinfectant wipes or sprays., 10
The crew cut is a type of buzz cut that became popular among college rowing teams, 68
the crown, 19, 21, 22, 63, 67, 68, 69, 73
the crown of the head, 21, 63, 67, 68, 73
the curling iron, 32, 34, 93, 96, 97
the curls are likely to be rough, 31
the depth of field wide, 153
the details of the haircut, 153
The end look of a haircut is determined by the angles, 3
The end of a piece of string, 24
the Fade haircut, 40
The fake hawk fade, 76
The fashion and beauty industry is ever-changing., 126
the fourth step is what you should do., 23
The good news is that you can dye your hair if you want to, 113
The hair clipper is made up of two razors, 6
The hair in type 4a coily is fine and can look "wiry" at times, 32
the hair is cut at X-degree angle, 26
The hair is now styled in a "shaggy cut.", 62
The hair of one woman and that of the other is very different, 26
The haircutter and customer, 50
the jaw and shoulder length, 36
The Lumberjack, 74
The man bun is a trendy haircut, 73
The mohawk is a bold look for a bold child, 81
The motor design is the most important part of the hair-cutting tool, 7
The motor is linked to the piston, 7
the nape, 7, 22, 23, 42, 45, 66, 72, 76
The new guard can get shorter, 58
the newest looks and techniques, 3
The number of teeth present, 5
the papilla, 13, 14
THE PREP, 146
The Psychology of Hair, 108
the quiff hairstyle, 75
The quiff hairstyle quickly, 75
The razor comb has two edges and a regular hair comb, 7
The right and left side of the hair, 21
The Role of Trust, 109
The root of the hair is in the skin, 13
The Rules for Crafting an Avant-Garde Hairstyle, 105
the scissor-over-comb cut, 7
the settings and better pictures, 153
the side, 15, 25, 43, 69, 70, 73, 75, 85, 106, 153
The skin is smooth and round hair grows right out of it, 14
THE SOFT-CUT APPROACH, 146
The strand test is a step that is very important to the process but is often missed, 114
The stylist can cut the hair shorter,, 4
The stylist can make even more beautiful, 3
The stylist's job is to figure out what the client wants, 2
The tapered cut, 72
The teeth can be found on the blades or both, 5
The third section should be the hair at the very bottom, 22
The Tools of the Trade, 3
The tools used for cutting hair, 3
THE TOOLS YOU NEED!, 146
The type of hair, 26
The undercut is a short to medium-length haircut for men, 71
The US Military made the fade haircut popular in the 1940s and 1950s, 70
the way of the blade and guard, 5
there are any allergic responses, 11
There are different ways to cut straight, 2
There are many reasons why hair patterns can change, 35
There are many ways to change the look of an asymmetrical haircut to fit your style, 103
There are no rules for avant-garde hair, 105
there's no real reason to make things more difficult, 26
There's no reason to hide those pretty locks, 32
They clip on blades with electric clippers., 64
Thick, 33, 69, 129
Thick Hair, 33, 129
thickening products and recipes, 34
Thicker hair can handle a little more heat and less movement, 91
thickness for the spiked top, 76
Thin and Texturize Strategically, 53
Thin Hair, 129
Thin or fine hair works, 82
think about how flexible the hair is, 15
Think about the people who will be looking at your portfolio, 151
think about using both digital and paper forms, 152
think Elvis, 75
Think of continuing your education, 112
Think of social media as a stage, 110
thinner and less dense, 33

thinner scissors, 7
Thinning, 3, 4, 17, 53, 63
Thinning hair is to make thick hair easier to handle, 17
thinning scissors, 53
Thinning Scissors, 4
thinning shears, 5, 17, 55, 63, 66
Thinning shears are like cutting shears, 4
thinning shears are mostly used to make hair thinner, 5
Thinning shears are used to get rid of bulk, 3
third finger, 43
thumb and fingers, 18, 33
Tie An Elastic Band A Little Down, 48
tie back the hair, 20
time off for employees, 128
Timely renewal, 128
tiniest draft, 13
TLC for Your Tresses, 93
Toni & Guy Academy, 141
Too Large Sections, 20
tool belts, 8
Tools and Equipment, 8, 9, 134
Tool-Specific Care, 136
Touch-Up Appointments, 117
traditional man, 69
Training, 125
Training and Awareness, 136
training opportunities, 141
training programs., 3
Transparency, 121
Treatment Plans, 120
treatments, 36, 119, 120, 121, 126, 132, 133
Trends and Innovations, 138
Trends and techniques change over time, 3
Trim Often, 46
Trim the hair into the shape you want without holding it, 44
Trimming, 4, 6
TROUBLESHOOTING, 129
TROUBLESHOOTING AND CORRECTION, 129
Troy Polamalu, 38
Trust the Process, 148
Try different lighting, 153
Turn the iron around 180 degrees., 94
Twist, 54, 97
twist the sectioned hair and clip it in place., 23
two blades on top of each other, 6
Type 1A, 27
Type 1B, 27
Type 1B hair, 27
Type 1B straight hair, 27

Type 1C, 28
Type 1C hair is the roughest and thickest of all straight hair types, 28
Type 2a, 29
Type 2b, 29
Type 2b hair waves are a bit tighter and clearer than type 2a waves, 29
Type 2b waves can get frizzy,, 29
Type 2c, 29
type 2c wavy hair, 29
Type 3a, 31
Type 3a curly hair is the best, 31
Type 3b, 31
Type 3c, 31
type 3c curls, 31
Type 4a, 32, 33
Type 4c, 33
Types of Advanced Workshops, 139

U

unattractive result, 132
Undercut fade, 73
Undercut Haircut, 71
Understanding Client Preferences, 108
UNDERSTANDING HAIR, 13
understanding how to change these geometric rules, 3
understanding of hair anatomy, 144
Uneven Bob, 54
Uneven lengths and textures can happen, 20
Uneven Sections, 20
uneven style, 99
unique and stylish, 99
Unique Asymmetrical Haircut, 103
unique characteristics such as texture, 144
unique haircuts, 3, 151
update your professional profiles, 128
updos can set a stylist apart, 126
Upgrade Your Updo, 108
upright against the floor, 26
upsetting, 39
Usage Instructions, 11
Use a brush suited to your hair type, 89
Use a butterfly clip to hold the sectioned hair in place, 22
Use a butterfly clip to separate the hair into three layers, 23
use a closeup lens to get clear pictures of small features., 153
Use a disinfectant solution to mop the floor often., 10

Use a Light Hand, 53
Use a lubricant like Vaseline to prepare your skin, 114
Use a nozzle, 90
USE A PRE-COLOR TREATMENT, 118
Use a Quality Camera, 153
Use a round brush, 89
Use a rubber band to hold the hair in place, 61
Use a sharpening stone or tool, 135
use a softbox, 153
Use a strong grip on the razor, 18
use advanced methods, 151
USE AN ANTIOXIDANT SHAMPOO, 117
use an apron or skirt, 10
use blunt cutting, 18
use clips or hair ties, 20
use different guard sizes., 18
use hair products and chemicals carefully, 11
use hair scissors to cut straight across your fingers, 74
Use hairspray, 94
use hand sanitizer., 10
use methods like texturizing and thinning, 53
use new methods, 112
use power strips with surge protection, 11
Use Quality Tools, 136
Use rake attachments, 65
Use sensible techniques to avoid pressure and injury, 11
use sites like Behance, 152
Use soap and water to wash your hands, 10
Use strong shapes, 107
Use Testimonials, 151
use the adjusting screw, 135
Use the comb's wide teeth for detangling, 18
use the hair clipper's guard with the lowest number, 77
Use the knowledge and inspiration gained from continuing education, 128
Use the right cleaning solution, 8
use the right items to add shine and reduce frizz., 153
Use the right products, 133
Use the Right Products, 47
Use your comb to smooth the fringe into place, 44
Use your fingers as a guide to cut straight, 77
use your middle finger, 52
Use your scissors like magic wands, 109
Use your stronger hand to hold the comb, 18
using a nozzle that focuses hair on the shafts in the section, 89
using a regular curling iron, 97
using angles and elevation, 26
using biodegradable capes,, 139
Using Curling Irons, 95

Using digital consultation tools, 145
using hair rollers, 22
Using Heat Tools, 92
using items to control the direction, 14
using new goods, 11
using the hair's natural splits, 20
using the idea of value, 111
using the same plan and design, 151
Using the wrong brush, 91
Using too high of a heat setting, 91
UV rays, 94

V

various directions, 144
Vertical graduation, 146
VERTICAL GRADUATION, 146
very cool and exciting, 99
very important message, 32
Vidal Sassoon Academy, 141
virtual try-on apps, 139, 145
Visual Aids, 119
vital components of a successful career in hair styling, 126
volume and movement, 2

W

Wait and release, 97
waiting a few years, 39
Warm Welcome, 120
WASH HAIR LESS OFTEN, 117
wash your hands right away, 10
Wash, Condition, and Style, 115
washing and dressing, 82
wave pattern, 24
Wavy Asymmetrical Bob, 100
wavy bob haircuts, 100
wavy cousins, 30
Wavy Hair, 18, 28, 37, 129, 145
wavy hair has curly strands, 29
wavy hair looks "wavy" instead of coiled, 38
wavy, curly, and coily hair, 2
we can do to improve our looks, 129
We use elevation as a part of hair cutting, 25
wear disposable gloves, 10
wear shoes that are easy and support your feet, 11
wedding hair, 151
Weight, 105
Welcome every customer with a smile and a good mood., 120

Wellaplex, 118
Wellaplex is suggested for all lightning services, 118
Wellaplex mixed with hair dye, 118
well-balanced diet, 34
Wet the hair with a spray bottle, 49
What are the main steps in sectioning hair for haircutting?, 19
what is a guideline?, 58
What Is Avant-Garde Hair?, 104
what the client asked for, 151
Where You Want To Cut, 48
Why is it important to section hair for haircutting?, 19
wide forehead, 15, 16
wide range of haircuts for both men and women, 7
wide-tooth comb, 39, 54
widow's peak, 15
widow's peaks, 15
wild volume is part of coiled hair's sexual appeal, 39
Will Ferrell, 38
Wipe down surfaces and mirrors, 10
wipe down tools to get rid of hair and other dirt, 9
Wispy bangs always look great, 34
WOMEN HAIR TYPES, 26
Women with thick hair can also have hair that is straight, 34
work hard and strive for greatness., 154
work like scissors, 6
work mindset, 152
working with cuts or sores, 10
Working with Hair Types, 129
working with wet hair, 20
Workshops and Seminars, 127
Workstation Cleanliness, 10
Wrap around, 97
Wrap the client's neck in a new, single-use neck strip, 10
write a short description, 151
Write comments from happy customers, 151
Write Descriptive Captions, 151

Y

Yelp and Google can help your image, 112
you build a safe and trusted space, 108
You can also add an extra layer of cleanliness with disposable neck strips., 10
You can also get the look by adding texture, 103
you can blow-dry your hair every day, 90
You can cut hair in many styles with the clippers, 64
You can do well in this exciting and satisfying field, 154
You can give your customers great haircuts that boost their confidence and style, 154
you can keep small problems from turning into big ones, 11
you can keep your curls looking great, 31
you can keep your roundness from standing out., 15
You can leave the bottom of the hair free, 23
you can make a business website, 152
You can make a stronger statement, 103
You can make your hair look beautiful by texturizing, 55
You can stand out from other stylists by focusing on what you do best., 151
You can still use hair waxes and pomades., 38
You can store bigger things like hair dryers, 9
you can try any thin haircut tip,, 27
You can use a printed portfolio for meetings, 152
You can use either a butterfly clip, 22
You can wear a lot of different haircuts, 129
You can wear your hair in a lot of different ways, 15, 27
You could ask your stylist, 33
you cut your hair at different lengths, 2
you need good lighting, 153
you need to divide your hair into three sections, 22
you need to have a deep understanding of geometry, 3
you need to know a lot about different hair types, 2
You should curl all of your hair, 96
You should set your goals, 151
you should write an interesting introduction that talks about your past, 152
you will get good results., 22
young guys, 80
Your bright hair coloring will make a statement once, 107
your clipper and shear, 5
your curls might become a little less curly., 31
Your face shape has a big impact on the hairstyles, 15
Your hairstyle is going to be worn, 105
your qualifications remain current and recognized., 128
Your resume should show off your unique style and attitude., 152
your resume should show that you are sophisticated, 151
Your work should show that you care and are dedicated,, 150
your workspace is set up, 8

Z

Zero degrees of elevation means hanging the hair, 25

zero elevation, 25
zigzag shape, 15
Zoning Permit, 124
Z-shaped pattern, 33

Made in United States
North Haven, CT
20 December 2024